WORK
THE
SYSTEM™

The Simple Mechanics of
Working Less and Making More

SAM CARPENTER

NORTH SISTER PUBLISHING • BEND, OREGON

First printing, April 2008
Second printing, September 2008

Published by North Sister Publishing Inc., Oregon
www.northsisterpublishing.com

ISBN: 978-0-9801127-0-2

Library of Congress Control Number: 2008901478

Text design by Gorham Printing, Centralia, Washington, U.S.A.

Dedication

To Linda, of course.

Acknowledgments

Dad, thank you for insisting on the English language basics and your steady, positive encouragement. This book wouldn't be here if it weren't for you; Ma, thank you for teaching me to speak out, and for encouraging me to write.

Sam Kirkaldie, my partner, for your calm strength; Andi Freeman, for your faith in me and our systems. You really "get" it, as you watch my back; Hollee Wilson, for also "getting it," and being on top of every situation, never, ever letting me down; Pattie Casner, for your superb work; for enduring the hard times; Lannie Dell, our longest-term employee: 18 years! For sticking it out through the difficult years; Sandra Packard, our 17-year veteran, for your insistence on perfection, and for weathering those storms; Linda Morgan, your dependability and calm demeanor are legendary; Carla Hoekstra, through ups and downs, and no matter what, for always being there to do-what-must-be-done; Mike Gordon, could there be a steadier hand? Denise Jones, for your non-stop, positive contribution; Dan Blomquist, master of the IT universe, and undisputed gadget champion of the world; Shannon Walker, your calm, steady let's-get-to-it comportment; Kathleen Conroy, TSR extraordinaire, (who, in 2007, processed sixty thousand messages with but a single reported error); The Centratel staff, for the smile in your voices. You are the cream of the crop and the heart of our success.

Lindsay Stevens, who, 20 years ago, gave me my first inkling that a business should be managed, not indulged; Reese Shepard, who insisted there be a plan; Roger Shields, retired banker, for smacking me in the head with your air-bat when I needed it most; Robert Killen, of Columbia River Bank: you gave me a break when everyone else equivocated; "RC" Christensen, President of Columbia River Bank. You cut me slack twenty years ago when the two of us were at our respective ladder-bottoms; Lane Powell, my mentor. You are deceased but I think of you often. You have marked my life; NYS Ranger School and faculty, for teaching me about common sense and hard work.

Linda Chestney, for primary editing; Sarah Max, for developmental editing; Bobbi Swanson, for indexing; Kathy Campbell, of Gorham Printing, for the terrific book design; Natalie Troyer, my assistant/publicist, for your hammer-down comportment; Anne Pietz, my wonderful mother-in-law, for your nit-picky proofreading.

To my daughter Jenny, for confirming that a penchant for living on the edge is indeed a genetic trait.

Ling Xu, for taking me into the heart of China; Khizar Abassi, your quiet strength in assisting me in helping the back-country people of Azad Jammu Kashmir; Ahsan and Mina Rashid, for showing Linda and me the real Pakistan; to my brother Steve Carpenter, who can put the abstract in a nutshell and do it with humor. Also, Steve, thank you for your contribution to the space shuttle illustration. You are the science guy—and, soon, let's make that trip to the Cape; Linda Carpenter, for your incredible patience and invariably on-target suggestions.

To the men and women of our military, thank you for your sacrifice. Your song is not sung enough.

Contents

*"One should choose the simplest explanation,
the one requiring the fewest assumptions and principles."*

—Sir William of Ockham, medieval philosopher

It's Simple Mechanics

I work the system. And not just one: I work *all* the systems in my control—social, work, financial, biological, mechanical. You have your own systems. Do you see them? Do you control them?

It doesn't matter if you are a CEO, employee, stay-at-home mom or dad, retiree, medical or legal professional, athlete, or student. Your life is composed of systems that are yours to control—or not control.

In the slang sense, someone who "works the system" uses a bureaucratic loophole as an excuse to break rules in order to secure personal gain. But winning the life-game includes *following* the rules because if we don't, any win is a ruse. My bet is you agree with these terms so be assured you will find nothing deceitful or unsavory in these pages. I'll take this qualifying thread a bit further to say the *Work the System* methodology has nothing to do with esoteric theory and doesn't concern itself with our Western culture's overzealous and too-sensitive PC sentiments. Politics or religion don't factor into the message either. This is about common sense and simple mechanics.

At the risk of committing a PC blunder, I call this a working man's philosophy.

Life is serious business and whether you know it or not, or whether you like it or not, your personal systems are the threads of the fabric of your life. Together, your personal systems add up to *you*. And if you are like most people, you negotiate your days without seeing them as the singular entities they are, some working well and some not working so well.

In the complexity that is your life, what if you could distinctly see each of these systems? Then, what if you could reach in and pluck a not-so-perfect system out of that complexity, make it perfect, and then reinsert it? What if you could perform this process with every system that comprises your life?

What if, piece by piece, you could re-engineer your life to make it exactly what you want it to be without having to count on luck, providence, blind faith, or someone else's largesse?

The foundational thrust of *Work the System* is not to educate you in the "10 steps to peace and prosperity," or to warn you of the "5 most common mistakes in seeking happiness." The method digs deeper than that. *Work the System* will cause a mechanical adjustment in your perception of life—a modification in the way you see your world. And when this quiet yet profound shift occurs (you will remember the exact moment you "get it"), the simple methodology will make irrefutable sense and you will never be the same.

The book will also provide a framework—yes, a compendium of do's and don'ts—to channel this new perspective so you can get what you want out of your life.

Long-Term Chaos

Readers who have experienced tough times will "get" this book. Those in their early years, who have so far cruised along unscathed, may not. The tough times to which I refer include prolonged physical and/or mental crisis where one stands alone against the blackness: A nightmarish childhood, war, disabling injury or sickness, crime/incarceration, addiction, untenable yet inescapable personal relationships, divorce with attending child custody battle, personal or public betrayal, financial calamity, mental breakdown, or endless work that drains and demoralizes.

Twenty year olds might not get it. Forty year olds probably will.

Two Viewpoints

In the broad sense, two viewpoints exist of how one can bring full, positive functionality to life. The first holds that the events of the past, and the resulting mindset, are determining factors in today's happiness; that we have been victims of unpleasant circumstance and we might have a chance at peace if we could face and then disarm the psychic monsters planted in our minds long ago. That's the Freudian stance.

The other viewpoint is the cognitive. It maintains that the thoughts we feed ourselves today are what matter most, and the events of the past are just that—in the past—and gone forever unless we insist on giving them new life by swirling them back into the only reality there is, the reality of this moment.

The cognitive approach is more practical than the Freudian, with the individual seizing control of the immediate thought process rather than wallowing in negativity from years gone by. So, call me a cognitive guy who believes what we do today will determine tomorrow, and blaming the past, or the world, or someone else is a debilitating way to travel through this precious one-time event called life.

Without question, blue-blood, old-school psychologists who see endless dour complexity in the human condition, will deride the simplicity of the *Work the System* message. Things are more complicated than that, they'll say. I thank them in advance for their oblique compliment. This is an elementary, dispassionate, drop-the-load-dispatch that describes lives as they really are: cause-and-effect mechanisms that can be logical, predictable, and satisfying.

No PhD necessary.

So, take the title of this book at exact literal face value, understanding you will be working *your* systems. In these pages, I challenge you to improve and manage them, to dissect and refine them one by one until each is perfect. (We'll call this process "system-improvement.") You will create new systems too, while discarding the ones holding you back, the ones that have been invisibly sabotaging your best efforts. Manage the systems of your life and move toward inner serenity, prosperity, and the best for those around you.

Leader and High Earner

Not too long ago I participated in Cycle Oregon, a weeklong bicycle tour. Seventeen hundred riders pedaled an average of 75 miles each day through remote eastern Oregon. At night we camped in ad hoc tent cities planted at various locations along the route: rural high school football fields, small town parks, or wheat fields. Seldom did we have cellular telephone coverage. That was just fine as we, en masse, divorced ourselves from the damn things for this seven-day break from the regular world.

At dusk on the last night of the tour, as my friend Steve and I were casually walking through the surrounding sea of tents, we encountered a group of thirtyish guys sitting around, drinking beer, being boisterous. As we passed, we overheard them laughing, waging bets about how many voice mail messages one of their group members would have the next day when he was back in cell phone range and able to check his messages. Clearly, back in the real world these guys worked together in an office. One predicted the total messages would be 250; another, 150. The young man on the receiving end of the jest was robust, clean-cut, and confident. He smiled at the fawning. That's all we took in as we walked past, but it was obvious this man was important in his work. He was well respected, a leader and a high earner—a success. People depended on him.

For 24 years I have been general manager and CEO of a small business. Centratel is profitable, has 30 employees, and a solid, loyal client base. It is certain the part I play is important: In *my* world, I'm also a "leader and high earner." Many depend on me, too.

The next day, at the beginning of the long drive home with my bike ensconced on my car's roof-top rack, I checked my voice mail box. There was one message. Left earlier in the day, it was a general and benign update from my chief operations officer who knew I would be interested in getting caught up on things when I was able to pick up my messages again.

Andi told me all was well in the office and she hoped I had a fun week away from things. "Drive home safely," she said. That was it. She didn't need to address the obvious: During the week, without a hitch and without an ounce of input from me, the business had functioned perfectly while it continued to churn out thousands of dollars in profits. It didn't matter I was absent.

Who knows what that voice mail-inundated young man does for a living but I tell you this: He is mismanaging things if his world can't proceed for a single week without his direct influence; if the myriad of systems in which he is involved all come to a halt when he is not available. Yes, all those voice mail messages attest to his status and importance, but in the bigger picture he is a slave to his job. And the people who depend on him are slaves to his presence. They wait for his next call and can't move ahead until he provides input. Because he fails to set up business systems, in his absence things come to a standstill in the same way a dam causes a river to back up into a lake.

I'd say he was about 30 years of age. I'm 58. People and circumstances change with time. Eight years ago, my life was just like his.

Hooked Up

Here's another, more general observation: In the past 20 years, the lure of instant gratification has gripped the youngest half of our population. For the hooked-up generation—those born after 1970 who are wedded to iPods and the immediacy/pervasiveness of the entertainment industry—it's a stretch to go backwards to consider the root of things. The gratification of the moment is a distraction from thoughtful contemplation of the reasons why events happen as they do. Today, unlike 30 years ago, a good "now" is available by just turning off and plugging in. For the young, slowing down to examine things is not entertaining, and that's too bad because *it is mandatory we understand the machinery of our lives if we are to modify that machinery to produce the results we want.*

Yes, *Work the System* is a throwback of sorts, back to an age when there was thoughtful preparation with no expectation of immediate payback. But having said that, know that an investment in the *Work the System* strategy will show quick tangible benefits. Maybe not tomorrow, but certainly within a few weeks….

Closed System Laboratory

Centratel is a high-tech telephone answering service. For 15 years it foundered, my personal life a reflection of its chaos. However, over the last few years, as I applied the protocols that are described here, my workweek has become a fraction of what it was, as my income has increased ten-fold.

Moreover, my life away from work is smooth and easy now, with plenty of extra time to do the things I have always wanted to do. In the morning I awake serene, looking forward to yet another day of quiet, steady improvement on all fronts. In the course of a week, I spend far more time reading, writing, going to the movies, climbing mountains, and riding bicycles than working.

My life is in control.

The nature of the telephone-answering service business, with its myriad of interacting systems, both human and otherwise, made Centratel the perfect closed-system laboratory for developing the *Work the System* methodology. It's logical and convenient to use my business as the explanatory platform for these chaos-to-order processes. And things can get too dry and theoretical without real-life examples, so describing the method within the framework of Centratel adds some life to the party.

The strategies described here are not just for the small business owner, but also for those who work in a management capacity for a business owned by someone else. There are lessons for the silver-spoon and self-made wealthy, too. We will be dealing with reality and reality works in the same way for everyone, everywhere, all the time, so when I offer a personal business illustration, read between the lines and find your own personal application.

And when I refer to my business and use the word "manager," understand the label also applies to personal life. We are the managers of our lives, and the foundational protocols described here are universal.

A qualifier: I don't adhere to the *Work the System* principles and guidelines every minute, falling down on the job now and then. Nonetheless, because I have structured my life around the methodology, the details of the day continue to take care of themselves despite any temporary distraction or physical/mental slump. My hyper-efficient systems keep things moving forward no matter what.

The same will hold for you too, should you buy into the method and choose to take firm control of your life.

SAM CARPENTER

August 2008

PART ONE

THE MINDSET

THE PRINCIPLES of the *Work the System* method are simple but it is not enough to memorize or understand them. They must be internalized, deep down. There is a difference between learning something new and undergoing a visceral epiphany. On a gut level, "getting it" is key.

For this reason, in Part One some repetition will occur as I approach the concepts from different angles. Trust that the epiphany will come soon.

CHAPTER 1

The Simplest Solution

Out of clutter, find simplicity. From discord, find harmony.

Albert Einstein

One should choose the simplest explanation of a phenomenon, the one that requires the fewest leaps of logic. Or one could say, "Keep it simple, stupid!"

My wife Linda and I live on the outskirts of a vibrant mountain resort town in the great American Northwest. Our house is not large, but it's open and bright, furnished in a pragmatic, people-actually-live-here way. For each of us, it is everything we have ever wanted in a home.

I sit at the dining room table in front of my laptop. Outside the window, the quiet of the late afternoon is tangible. It's June. The lawn is lush green and is the launching pad for a half dozen huge ponderosa pines towering above the house. The weather is warm—another perfect, cloudless day in Central Oregon. Yesterday was like that and tomorrow will be the same.

It's peaceful. Linda sits at the table next to me, and we chat.

Meanwhile, in town, my telephone answering service business churns away whether we're thinking about it or not, providing more than a good living for us. It wasn't always this way. Fueled by a natural propensity to be scattered and unfocused, for 15 years my business experience was a chaotic morass of endless work, fire-killing, debt, health problems, and bad relationships.

Over the past few years, my life has moved from tumult to focused calm. Eight years ago, at a single point in time, I experienced an unexpected shift in perception that began the transformation of my life. Now, truly managing my small business and my life, I am no longer enmeshed in minutia but am an arms-length observer of it. The numbers are good: Compared to just a few years ago, my workweek is two hours instead of 100, and my earnings in a month exceed what I used to make in a year.

My health is back, too: I'm climbing, cycling, and skiing again.

As for the subjective? It's no stretch to say my life has ten times more peace and freedom. Much of the time, as my day slides by, I feel like an athlete in the zone: powerful, relaxed, and efficient.

Getting to this place wasn't hard to do once I tweaked my mindset to view each day from a more intimate angle. Since seizing upon this deeper reality, I have been able to channel my efforts to get what I want from life. Did I have to work hard? Yes, for a short while, there was some hard work. But in comparison to the nightmare of my previous life, the effort was not much and I was happy to do it, especially as the results began to roll in.

How I got to this place—and how you can do the same—is the grist of this book.

I direct *Work the System* to those who have the following chronic internal dialog: "There are things I must do *right now*, and there is barely the time/money/energy to do them. Oh, these tasks will be completed. I will bulldog things through, and as usual, they will be completed just in time—but the results will be of marginal quality and my body and mind will continue to be stretched to the breaking point. *I'm tired and stressed and can't seem to shake free of living on the edge, and I worry about my frame of mind and my health. There is too much chaos around me, too little control, and never enough money—things are far from what they should be."*

If you own or manage a small business, have a job, or are a student, there's a good chance the above dialog caught your attention. In our Western world, the I'm-just-barely-hanging-on self-talk is endemic to every class of people and every age group.

I'm a low-key guy. Not a lot of flash, no frills, and no advanced college degree. I've run the standard gauntlet of ups and downs, successes and failures, and like a lot of folks, worked hard all my life. It is clear to me that pragmatism increases with age; that life is trial and error, and lessons can be learned from being banged around. Further, I'm not afraid to face cold reality and I exhibit a knee-jerk suspicion of unsupportable theory.

I have a single, limited time-span life and I treasure this life-gift. My life is managed now, planned and maintained. Work or play, it gets my full attention.

No, of course I haven't got the world neatly tied up in a bag (who does?) but I have found a way to take control; to make the days of my life orderly and calm.

Almost always now, I wake up in the morning alert, strong, and happy.

Complex Jumble?

What about you? How do you describe your own day? Is it an amorphous, complex jumble of events or is it a relaxed and ordered sequence of happenings? Is it chaotic or is it under control? Do you have enough money? How much time do you spend with friends and family? Through the day—and through your life—are you in an endless race around a circular track, or are you climbing slowly and steadily to a mountaintop?

In your life, are you getting what you want? If not, could it be a personal management problem?

Don't confuse these questions with right, wrong, good, or bad, and don't inject some abstract theoretical, political, or religious aspect. Keep this mechanical, and especially, keep it simple. And take heart. If you tend toward the "amorphous, complex jumble of events" condition, rest assured you already have 100 percent of the necessary resources to eliminate this too-common story line. You'll just need to assemble the pieces of your day in a different way.

The *Work the System* method is almost silly in its simplicity but nothing less than profound in its capacity to transform. Per Sir William of Ockham (1288-1347), the simplest solution *is* invariably the most correct solution. Here, as I begin to discuss recognizable events and scenarios, habits, goals, successes, failures, and plain common sense, you will relate to the *Work the System* methodology because it is believable.

Yet, what I describe in these pages is not apparent to the casual observer.

This book is not about feel-good, pie-in-the-sky promises. Here, there are no new-think premises nor is there pseudo-intellectual blathering. You will not be asked to write down tedious lists, memorize odd platitudes, repeat affirmations, make daily journal entries, publicize your newfound direction to your friends and family, or worst of all, wait to see if yet another mysterious theory will make things better.

This isn't a matter of blind faith.

It is about simple mechanical improvements that will combine to transform your existence.

So, do you think sheer energy, clever thinking, and unbounded enthusiasm are enough to deliver you the freedom and income you want? If so, think a bit further. Certain structures—certain *systems*—must be in place before these important attributes can take you where you want to go.

Freedom and wealth occur *after* the mechanics are in place.

With the *Work the System* method, is there something you must do, work that you must perform in order to find peace and prosperity? Yes, you will produce some written documentation. And, if you manage people, you will teach them your new vision. But you're working and directing anyway, right? Now, you are doing whatever it is you do and that takes a certain amount of time and energy. The *Work the System* method asks you to channel these same allotments of time and energy away from the endless churning of immediate survival tactics, and toward incremental step-by-step building efforts that lead to freedom, prosperity, and peace.

And think again about racing around an endless circle versus a steady upward climb toward a goal. Effort is required either way, but know it is the climbing you want. Instead of expending precious time and energy on getting-nowhere tedium (which is the hardest and most frustrating work of all), you will expend that same time and energy in a step-by-step steady climb that will provide a geometrical return on investment.

The *Work the System* method deals with a mechanical fact that most people overlook—a "can't see the forest for the trees" myopia. The system-based protocols discussed here are quietly used in large, successful businesses and organizations everywhere, but are not often present in small businesses. And although the principles of the method are scattered among scores of business, religious, and pop-psychology writings, here they are grouped together in an everyman's methodology that is rooted in one fundamental truth: *A life's mechanical functioning is a result of the systems that compose it.*

And the simple crux of the *Work the System* method? It's this: If it is true "a life's mechanical functioning is a result of the systems that compose it," then getting what one wants in life lies in continuously improving those systems.

Consciously Paying Attention

All of us have recurring personal systems we employ to good advantage. We have many systems "down pat," systems that are efficient and quick because we have honed the details to perfection. We have perfected driving a car, fixing breakfast, and attending to a repeated minor challenge at work. Why are we expert in these small processes? Because they are simple, yes, but mostly because at some point we *consciously* paid close attention to those processes; we analyzed and adjusted them so we could do them with little effort, almost without thinking. But for many people, there is no deliberate effort to isolate and study the sequential workings of more complex wide-angle areas like careers and relationships. Some of us just float along without direction, wasting time and energy revisiting the same problems over and over again.

In order to tackle the more involved challenges of our lives—the challenges that have stymied us because of their complexity—the *Work the System* methodology expands perceptive, investigative, and analytical skills we already possess. *There is nothing new here, just a new approach.*

Your Mental Posture

The *Work the System* mindset is different from the mental posture most people pack around from day to day. *Instead of seeing yourself as an internal component of circumstances, enmeshed within the day's swirling events, your* Work the System *vantage point is "outside-and-slightly-elevated" from those events.* The day's happenings are visible as separate and individual elements, arranged in logical sequences. You are an observer looking down on things, examining the comings and goings of the day as if they are tangible, physical objects. Things are simple and understandable. Wherever you look, the machinations of the world make sense: Step-by-step, one thing leads to another as the systems around you continuously execute.

You constantly work on those systems. You make them better, one by one. Over time, complexity and confusion decrease to be replaced by order, calm, and rock-solid self-confidence. There is little fire-killing, little confusion, and as you continue to peer down at your handiwork, you feel an intense self-respect and you are proud of what you've accomplished.

I Come to You as a Project Engineer

With roots in the blue-collar, my personal background is a mixed bag: land surveyor, heavy-equipment operator, factory worker, door-to-door salesman, technical consultant, hamburger flipper, house painter, department store sales clerk, construction superintendent, project engineer, ditch digger, sales professional, builder, janitor, journalist, public speaker, book publisher, retail store owner, lab technician, logger, mill worker, stock and commodities investor, writer, photojournalist, telecommunications entrepreneur, real estate salesman, kitchen worker, handyman, corporate CEO, and business owner. I founded and continue to oversee a nonprofit organization that assists earthquake victims in northeast Pakistan and Azad Jammu Kashmir (see **kashmirfamily.org**). Through my business, Centratel (**centratel.com**), I am especially expert in the practical methodology of telecommunications: taking information, processing it, and then passing it on. I have been doing this for 24 years.

My overall life-role is as a project engineer: someone who accepts a problem, develops a mechanical solution, and then makes that solution work in the real world. I'm a project engineer in every aspect of my life including the personal roles of father, son, husband, and friend.

Metaphorically, here's my day: After a solid night's sleep, I bounce out of bed, shower, eat a big breakfast, and plow into things full bore, plunging deep into the new day. Today I am working with my crew to build something tangible out of the design I created on the drafting table just yesterday. I'm on the job in clean jeans, work boots, and a decent shirt. My persona is relaxed, with a slight smile on my face just under the surface of my focused comportment.

Again, metaphorically, I pull the levers and push the buttons of the unfolding day. My crew and I are lighthearted, relaxed, and efficient—and we're fast—*work feels good* and time flies as we cut a wide swath, making positive things happen, translating the improvements described on yesterday's paper design into the reality of the physical world today.

We're creating something worthwhile. We're permanently improving things.

A couple of years ago I was in an accident. I was charging down a city street on my mountain bike, returning home after a long, hard ride in the backcountry when a sixteen-year-old driver veered across my path. I slammed into the side of her SUV and was launched over the roof, landing on the pavement on the other side. To this day, I don't remember either of the impacts.

I was knocked unconscious, coming awake only as I was loaded into the ambulance. On the way to the hospital, the paramedic asked my name. I answered correctly. Then she asked who was close to me; who she could call to inform that I was going to the hospital. I told her "Linda." Then she asked me where I had been on my bike and…*I just couldn't remember.* It was several hours before I could put the pieces together; to recall the details of my ride.

From this experience, a lesson was hammered home: Our minds and bodies are complex *mechanisms*. They are machines that perform—or don't perform. They are indescribably complex collections of sub-systems, operating via countless sequential and cooperative protocols. Our minds and bodies work well most of the time, but because of the occasional mechanical glitch within a sub-system, sometimes they don't work so well.

We should never take for granted our connection to the reality around us; never underestimate the tenuous grip we have on our worlds. We must handle our bodies and minds with care, yet challenge them so they stay strong, while we are careful about upkeep and maintenance. *We must attend to them and never take them for granted.*

Changes in Your Life

Because this isn't a mystery novel, and because preparation is at the heart of the *Work the System* method, here's a two-part summary of how it will affect you and what it asks:

First, here are four general points about how the *Work the System* process will impact you personally:

1. **You will undergo an elementary yet fundamental shift in perspective.** This will come to you as a stark awakening in a moment of time rather than over a long, drawn-out learning experience. After it happens, moment-to-moment through your day, you will dispassionately observe the human and mechanical systems that comprise your world. These systems will stand apart from each other, starkly visible and sharply defined.

2. **There will be no turning back.** You can't go back! So point two is a warning of sorts. Because of the obvious truth of it, this "systems-perspective" is something you won't be able to shake.

3. **You will not be swallowing unsupportable theories of reality.** This is because there is nothing new here. It's just a matter of tweaking your perception of life's mechanical workings. Plenty enough reality exists without having to delve into esoteric, unsupportable, feel-good theory. Deep down you will know the truth of the *Work the System* method because it makes logical sense and it feels correct. Be assured that you won't sound flighty when explaining your new point of view to those around you. You're not going to lose your friends and family because you are not going to ask them for anything. You have nothing to sell. Instead, should they ask, you will explain what this is about and they will be intrigued with what you have to say.

4. **There is some heavy lifting**. Yes, you will undergo an exciting change of perspective but that is not enough. Especially at the beginning, some heavy lifting is required as you create documentation. That's OK. It's a superb investment because the result will be freedom, a relaxed persona, and plenty of money. It could be the best investment of time and effort you will ever make.

Here's the second part of this nutshell-summary, the three steps of the *Work the System* method:

1. **Documentation**: Creating written goals, principles, and processes that are guidelines for action and decision-making. This is the one-time heavy lifting. It won't take long.

2. **Separation, dissection, and repair of systems**: The satisfying process of exposing, analyzing, and then perfecting personal, work, and relationship systems. This effort includes creating new systems from scratch as well as eliminating those that are unnecessary or are holding you back.

3. **Ongoing maintenance of systems**: Greasing the wheels. This is easy because the positive tangible results of the *Work the System* method are motivating. Because it's obvious the systems you create and maintain are doing more and more of your regular daily work, you will continue to make adjustments in order to keep them working at peak efficiency.

Per Ockham's Law, the simplest solution *is* invariably the best solution, and the operating principles of *Work the System* are indeed, absurdly simple. (For more thoughts about Sir William, see Appendix A).

A PAUSE TO ADDRESS THE HOLISTIC

Is there a "holistic" or "global" side of you that is balking at separating things out and then examining them individually? You say "everything is connected and we're all one," and, "we must stop seeing ourselves as separate from the world around us," and, "our bodies and our lives are of unfathomable complexity, way beyond human comprehension." That's fine for the big picture. I tend to think that way myself when I am relaxed and daydreaming. But for now, here in the material world where you must navigate moment to moment, put all that aside and go with the case for separation and simple mechanics.

Understand that fixing an entire scattered conglomeration of a life in one fell swoop is impossible. It can't be done "holistically," despite the rightness that term suggests. Fixing anything of complexity requires proceeding one step at a time, one component at a time—a decidedly non-holistic approach.

I prefer not to use the term "holistic solution." Instead, I like the term "holistic result," which suggests that each component system within the organism is functioning at peak capacity, resulting in an organism that is superb in fulfilling its purpose.

So it's OK to take things apart to examine them, to get things straightened out piece by piece. You can view things holistically later, when you're not working on the details. There will be plenty of time for that.

The Movies at Home

Sometimes a more efficient system is right in front of us and all we need is a nudge to get the new process up and running. Here is a simple illustration of trading a cumbersome system for one that is efficient and fast. It's a scenario that perhaps you have already experienced. As you read, begin to think in terms of systems....

Going to the video store was an exercise in futility because the movies we wanted were seldom in stock. Returning them was a pain and paying late fees made me want to kill something. Our "let's get a movie" system was bulky, time-consuming, and frustrating. So we dumped it.

The new system we adopted is Netflix®.

Now, ordering and returning movies is effortless and

can be done anytime. No longer are we part of the out-dated video store system that demands time and travel, the luck of the draw in finding the precise movie we want, navigating hoards of people, waiting in line, and late fees. Now we order movies online, watch them when we feel like it, and when we're done, pop them into the postage-paid envelope and then the mailbox. Netflix, upon receiving a movie back from us, sends the next movie we've designated in the online queue. Despite the three-day turnaround via the postal system, we always have a movie at hand because we signed up for two movies in process at any one time. The Netflix system is simple and does the job at a reasonable cost. (Note: as of this writing, Netflix now offers 10,000 titles on-line, without the need for DVD shipment back and forth.)

Note that we were integral to the old video store system which did not often produce the results we wanted, and in any case, demanded time and travel—mandatory components of the video store system. With our new online system, there is no travel, no hassle, and we get what we want every time. We are not internal components of the Netflix system but instead remain outside of it, directing it. Mostly automatic, the new system does the majority of the work with little input and time required from us.

CHAPTER 2

THE DARK SIDE
OF FLOWER POWER

*There are some people who live in a dream world,
and there are some who face reality; and then there
are those who turn one into the other.*

Douglas Everett

Control is a Good Thing

To *get what you want, you must have more control.*

For many, hearing any version of this statement evokes the robotic response that seeking control is a bad thing…one should go with the flow, relax, stay loose, and not worry so much about details. Seeking more and more control can only mean one is devolving into a nervous "control freak." There is an almost cosmological sense—a hangover from the '60s—that "we're all one," and the problems in our lives and the world around us are due to people who don't share our brand of let-it-be spirituality. If my boss, my spouse, my parents, my children, my neighbor, and my government would just lighten up and be sensible—like me—then everyone could be happy!

Confident in the truth of it, we are eager to proclaim that the states of our lives—and of the world—are not good. We exhort that people are too uptight, too concerned with tiny details.

Allow me to retort.

Notwithstanding the possible metaphysical truth of the "we're all one" mantra, it's my contention that being in command of the details of our lives is mandatory if we are to find personal peace and success—if we are to find happiness. Conversely, while we're focusing on those things that are in our control, we must "lighten up" about those things that are *not* in our control. If we attempt to control events we can't influence, we are in for disappointment.

Is it difficult to determine what we can and cannot control? No, it's not.

And before continuing to disparage the '60s, I should say that my generation did bring along a great and useful truth. "What's happening now" *is* the most important thing. But I also know the satisfaction I feel in any particular "right now" has much to do with the details I've managed in days past. Yes, I try hard to "be here now," but I spend some of that "here" time focusing on actions that will ensure future moments will be serene and efficient. Make sense?

Wallowing

With my younger brother as an ally, I was brought up in my grandparents' house in a small town in upstate New York. It was a chaotic, unsettled household.

At 17, I was out of there, on the streets of the Haight district in San Francisco. It was the "Summer of Love" of 1967 where I discovered an intriguing escape from the not-so-perfect family situation back home. For two years, I traveled around the country, wallowing in sex, drugs, and rock and roll. (Well, maybe not that much sex).

I found myself at the Woodstock Music Festival in the summer of '69. Far out, I thought.

As I fruitlessly sought a better state of mind, two more years wafted by in a blur of pot and whatever other substance was handy. I was the poster child for the free-wheelin' '60s.

In my self-imposed stupor there was little I didn't complain about. I tried college but dropped out my second year, distraught in my loneliness and with my vision of a world gone mad. In 1970, in a Washington, D.C. political demonstration, I was tear-gassed. Literally, as the mist of gas rained down on our heads, I met the woman who was to be my wife and the mother of my two children. Within weeks, with my new love in tow, I revisited the by-now dangerous street life of San Francisco. We lived on those streets for two months and then returned to upstate New York.

Through it all, I balked at everything that didn't align itself with my idea of rightness, chafing at the unfairness of it all. I ranted that too many selfish people were controlling things; selfish people who were conspiring to ruin my life.

Of course, I was a beacon of equanimity.

In truth, I was a pain to everyone around me while my life was a series of dead-end jobs and fleeting relationships with unhappy people not unlike myself. Profoundly unhappy, I was a narcissistic complainer, haunted by self-imposed psychic hooligans.

In the middle of all this, I married my tear-gas love. Not surprisingly, my bride was equally frustrated with the unfairness of life. We were two peas in a pod, loud and bold, convinced of our rightness and everyone else's wrongness.

But after six years of wallowing in this fog-existence, one August day the chains fell off. That morning, yet again hungover and depressed, I sat at the kitchen table in our dumpy apartment. At the age of 24, I was working a minimum-wage seasonal job as a garbage collector and public restroom cleaner in a recreational campsite. I was late for work that day but sat there immobile, looking inward. I declared to myself, in not so many words, *This is over. I'm not living like this anymore. Until now, my point of view has been wrong. No longer will I try to change the world by whining about it and fighting it. There is very little outside myself I can control so I will stop agonizing over those things. Anyway, I haven't even been able to control myself! Today it starts. This moment my responsibility is to go out the door and show up for work, but after work I will make a phone call to arrange to go back to school this fall to learn something that can be used to create a future. I'm cleaning things up. From now on there will be no more complaining; no more blaming. Rather than reject the world-package as it is presented to me, I will get inside it—as it is—and see what I can do with the parts of it that are in my control.*

Little did I know my desperate acquiescence of "the system" in my mid-20s would be the first step toward writing a book 35 years later that would point out the beauty of systems and the freedoms they can provide. But unlike my preoccupations back then, what I write about here has nothing to do with politics, esoteric theory, or right or wrong. It's about simple mechanics.

So that afternoon in the late summer of 1973, I stopped bucking the world around me, made a phone call, and enrolled in a technical trade school. Two weeks later, we relocated north to a tiny town in the Adirondack Mountains where I would attend the New York State Ranger School to study forestry and land surveying. (In my early teens, it had been my dream to live in the Northwest, to work in the great forests and mountains. Maybe now, I thought, this juvenile fantasy could happen if I learned a skill that could be used in those forests and mountains.)

I put my head down, worked hard through the winter and graduated the next summer with a technical degree. Continuing to pay attention to the details, we headed to Oregon with our five-month-old son. Leaving the entire immediate and extended family behind, we had $400 in our pockets and everything we owned packed into a homemade trailer attached to the back of the Plymouth. I had made a stand. *I was improving my life—and the lives of the two people who were depending on me—by expending my energy only on the details that I could control. The fog in my head had lifted due to an absurdly simple adjustment in my thinking process.*

But, despite those first positive steps at dealing with the real world by focusing on what was truly in my control, I had not yet recognized the next necessary "systems-perspective" step that would lead to actually getting the peace and prosperity I wanted. In this ignorance, I would carry some very heavy baggage for another 25 years.

The Futility of Meadow Dancing

The best illustration of the baggage I carried is a photo taken at the Woodstock Music Festival (officially, the Woodstock Music and Art Fair, the famous gathering of 500,000 in rural upstate New York in 1969). It's one you may have seen. There is a lovely, slender, long-haired girl of maybe 18 years of age. She's beautiful, dancing in a meadow in a long, sheer dress. There is a flower wreath in her hair and she's laughing as she whirls with her arms stretched above her head in a casual way. Her thin, handsome, pony-tailed boyfriend is dancing, too. They share a blissful peace-joy ecstasy and anyone who sees that photo would, at least for a moment, want to be one of those two young people.

The image is a declaration of pure bliss with the clear message that unrestrained freedom and happiness *are* attainable, and the path to that place requires no more than a carefree and unrestrained comportment, hip music, and an unlimited supply of drugs. With a broad metaphorical brushstroke, the message of that photo is that happiness is available as soon as we drop our uptight preoccupations and "dance in the meadow."

Let it all hang out. Stay loose. Go with the flow.

Back to the real world. The photo is enticement for a state of mind that exists only for brief moments. Its message is a sham. One can't just "lighten up" and then expect ongoing happiness. Life isn't that way. But many of us who evolved from that era think it *should* be that way and so we approach life in perpetual disappointment with a world that won't conform to our expectations. Forty years after the '60s, that silly let-it-all-hang-out perspective has carried over to our children and beyond. We share a culture of chronic disappointment and it's no surprise many of us are crass, self-absorbed, and narcissistic. We bask in wealth the world has never known but wonder why our lives are chaotic; why we are unsatisfied.

We obsess about our yearning states of mind as we grope for personal peace.

(Don't get me wrong as I make my points here. I don't like focusing on negatives, and this is a bit painful for me as I discuss the unhappy contortions of my generation. But it's a necessary discussion for understanding the *Work the System* premise, so I *have* to start here—in the negative—in order to set the stage for the rest of the book, which I promise you will find uplifting.)

So Dissatisfied

In the western world, 10 percent of adults are alcoholics, 70 percent drink copious amounts of caffeine, 25 percent are addicted to tobacco, and over 5 percent rely on anti-depressants. Throw in the other legal and illegal mood-altering drugs and it is safe to say that each day, 98 percent of us ingest at least one mood-altering substance in our endless search for better states of mind. Of course, many of us are multi-substance users, for instance, consuming caffeine in the morning and alcohol at night. One substance counters the negative effects of the other and we have the classic, endless loop of Western chemical mood adjustment.

So, we finger-point and complain and wonder at our dissatisfaction.

It's too bad we do that because it's not just a waste of time, *it's a diversion from what needs to happen.* Personal excuses, generalizations about the alleged dire state of the world, and under-the-radar and overt attempts to change the people around us are ineffectual to the point of paralysis. *These preoccupations are distractions from the personal actions we could take that would produce what we want in our individual lives: peace, prosperity, and control of our destinies.* And pursuing personal peace, prosperity, and control are noble goals because the sure way to realize them is to contribute to the people around us.

So, what about the generally accepted notion that someone who seeks firm control is an unpleasant personality, someone who needs to loosen up? With some rare exceptions, I contend that this ubiquitous assumption is wrong. Despite the almost visceral societal belief to the contrary, *there is a direct connect between happiness and the amount of control we attain.* But, let's be clear: Happiness is not found in the control we have over others. It's found in the control we have over the moment-to-moment trajectory of our own lives, and more exactly—here we get to the root of things—the control of the personal systems that are ours to adjust and maintain.

The solution to getting what we want and making a contribution is not in complaining about the world condition or ingesting the perfect drug. And it's not about acquiring more things or being popular or famous. The solution is rooted in adopting a different perspective—a different way of seeing, thinking, and processing things—and it's about facing the world cold-turkey, courageously questioning the sacred status quo as it relates to our own selves. It's about sorting out what's going on within our individual areas of direct influence.

The thinking process is a linear system and my contention, as illustrated in the dancing girl story, is that many of us make a fundamental error in executing that process. Albeit tongue in cheek, I like to call this chronic thinking error the "Dancing-in-the-Meadow Syndrome."

YOUR CIRCLE OF INFLUENCE

A metaphorical concept made popular by Stephen Covey, the *circle of influence* describes one's ability to have an impact. In years past, my circle of influence felt like it was maybe two feet in diameter as I was hardly able to influence and control my own comings and goings due to whatever psychological funk was swallowing me up in the moment. Nowadays, my circle is miles in diameter as my day effortlessly sails by and I am able to accomplish nearly all of what I set out to accomplish, and as good news travels to me from areas I didn't even attend to that day. This impact gives me enormous satisfaction as the wheels of progress keep turning due to my previous input and not because of my immediate presence.

Metaphorically speaking, and use your imagination here, describe your own circle. How large is it? Could it be just six inches in diameter? If it is, when you look down—is the six-inch circle hidden underneath your feet? If the tiny circle has height, say 12 inches, do you barely balance on it? Is all available energy and attention focused on just trying not to fall off?

If that is your situation, your tenuous balancing effort doesn't leave much time for anything but complaining.

Wherever you are, whatever the size of your circle, focus on making changes *inside* of it, not outside. Don't spend precious time and energy analyzing and dissecting big-picture issues you can't affect. Instead, spend that time and energy on the things you *can* affect, those things within your circle. Do that, and your circle will expand in size.

Life Is a Streaming Video, Not a Snapshot

Outside of brief moments within that encapsulated era, the unbridled approach of the '60s was just another great idea that didn't work. *It was a theory that didn't consider how we are, but how we thought we should be.* If the Woodstock meadow-dancing photo had instead been a documentary movie, the hours and days surrounding that dance would tell a different story.

The truth of Woodstock? The non-stop music was good, but few bands played their best due to the confusion and pervasive drug ingestion. Yes, it was peaceful, but after that first glorious day it was cold and wet and we sat in the mud shivering, drenched, hungry, and thirsty. In the rain, a half million of us worked hard to relax, insistent in our success at being together outside "the system" for nothing more than music and love. "It's all we need!" we told ourselves over and over again. We had jumped outside the everyday world, but in our T-shirts, jeans, and little else, we were unprepared as the chilly torrent hammered down.

It was no contest as soft theory met bareknuckled hard reality.

With the inevitability of a wave washing into shore, the enthusiasm faded as the filth that comes with neglected crowds began to accumulate.

After two days of this, as a general paranoia began to sweep through the wet, shivering, drug-hungover hoard, my friend John and I got out of there. We left despite the fact that Jimi Hendrix hadn't yet taken the stage. It was that bad.

As we headed home in my beat-up old car listening to the radio, we were reminded of Vietnam, racial unrest, and political deviousness. And beyond those negatives, we each had dropped out of college and that meant having jobs. We both worked graveyard shifts in a paper mill, and as we drove north, exhausted and depressed, we pondered the awful midnight shift looming ahead. Any joy we experienced at Woodstock was within a narrow sliver in time.

John was 18 years old; I was 19. We were college-dropout-party-guys and proud of our chaotic lifestyles. We never thought of the relationship between our self-absorbed, uncontrolled lives and our unhappiness. As I think back and make judgments, it occurs to me the ones who were creating something worthwhile were the "straight" kids. They were not immune to down times, but in their willingness to conform to the reality of the world, they were more in control, and yes, happier.

The lure of dancing in the meadow is an invitation to illusionary bliss. Truth is, orderliness and attention to detail are the roots of peace. Proof? Consider the indisputable reverse-logic: In any setting, the opposite of peace—disorder—always leads to desperation.

So today, too many of us are distracted in the static snapshot of how we think things should be instead of working with the mechanics of the world as it is. *Life is not a snapshot; it's a real-time, streaming video—and the video plays on whether we participate in it or not.*

Distracted

So, 40 years later, what is the relevance? For those who still buy into the '60s mystique, an unfounded assumption smolders. It whispers there is chaos all around, that systems and organization are bad, with big brother right there behind the curtain, steering things in the wrong direction.

This thread of paranoia leaves too many of us obsessing about things that are out of our control, and the obsessing distracts us from taking the actions that would truly make us free! It's not "the system" that holds us back, it's a flaw in our perception. As we focus on events outside of ourselves we can't control, we overlook the imperfect aspects of our own lives that we *can* control. We don't recognize that *recurring personal pain is not the result of a flawed world, but a result of our own flawed personal systems—systems that we can repair!* We don't grasp that experiencing peace and prosperity—nothing less than freedom—comes from paying strict attention to the details of our own lives.

If we don't overtly take control of the churning forward flow of ourselves, the mistake of a lifetime is just around the corner and ready to flatten us when least expected. More endemic and less dramatic, small inefficiencies will take us to the same dark place. *Life carries on whether we like it or not, and this churning flow is at our command only if we pay close attention to the details.*

Back in 1974, as the three of us headed to Oregon, what I still didn't understand was that the successful people in life, the people who create and build and contribute—the ones who have poise, freedom, and wealth—are self-disciplined, organized, and methodical. I didn't understand that peace and prosperity arrive *after* the mechanics.

Illustrations

At the end of most chapters are real-life illustrations of various aspects of the *Work the System* method. Some relate to the previous chapter, some don't.

The examples will remind you that the essence of the *Work the System* method is a new perspective. Instead of wallowing in the middle of it all, the new vantage point is "outside-and-slightly-elevated." Only from an exterior vantage point can systems be examined and adjusted to perfection.

Use the scenarios to think about systems in your own life.

A Dearth of Systems

Woodstock: From a systems-perspective, what happened there? One system that worked well was the system that delivered the music. The technicians were adept and the equipment functioned adequately. The musicians showed up which meant the transportation system worked—the entertainers were delivered by helicopter. The location (Yasgur's farm) worked.

What systems did not work? Outside of the above, you name it: The ticketing system failed with all the surrounding fences coming down early in the process—a disaster for the promoters who sponsored the event. The sanitation and medical systems were overwhelmed and borderline dysfunctional. If overt police protection had been required, it would have been mayhem because there was little more than a tiny contingent of informal private security guards.

The musicians, the "music-generating systems," were too often flawed: Many were drug-impaired and did not perform to their best abilities. The dysfunctional-system list goes on. Every system having to do with regular day-to-day necessity was not up to the task: communication, commerce, protection, food, water, emergency medical care, etc.

Of course, from a personal systems-perspective, few in the audience were physically prepared, even in a rudimentary way. To compound things, drug use was hampering rational thinking. Everyone was in the middle of everything, and chaos was a breadth away, held back by no more than the luck of the draw.

One day of peace and music? Yes, OK, that's true. Two days? Well, the drugs helped maintain a calmness, but things were stretched. Three days? Whew! It was an exodus *out* of there! If there had been four days? For those die-hards who might have remained, it would have been a sordid, nasty affair.

Yes, it's true. It was the love and goodwill of the people that made the festival work. But that sliver of "bliss-time" was narrow and can't serve as an example of how a life can be lived day to day. "I love you, man" is not enough for the long term. There must be fore-thought, organization, and rational thinking, and that means well-attended systems.

It's mechanical, just the way of the world.

CHAPTER 3

A SYSTEM
OF SYSTEMS

King Arthur (after Arthur cut off both of the Black Knight's arms):
Look, you stupid bastard. You've got no arms left!"
Black Knight: *"Yes I have!"*
King Arthur: *"Look!"*
Black Knight: *"It's just a flesh wound!"*

Dialog from the 1975 movie, *Monty Python and the Holy Grail*

Read Between the Lines

Here I discuss my company, Centratel, but keep in mind this is about more than problems, solutions, and systems within a business or in a job. As we go through the details it is important for you to read between the lines to understand the picture I paint is also applicable to personal life outside of the business/work environment.

To explain the *Work the System* framework, one reason I use Centratel as an illustration is because it is an easily understood "primary" system that is composed of sub-systems—Centratel is a closed, "system-of-systems." It provides simple, real world, cause-and-effect depictions. Again, dig deeper than the specific business scenarios I describe and see that the principles are universal and therefore applicable to your own most important system-of-systems: *you.*

Work the System Glossary

Let's speak the same language. I will use all of these terms in Part One although some of them are not tackled in-depth until later. Review them carefully now. I define these words and terms as applicable to the *Work the System* method. These are "building block" concepts so I do not present them alphabetically, i.e., in many cases you'll need to understand concept A before you tackle concept B.

- **Recurring:** A process that happens over and over again.

- **System, Sub-system:** A package of sequentially related actions and/ or events that has a singular purpose. A linear process. Here, we are interested in *recurring* systems. Note that the terms *system* and *sub-system* are interchangeable depending on context. From Wikipedia: "From *Latin* systēma…is a set of *entities*, real or abstract, where each entity interacts with, or is related to, at least one other entity."

- **Primary System or System of Systems:** Composed of sub-systems; a whole, encapsulated entity with an ultimate purpose; an organism to itself, such as a personal life, business, job, car, or relationship.

- **Work the System Mindset:** The crystal clear internal understanding of the mechanical way the things of this world operate. Typically arriving as an epiphany in a moment of time, this viewpoint makes it easy to isolate systems for examination and modification.

- **Work the System Methodology:** The mechanical process of establishing goals and then perfecting the systems that will attain those goals.

- **Working Man's (and yes, Working Woman's) Philosophy:** A set of beliefs stemming from the hard, cold, sometimes dirty realities of the job site—the job site of a life where a carefully composed blueprint directs the assembly of individual pieces into a superb end-product.

- **System Management:** A focus on maximizing the efficiencies of systems in order to prevent recurring problems, increase production, and garner more personal time. It is the opposite of fire-killing in which one tackles a problem while not considering the root cause of it.

- **System-improvement:** The heart of the method. A search-and-repair process; the system management effort of tooling a system into perfection and then, for business or work, documenting that system so its perfect functioning will recur. It is the day-to-day mindset of a manager; the prime responsibility of an organizational leader. For a personal life, it's an imbedded inclination to seek out and identify personal systems, then to hone each to perfection.

- **Strategic Objective:** The first of three primary *Work the System* documents. It's short, a single page in length, an individual's thought-out and carefully constructed "guidebook." It defines overall goals, describes methodology, and prescribes action. It gives direction for making major and minor decisions. An essential instrument for a business and for personal life. (See Chapter 13).

- **General Operating Principles:** The second of the three primary *Work the System* documents; A two- to four-page collection of "Guidelines for Decision Making" that is congruent with the Strategic Objective. Essential for the work environment and in a simplified and shorter format, for one's personal life. (See Chapter 14).

- **Working Procedures, Procedures:** The third of the three primary *Work the System* controlling documents. These are instructions that describe how the individual systems of the company or the job are to operate. They are end-products of the system-improvement process. Written Working Procedures are not necessary for personal life. (See Chapter 15).

- **Job or Profession:** One has to show up in order to earn money.

- **Business:** One does not have to show up in order to earn money.

- **Off the Street People:** As a business owner, or for anyone in a business management position, these are the people who will "do the work." They could be laypeople or professionals, depending on the situation. They are not mind readers and may not be experienced in the given field. But because of thorough documentation and systems strategies, they don't necessarily need specific experience in order to perform superbly.

- **Outside-and-slightly-elevated:** Opposite the common vantage point in which the viewer is integral to the workings of his or her day. The essential perspective of the *Work the System* methodology is external, looking down. The view downward also encompasses the viewer: Objectively, we see ourselves down there, too, as separate and distinct.

- **Linear:** For our purposes, this is how most systems execute themselves, in a 1-2-3 step progression. Yes, there are always minor external and internal variables which prompt physicists to construe that most systems are, strictly speaking, non-linear. But, here in the real world, we are streamlining things so events can be understood and manipulated. A linear system is not chaotic. Within its context it is logical, reliable, simple to understand, and simple to improve.

- **Tweaking:** The opposite of neglect. The elemental, boots-on-the-ground mechanics of making incremental system-improvements that ultimately produce hyper-efficient primary systems.

- **Project Engineer:** The role of a business owner or manager who adopts an outside system-improvement/management posture rather than an inside, doing-the-work role. For a personal life, it's real-time positioning in which one's systems are contemplated, analyzed, and then controlled. (See Chapter 11).

- **Error of Omission:** A less-than-perfect situation that occurs because someone didn't do something. It is the cause of the majority of problems in the world and in personal lives.

- **Perfect:** 98 percent accuracy. In the *Work the System* world, 98 percent is "perfect" because trying to achieve that additional two percent demands too much additional energy. It's the law of diminishing returns in action, and it's a catch-22: The enormous energy required for this additional tiny increment of improvement is in itself imperfection because that energy could have been put to much better use elsewhere.

- **"99.9 Percent of Everything Works Fine":** It's the truth! Note the unstated premise that there is a penchant for efficiency in the world; that systems *want* to work perfectly.

Answering Service Overview

For 15 years Centratel struggled for survival, always at the brink of disaster. Why did this "system of systems" begin to prosper in year 16? Focused attention, terrific staff, targeted marketing, and a consistently high quality product went a long way, but they were not the *cause* of the turnaround (and were, instead, *byproducts* of the cause). The root cause of the turnaround was the discovery and application of the principle that management must focus on improving systems, not in performing the work or in repeatedly killing fires.

Hear this: *Consistently high quality products or services, a stable staff, and profitability are the RESULT of the quality systems that produce them, not the reverse.* We'll get to the details about all that soon. First, here is a quick background sketch of Centratel.

Centratel is a high-tech, national telephone answering service. As I write this, our gross yearly revenues are just over two million dollars and the company employs 30 people. As a third party "outsourcing" business, a telephone answering service (TAS) employs telephone service representatives (TSRs) who process incoming telephone calls (from "callers") for various businesses (clients). Any answering service's purpose is to take messages from the client's callers and then deliver those messages to the client. Clients include medical and veterinary clinics, funeral homes, property management companies, HVAC operations, high-tech firms, and the like. These are businesses that must provide 24/7/365 human interaction to their customers or patients. Since these businesses can't cover their phones 24/7, they must employ an answering service to screen and process after-hours calls. A smaller group of clients use an answering service during daytime hours when incoming phone traffic is more than they can handle, or if they don't have a physical office.

At Centratel, up to twelve TSRs (depending on call traffic) sit at workstations and field one call after another, with the incoming calls arriving randomly from any one of approximately 1,000 accounts. Sometimes, when traffic is heavy, calls come in like machine gun fire. One call will be from a nervous husband whose wife is on the way to the hospital to have a baby; the next call from the panicked owner of a horse that has colic; the next from an apartment tenant who has accidentally locked herself out of her apartment. You get the idea.

Our TSRs take messages, record them in a database, and then deliver them in a variety of ways including pager, cell phone, voice mailbox, e-mail, or fax. It is an unbelievably complex enterprise, with multitudes of human and mechanical systems working simultaneously. Caller, client, and TSR communication is constant and nearly always time-sensitive. At Centratel, each of our accounts provides unique and exact instructions on how to handle callers and process messages.

So, within any TAS business there is enormous opportunity for error, and without strict system protocol and superior staff, it's an understatement to say it's a seething breeding ground for chaos.

The TAS industry stretches back to the first days of telephones. As they were then, answering services are now: non-stop operations. This all-the-time activity engenders another interesting challenge: odd working hours for TSRs as they come and go from the office at all times of the day and night. It can be a tough way to earn a living, a major personal challenge for those who work the odd schedules. Our more senior TSRs have worked themselves into traditional daytime shifts but new people must earn their stripes, enduring the tougher schedules until they can move into better slots that open due to staff attrition and company expansion. In any case, the pay and benefits are very good at Centratel, close to double industry averages.

It's a fascinating industry but it is in decline. In 1975, the total number of TAS businesses in the United States was over twenty thousand, most of which were small mom-and-pop operations. Now, survivors are larger—but perhaps only two thousand total—and as a percentage of the overall population, the number of TAS clients has also decreased considerably. Cell phones, paging, voice mail, the internet, and telephone company switching options have cut deeply into the industry. Nevertheless, plenty of businesses still require a real-live human being to process their incoming calls, and the market will not be disappearing any time soon.

More than two decades ago, I contemplated entering the TAS business for three reasons (and these reasons are still good general considerations for anyone going into business).

First, it intrigued me that it was all about people and communication.

Second, revenues would be passive. If managed properly, I would not have to be physically present in order to receive income. I was young and new to business, but it seemed to me that making money without having to show up to do the work would beat being a doctor, attorney, teacher, psychologist, working man, or any number of occupations where the individual who provides the service is the centerpiece of the endeavor.

Third, revenues would be recurring—clients would continuously use our services and pay us over and over again. With clients paying monthly, generating new income would not be a full-time, daily challenge. I reasoned, if the product was superior and our clients were happy, the money would constantly flow.

Centratel

So, on December 1, 1984, at the age of 35, I bought Girl Friday Telephone Answering Service, an ailing TAS in my hometown of Bend, Oregon. The total purchase price was $21,000, the downpayment, $5,000. There were 7 employees, 140 clients, and 400 square feet of office space.

Now the owner of a business, I changed the name of the company to reflect the changing times, and—per the arrogant cockiness that surrounded me in those days—announced to anyone who would listen that we would someday be the highest quality telephone answering service in the United States. Despite my bravado, I had no idea how we would achieve such a goal (and as I think back on those days and how I went about things, the words "brash" and "clueless" enter my mind).

Events did not unfold as anticipated.

The business was a disorganized nightmare and my personal life, what there was of it, devolved into shambles. Within a year, I went through a divorce and then proceeded to do my best to bring up my two children as a single, custodial parent.

Although always on the brink of disaster, Centratel grew in volume—but profits never increased. It was an epic struggle and as the first years passed, the "Best in the U.S." goal disappeared behind the cloud of chaos.

For a decade and a half, I endured moment-to-moment turmoil, working long, long hours, often in excess of 100 hours a week, always just scratching by financially. I got sick from the pressure but powered on anyway. The only thing that would stop me would be if I dropped over unconscious from stress and sheer fatigue (and after 15 years of relentless pressure, this became more than a possibility).

Then, as previously mentioned, I had an unforeseen insight and began to apply the *Work the System* principles to my business and my personal life. An earth-moving event, the new vision deeply affected me, subtly changing the way I perceived the world. With this new outlook, all aspects of my life improved as the turbulence subsided. It became a different world at Centratel and at home.

Just after my "enlightenment," I brought a partner into the business—a good man, an acquaintance I had always respected—and I was no longer in it alone. Now I had a second set of professional eyes, and with his stock purchase, a financial boost. Coincidentally, my partner's name is Sam, too.

The next few chapters describe the odyssey in detail. As you read, think of parallels in your own life.

Installing a Preventative System

Sometimes we install a system and it doesn't do much. We achieve the desired effect by the mere existence of it.

At Centratel, we knew a few of our employees spent time "cruising the net" on company time. It was impossible to track these sleight-of-hand excursions and the closest we could get to managing the problem was to walk around a corner and find a staff member covertly close a non-Centratel screen upon our approach.

So, we installed special software that tracks and logs internet activity.

The software solved the problem instantly and completely. We track everyone's activity including who goes where, and how much time is spent "cruising."

Have we ever tracked down bad behavior with it? Yes, when we first installed it without announcing what we had done, the usual suspects emerged. Did we say anything to them? No, it wasn't necessary because we knew that once we announced the installation, and noted it in our Employee Handbook, the people who were abusing the system would change their behavior. Did they? Yes.

Have we had subsequent abuses? No. We check the logs each month but there is never a problem.

Another example of the installation of a preventative system? Drug testing. And, police and military.

With these systems, the preventative aspect is key. The systems are intended to halt problems before they occur.

CHAPTER 4

THE ATTACK
OF THE MOLES

Guy Fleegman (Sam Rockwell): *I don't like this. I don't like this at all.*

Gwen DeMarco (Sigourney Weaver): *They are so cute!*

Guy Fleegman: *Sure, they're cute now, but in a second they're gonna get mean, and they're gonna get ugly somehow, and there's gonna be a million more of them.*

—Dialog from the 1999 movie, *Galaxy Quest*

Surviving

All answering services perform the same function for their clients, and my newly purchased TAS was no exception. At all hours of the day and night, our TSRs took incoming calls from our clients' callers on Lily Tomlin-like, mechanical "cord boards," recording messages on small printed forms we called "message slips." When clients called in, the TSRs read the written messages back to them. It was the mid-1980s when, for much of the business world, word processing and computer database management were little more than future concepts. We were a "mom and pop" service, and for a "flat rate" of $35 to $45 per month, we processed as many calls as the client could send us. During the day, two TSRs handled calls. After hours, one.

From the beginning and for 15 subsequent years, I managed all aspects of the operation myself.

From the first day of ownership, it was a madhouse as most of our clients had taken advantage of the flat-rate arrangement and used our TSRs as their full-time telephone receptionists. Our staff was overwhelmed with call traffic and so the quality of call handling was abysmal. At first, because I had no understanding of the internal mechanics of the answering service business, all I could do was watch and wonder.

When I bought the business, the monthly total gross revenue of $5,500 was not enough to cover wages, rent, telephone company costs, and everything else including supporting myself and my two children. The business had been mine two months and disaster was already at hand. ("Disaster at hand" was to become a serial catch-phrase over ensuing years). Standing by without taking action would be a quick ticket to failure, so with my staff, and my eight- and ten-year-olds depending on me, I had to do something immediately.

Here, my brashness would be useful.

It was a fortunate irony the business was in terrible shape when I bought it—some positive aspects lay hidden. After just a few weeks the major problems were obvious even to me, someone with zero knowledge of the industry. It was clear I must immediately correct the most glaring inefficiency: a customer-pricing schedule that was too low. The fortunate part was the service rates were extremely low—we could raise them significantly and still remain competitive.

I informed our clients by letter that service rates were going up and we would start charging for the actual call traffic we handled for their individual accounts. I told them a large price hike was the only choice if we were to stay in business.

So we dropped the "flat-rate" billing plan and began counting message slips, billing each account for actual messages processed by TSRs.

On average, this *tripled* our customers' cost, and immediately one third terminated service, while others cut down the call traffic forwarded to us. The decrease in incoming call traffic allowed our TSRs to spend more time on each call, and because they were less rushed, the quality of service improved a bit—the first of many incremental quality improvements that were to accumulate over the years ahead.

As a sidelight, and to illustrate just how low our service rates had been, even with the 300 percent increase, our prices remained significantly lower than our much larger local TAS competitor.

Despite losing 30 percent of our total client base, our gross monthly revenues doubled overnight to $11,000.

The huge increase in gross revenue was terrific, but equipment had to be upgraded and wages raised. So, even with the additional income, the company was still not profitable. We raised rates again in six months and then again six months after that. One year later we did it again. Nonetheless, we continued to struggle.

This just-barely-hanging-on predicament endured. Over the next decade and a half, we couldn't get ahead even though we managed to multiply the gross income by a factor of 12. Our revenue growth was due to rate increases as well as the new clients we gained because of our growing reputation for quality—quality that had risen from terrible to marginal (but marginal quality was better than our local competitor who remained at the "terrible" level because of their own self-induced chaos). The rise in income was always matched by increases in operating costs. The largest increases were in wages, health insurance, retirement, and other benefits to the TSR staff.

Within three years of buying the company, we moved to larger office space. We stayed in that location for 12 years and then moved to an even larger space. We continued to grow, but the turmoil and cash flow problems increased.

For almost two decades, my small salary didn't change while my 60-80-100 hour workweeks continued unabated. I had no life outside the business, and any personal time went to my children.

As the years passed, I learned the ropes and prided myself on being expert at every facet of the business, able to perform any function. In moments, I could move from scheduling staff, to handling customer complaints, to solving telephone company problems. I could interview a job applicant for a TSR position one minute, and in the next, put together a plan for adding a computer system. I could prepare payroll while I signed up a new account and then head to the bank to plead my case for yet another small loan.

I did it all, including being there for my kids (and as a single parent of children in school, the task-juggling at home rivaled the task-juggling at the office).

What a feeling of power, as I simultaneously solved multiple problems. I was a master of survival-juggling! How heroic!

But in my arrogance, and swept up in the endless fire-killing, I was spinning my wheels and headed for destruction.

THE NUMBERS ARE GLOOMY

Statistics show that of one hundred new business start-ups, only twenty will remain after five years. Then, in the next five years, four of that remaining twenty will still be functioning. In another five years, three of those four will disappear, leaving one out of the original hundred. That's a ninety-nine percent small business fatality rate over a fifteen-year period.

Gauge your own situation and look ahead. Are you an employee of a small business? If so, the numbers are not on your side. Or, do you own a small business? If so, there is hope because you have the power to get inside and direct it.

Too often, what ends a business or a job, or casts an onerous spell on a life, is "death by a thousand cuts." This is relentless erosion caused by recurring inefficiencies and their offspring: fire-killing and distraction. These time-wasters undermine efforts to create and sell a good product that has a viable market. And in personal life? You've seen it in those who can't seem to break out of the bad-luck syndrome. For business or personal life, it's not mysterious bad luck that takes people down. It's serial inefficiency. The great news is that inefficiency is easy to correct if one can see the cause of it.

This Survival Thing Is Killing Me

With the exception of whatever happened to be going on in my mind on any given day, there was no direction for the company. Centratel grew because of a booming local economy and my knack for foiling the reaper at the last minute.

Through those years I was the constant factor in the management equation, single-handedly fixing whatever needed to be fixed, smoothing out the rough spots, and keeping the ball rolling no matter the day of the week or time of the day.

Long-term planning didn't happen and routine maintenance was no more than a vague concept for the future. My role was fire-killer. If a problem came up, I would take care of it. I always took care of it. Who could argue with those noble theatrics? I trudged on.

As the ten-year anniversary passed, my days spiraled downward into ever deepening chaos. I leaped from one predicament to the next as crises multiplied. The days were crammed with cash flow crunches, chronic staff absenteeism, and a myriad of customer complaints. The office temperature was too cool—or too warm. We would run out of critical office supplies and not have the time to leave the office to replace them. Turnover among TSRs was incessant as scheduling was haphazard, put together at the last moment. In year ten, we went through over 60 new people—and my total staff was 12. TSRs would start work, stay for a week, and quit. My employees were unhappy, and the same held true for our clients as they endured a still marginal quality of service.

Making payroll was always a challenge and every two weeks it was a last minute, hold-your-breath epic as we gambled that all payroll checks would clear. Twice they didn't, and I went to employees' homes with cash to cover their bounced checks, pleading with them to give me another chance and come back to work *right now*.

I was the heroic jack-of-all-trades, the master fire-killer who would work as long and as hard as necessary.

The years drifted by. My teenagers would wait for me at home as I flailed around at the office late into the night, killing one fire after another.

I would finally come home, check to see if they were sleeping OK, and then stumble into my bedroom and climb into bed. I would lie there exhausted with that deep, deep fatigue way down inside the chest.

Bills were not paid on time, both at Centratel and at home. Collectors called day and night. Checks bounced, and NSF-check fees accumulated, sometimes over a $100 at a time. The people at the bank felt sorry for me as they marveled at both my endurance and my ineptitude in keeping the money straight.

For awhile, my two teenagers shared the office space with me because we could not afford a place to live. They went to school during the day, and at night slept in a bunk bed in the back room of Centratel's small office. When I could, I slept alongside them on a cot.

The years passed, and the kids went off to college.

Then, in one long stretch of seven months, I answered calls as the sole TSR on the midnight to 8 a.m. shift *every night*. Here's the kicker: During those seven months, Monday through Friday of every week, I also worked in the daytime from 8 a.m. to 5 p.m., taking care of 100 percent of administrative and management tasks. This meant each weekday my shift began at midnight and ended no sooner than 5 p.m. the next day. Weekends were a relief because I only had to work the midnight to 8 a.m. shifts. My workweek exceeded 100 hours.

During those months I was sleeping just a few hours each night and never in a single stretch because, as midnight TSR, it was necessary to wake up each time a call came into the service. Throughout the shift, the medical and veterinary emergency calls came in at a steady pace. Lying on the floor with a pillow and blanket, there was the occasional straight hour of sleep. After my seven month stretch of graveyard shifts, when I fell back to my normal 80-hour workweeks, it was impossible to sleep through the night even when there was the opportunity. My body had become hard-wired to perform a day's work with three hours of sleep.

Of course, there was no social life. I didn't have time for friends.

I wondered how soon my physical and/or mental collapse would occur, but there was no relief due to my intimate involvement with every aspect of the operation. The business would immediately fail if I wasn't there moment-to-moment. Everything depended on me.

For the body and the mind, few things are worse than long-term sleep deprivation, and eventually I succumbed to the stress. It was a depression/exhaustion that inhibited every thought and action. My performance became clumsy in the face of escalating problems. Things were getting worse by the day, and after 15 years of accumulated trauma, the end was near.

If things were so bad, why didn't I throw in the towel and get a regular job? I was terrified of rejoining the work force as someone's employee. The thought of having to get a job sent shivers down my spine. After all those years of being on my own, working for someone else would be a nightmare for me *and* for my employer. I rationalized, if I am in Hell, at least it's *my* Hell.

Working Hard: A Distraction from Reality

I had no idea what to do other than what I had always done, to dig in and take care of whatever came up. I had become expert at handling every detail of the TAS business, but it was horrible and the fire-killing got worse.

I kept at it. My existence was like the Whac-A-Mole® game in which little grinning-faced moles keep popping their heads up in any one of a dozen holes. I would whack one mole and two more would emerge. My hammer would respond in a flurry and the mole heads would be rammed back down into their tunnels, one after the other. It was a beautiful performance; a remarkable demonstration of dexterity and power.

But despite the heroics, the game was distracting me from seeing what was necessary to fix my business and life. Centratel's daily disaster control was diverting me from facing the reality that I was playing a game that should not be played; a game I could never win.

A Potent, Visceral Reminder from the Folks at NASA

A space shuttle craft is arguably the most complex machine ever built by man—and a launch is perhaps the most magnificent display of human system control. I never miss an opportunity to watch the event on TV, real-time.

For maximum impact, it's important to watch a launch *live* on TV, as opposed to watching snippets on the evening news. One day I will travel to the east coast to see it in person, probably with my engineer-brother, Steve....

As you watch a launch, consider the precision of the countdown which relies on thousands of simultaneous and automatic monitoring processes, all overseen by engineers and technicians. The launch executes and tens of thousands of active systems, both on the craft and on the ground, execute independently and in concert; each a precision entity unto itself.

As the engines roar to life and the craft lifts off, questions arise, "How could this take place? How is this possible?"

At the date of publication of this book, there have been 123 flights of which there have been two spectacular, horrible failures. (Allegedly, one or both failures can be explained, to a large extent if not completely, by internal political failures to implement actions based on data that was already available). Yet, considering the incredible complexity of the endeavor, and acknowledging the human penchant for error, one could legitimately wonder why there have not been more failures than these.

Like countless minor failures of the past, these tragedies provide space shuttle engineers information to use to prevent future problems. As time moves on, the chances of minor and overt failure decrease steadily as the space shuttle system is tweaked ever closer to perfection.

Are space shuttle system-improvements, most based on advancements in science, engineering, and mathematics—but many based on previous failure—the result of an outside and slightly elevated vantage point? As you watch the next lift-off, consider that question while you marvel at the miracle: The keynote celebration of human potential, and a potent, visceral illustration of the beauty of the countless systems that comprise our existences.

CHAPTER 5

Gun-to-the-Head
Enlightenment

It is Often Darkest Just Before Dawn.

Sojourner Truth

Despair

For 15 years I pounded my small answering service into some kind of subservient yet mocking submission, carrying on like a perpetual motion machine. But, of course, it was tenuous. Everything *did* depend on me, and if I let up for one moment my world would come crashing down. It was just a matter of time.

Then, on the heels of my seven-month double-shift epic, I hit a brick wall. In my arsenal of last-minute bailout strategies, there was no solution to the deathblow crisis looming just ahead—the inability to cover the next payroll. On payday, my staff would walk out when there were no paychecks, instantly ending my business as our clients raced elsewhere to find another answering service to handle their calls. In a single moment, Centratel would close its doors and everything I had accomplished in the past decade and a half would be lost, not to mention that my staff of 16 would be jobless and my 300 loyal clients would be in crisis.

I was a mentally and physically wrecked 49 year old single-parent facing financial and career oblivion, and it was more than an interesting coincidence the imminent end of Centratel was dovetailing with my almost certain mental and/or physical breakdown. I was desperate, and the doomsday clock was ticking.

THE WHAC-A-MOLE® GAME, PER WIKIPEDIA

"Once the game starts, the moles pop up from their holes at random. The object of the game is to force the individual moles back into their holes by hitting them directly on the head with the mallet, thereby adding to the player's score. If the player does not strike a mole within a certain time or with enough force, it will eventually sink back into its hole with no score. Although game play starts out slow enough for most people to hit all of the moles that rise, it gradually increases in speed, with each mole spending less time above the hole and with more moles outside of their holes at the same time. After a designated time limit, the game ends, regardless of the skill of the player. The final score is based upon the number of moles the player struck."

The Dawn

The payroll was less than a week away when, yet again lying awake in bed late one night, exhausted, I stopped thinking about work details, business philosophies, elaborate theories, or some last minute divine intervention. It was the end, and there was nothing left to examine or ruminate about; nothing left to salvage… except one small thing. In a last gesture of raw defiance, at least I could end things with some self-respect. As a final, last-gasp effort I would either save myself or go down in a blinding flash. This would not end with a whimper. Since everything was lost anyway, why not enjoy one last moment of control?

I lay there in the 3 a.m. darkness of my bedroom and reviewed the blinding-flash possibilities. But something was odd. I was at peace for the first time in years. How could that be? Then, in this bizarre, defiant/relaxed state of mind, questions arose. Without coaxing, and for no apparent reason, two simple, pragmatic questions came charging out of the blackness; general questions that had nothing to do with the specifics of the immediate crisis, questions I had never asked myself before.

"What have I been doing wrong all these years?"

And, this: *"Since the end is coming, what is there to lose if I abandon past assumptions and look at things from a completely different angle?"*

My "what is there to lose" posture was the catalyst. The certain end of Centratel opened my perception gates and gave me the freedom to consider anything. No matter how outrageous, any new idea was an option because there was no further possible downside. I had a few more days to stretch into unknown territory and do some experimentation, because... what did it matter?

Then, answers came.

Physically and mentally sapped, and knowing there was everything to gain and nothing to lose, I underwent an enlightenment of sorts. It sounds corny, but in my mind, I rose out of the jumble that was my life, no longer an integral part of it. Floating upward, "outside-and-slightly-elevated" from the chaos, I gazed down at the details of my business, spread out neatly as if on display on a tabletop. From this bird's-eye perspective, it struck me that *Centratel is a self-contained mechanical device!* It is nothing more than the sum of an assemblage of sequential systems—answering the phone, sales, payroll preparation, scheduling, handling complaints, etc.—each executing in linear 1-2-3 step fashion whereby one step follows another step until the sequence for that particular system is complete. Instinctively, I knew the rest of my life operated in the same way, an assemblage of separate and independent systems, executing in predictable, reliable sequences according to their own individual construction. (Yes, I thought, of course these systems intermingle and affect each other—a holistic assemblage to be sure—but that holism can't mask the separateness of them; the beauty of their individuality.)

My thoughts raced at light speed as I marveled at the simple beauty of it. I understood that my previous vision of the world had been wrong. *The world is not a chaotic jumble of people, objects, and events clanging together in disarray. The world is a place of order and logic; a place of predictability. The world is a collection of logical systems!*

For the first time, I saw Centratel as an enclosed package—an independent, "primary system"—a separate entity, like a human body, airplane, tree, or city. And the primary system called Centratel shared a commonality with all other primary systems in that it was the product of the sum of the myriad of separate sub-systems that composed it.

The logic of it was crystal clear; exquisite.

I saw all of life for what it is: an elaborate collection of linear-executing, 1-2-3 step systems. A line from an old rock song by The Fixx suddenly made sense, and although most of the lyrics are obscure and metaphoric, having to do with a love gone wrong, the chorus is haunting. It went on and on in my head as I lay there: "One thing leads to another. Yeah, yeah. One thing leads to another…"

So, late that night I looked down and saw that my fire-killing mode had been reactionary, defensive, and incredibly inefficient. *I had taken the wrong stance because the mechanics had been invisible to me!* All I did was kill fires, unaware the fires were the products of invisible, dysfunctional sub-systems. These sub-systems had lives of their own and were acting out their 1-2-3 sequences without direction, producing results that were unpredictable at the least, and debilitating at the worst. *My business was out of control because I had been coping with the random products of undisciplined systems.* This was why my role at Centratel was that of a mole-whacker.

My life was chaos not because I was some kind of loser or unfortunate victim of circumstance, but because many of the sub-systems of my life were not being managed. Out of control, these inefficient sub-systems composed the dysfunctional primary systems of my life: my business, health, and relationships.

Who is in Charge of All This?

Exhausted yet exhilarated, I lay in bed floating above it all, looking down on things, savoring the delicious new vision. It was borderline mystical, a sort of near-death experience, but without the tunnel and bright light. For the first time it was clear that my previous perception of reality had been murky and undefined.

How does it go: "One thing I know: Once I was blind but now I see"?

From depths beyond my physical and mental despair, and liberated from my self-absorption, more questions surfaced, ones I had never considered before:

"Who is in charge of all this?" and, *"How does this world continue to function day after day, year after year, millennium after millennium?"*

The answers to those odd questions came fast and hard.

I was startled to grasp there is no human "King of Everything" who directs the goings-on of the world. On its own, and no matter what, this earth keeps turning and life carries on in an overall structured and organized pattern, and...*no one is in charge!*

I floated in my thoughts and wondered at the silent, invisible background organizational strength that keeps things chugging ahead like a train, despite our human race's best attempts to derail the process.

Cyclically, methodically, and for whatever reason, this complex world moves along on its own, adjusting, balancing and counter-balancing. And at the root of it all, and in the middle of it all, uncountable separate linear systems are at work.

The indomitable laws of nature ensure systems work perfectly according to their construction: On this earth, gravity works all the time, everywhere. Over here, one plus one equals two, and over there, one plus one also equals two! The laws of nature cause the mechanics of the world to be dependable and predictable, and the gift with which we humans have been blessed is the ability to get in the middle of it all and to manipulate it; to direct our lives to be what we want them to be; to use the laws of nature to our advantage.

And no one human, or group of humans, is in charge!

The World Is 99.9 Percent Efficient

This systems-rationale is not another feel-good, think-positive invocation, and it's not about faith. It's about stone-cold mechanical reality.

Think about the systems of our lives and then do the numbers. We wake, shower, eat, dress, go to work, and proceed through the day to return to our loved ones in the evening. Then we watch TV, read, and we go to bed early—or we stay up late. At some point we go to sleep, and then we awake again the next morning. Everything works fine 99.9 percent of the time.

That's the cursory overview. Break it down and sequentially note the other events of the day's chronology. It will be thousands of items long as it includes contributing components such as the coffee maker that works every morning; the car that—despite all of its internal intricacies—operates with the turn of a key and then the turn of the wheel; the office we occupy; the complexities of the work we do; the paychecks we receive for doing that work. Consider the process of sharing information back and forth with those around us: one-on-one, voice mail, cellular phone, e-mail, the written word… each is a system and 99.9 percent of the time each works flawlessly!

Envision the system we call TV: We only have to push a button when we want to watch… and this incredibly complex mechanism jumps to life every time! Beyond the physical TV itself, consider the myriad of organizations that puts together the programming that appears on it. Then, switch gears and think about the lawn mower, the water that flows from the kitchen tap, the ubiquitous electricity that comes to our homes to give life to a host of devices, each a complex system of its own.

Contemplate the clothes we wear, the shopping we do, the work we perform. Consider the gas pumped into our cars at gas stations. In some faraway place, sophisticated mechanisms extract oil from the ground. Then people transport it via high-tech boats, trucks, and pipelines to refineries where the oil is converted into gasoline via complex refining processes. Next, truckers deliver the gasoline to uncountable convenient locations so we can pump it into our cars whenever we feel like it. We never think twice about the intricacies of the drilling/refining/delivery systems, this process of pulling oil from the ground, turning it into gas, and getting it into our cars. And this is just one of the millions of systems that touch our daily lives.

And of course, what about the human body? Consider the amazing complexity of chemicals, electric signals, and mechanics that make it work.

Do these complex systems sometimes fail? Of course! Nonetheless, it's a numbers game, and it is unquestionable that the systems of our lives, taken together, work perfectly more than 99.9 percent of the time.

So far, I have mentioned human systems which are just a fraction of the total systems at work in any given second. Uncountable natural systems add to the numbers and dwarf what man has created, and they all work perfectly according to their scripts.

Once one accepts the world's beautiful systems-dance for what it is, the mystery of it goes even deeper: Consider that primary systems depend on sub-systems and those sub-systems depend on sub-sub-systems branching outward and downward, further and further, to sub-primal levels.

Stop for a moment and attempt to draw it all in. The depth and intricacy of life's fabric is astonishing beyond comprehension.

Try to grasp the beautiful intricacy of life's workings and know that all by itself this world gurgles and percolates along with no overall human supervision. The countless systems that comprise life churn on and on while most of us remain oblivious to the perfection of it; to the mystery of it.

It's interesting that the two most opposite groups imaginable share the wonder of the world's miraculous workings: scientists and the religious.

I am not promoting nor discounting the existence of a supreme being's controlling influence in maintaining this powerful, intriguing efficiency. The point here is that, for whatever reason, the wonderful flow of life carries on exquisitely without some human's direct and overt guidance. The sun comes up and later goes down. Grass grows in the spring and lies dormant in the winter. The tides rise and fall. We go to bed at night to wake up in the morning. The toaster works! The car works! Love comes, love goes, and then it comes again. We live, then we die, and another is born. Systems, systems, systems—everywhere!

A Propensity for Efficiency and Order

I asked myself, could it be the common presumption the world is not functioning well—the world is a mess—is *wrong*? Yes, I realized, that presumption *is* wrong, because in any given life, on any given day, countless events and connections—systems—work perfectly. We don't notice them and so we take them for granted, never appreciating the impeccability of it all. Moreover, the tiny number of systems we consider flawed seem that way only because they are not what *we* want them to be, as they stand in stark contrast to the massive perfection all around them. *We hyper-focus on personal, mechanical, and geo-political systems that are not to our liking and conclude imperfection is the default way of the world.* Swallowed up in this, we see perfection as an anomaly; imperfection as the norm.

That conclusion is backwards.

Overall, the systems of this world work absurdly well: 99.9 percent of everything works just fine, and as I said, even the parts we consider imperfect are that way only because *we* think those parts should be different. (In truth, the world is 100 percent perfect if we discount what *we* want. However, for our purposes, let's not discount what we want. For practicality, let's characterize the world as 99.9 percent perfect...)

I'll say it again, to compound the wonder of the perfection: No single human being—and no committee for that matter—is in charge of all this. The universe, the world, and humanity flow ahead, fueled and directed by the laws of nature or who knows what.

I lay in bed in wired stupor, thinking, since this world relentlessly churns ahead within a framework of countless efficient systems, and since there is no human King of Everything, there has to be an underlying cosmologic propensity toward efficiency and order. *Something out there prefers things to go smoothly.*

God?

This new understanding was the reverse of my previous vision of things in which I saw the world as a place of barely controlled mayhem, tenuously held together by its human masters. I had visualized perfection—a rare thing—as an occasional harmonious chord in a universe more comfortable in its cacophony.

My mind raced, and it struck me that *if the universe has a predilection for order, it should be a simple thing to "climb on board."* Since system inefficiencies comprise such a small percentage of the things of my life, and because I have free will, I should be able to methodically isolate problematic systems and then, one by one, manipulate their mechanics to make them efficient. It should be easy because cosmological bias is on my side—and this bias is not just rooting for efficiency, it's *demanding* it.

The Power and the Why

Is there a real-time analogy for the relentless power that propells the systems of the world? Yes. Find train tracks and stand nearby while a train slams by at full speed. Feel the overwhelming strength and inevitability of it. As the enormous mass of the train surges, feel the invincibility. This is an in-the-guts sense of the universe's mechanical potency and purposefulness. It's *that* deliberate.

The world's turning is powerful and systematic and *that* is the point. *Why* it behaves that way is the human mystery—the ultimate question—but is not the issue at hand. What matters here is this: Despite the common assumption that chaos reigns, truth is, the mechanics of the world work very, very well. And if we can proceed from the premise there is a proclivity for powerful efficiency, rather than society's general assumption that all-is-chaos, we will stop fighting things. Instead, confident and deliberate, we can dig a bit deeper and, step by step, construct the lives we want.

Gumming Up The Works

Of course, it must be said that although there is a regulatory force disposed to keep systems flowing, human freewill enables us to cause havoc on personal and global scales. When a system doesn't produce the outcome we want it to produce because of something we did or didn't do, we must recognize this is the down-side of the human race's gift of being able to influence and control systems.

Dysfunctional systems may comprise just a small percentage of all systems, but for the record, let's state the obvious: We humans are inclined to disrupt things, and for this reason there have been and continue to be horrible problems in the world. The worst of it? In the last century, in fits of narcissistic insanity, tens of millions of people were slaughtered by Hitler, Mao, Stalin, Mussolini, and Pol Pot. These were human systems gone haywire.

And still, the agony continues, at its most virulent in third world countries.

Then there is the self-generated personal pain of our own making, residing within our own thought processes. Add to this the self-inflicted damage caused by the neglect and abuse of the body-systems that we inhabit, not to mention no-fault set backs such as accidents and genetic irregularities: the Forest Gump, "s**t happens," scenario (a brief yet profoundly meaningful phrase).

Large or small, cultural genocide or a missed appointment, the things that go wrong are due to component failures within systems. Within a system, something is not right. Something is gumming up the works.

Despite all this, and notwithstanding the general media's allegations otherwise, the majority of lives move from beginning to end with a minimum of true, overt anguish. When there is trauma, it is most often short-lived. For most of us, pain is a small slice of the pie, and when it happens, it is usually the result of self-inflicted mental anguish and fear—negative constructs within our thinking, not overt external, physical pain. Yes, again, of course there are the notable exceptions. I am not a Pollyanna.

So, because the universe's overwhelming inclination is toward stability and efficiency, the events that go wrong in a typical life are but a small percentage of that life's total events. Systems *want* to be efficient. If a system could talk, it would say, "My single goal—and I am passionate about it—is to accomplish the task that I was built to accomplish!" This means that our personal efforts to make things right are aided by an enigmatic power that works hard to propel those efforts to success. *Within one's life, getting things to work swimmingly is not a difficult task if one pays attention to the mechanics of how things work.*

Late that night, lying awake in bed, I realized the force *is* with you.

SAFETY, COMFORT, AND PC
IN THE FIRST AND THIRD WORLDS

Why are there major differences between life in the Western world and life in, say, Afghanistan or Rural China? Why is life in the West easier than life in the East? A part of the answer is that, in the Western world, there are far more safety and protective systems than in the East, therefore our lives are less in jeopardy. A simple example: In the West, we wear seatbelts in our cars 99 percent of the time. It's the law—and the law is a system. In the many times I have been to the rural far East, I have seldom seen a driver or passenger buckle up. In most third-world countries, there are no enforceable seat belt laws. (Are seat belts actually *in* the cars? Yes, they usually lay buried in the seat cushions—but sometimes the driver has altogether removed them…)

Another example: Here in the West, there are quick and severe penalties for anyone's non-cause, assertive aggression toward another. In much of the East there are few protections and justice systems can be corrupt and impotent, causing person-to-person and governmental crimes to go unpunished.

And the flip side? It is telling that the annoyance of the politically correct is nowhere but in the West. This is a result of a culture trying too hard to regulate. It's system-thought taken to the extreme by manipulative people whose basic needs are satisfied and who have the time and energy to attempt to channel the thoughts and actions of others. To the rural Asian, there is no PC thinking, as life is negotiated via just a few systems, systems having to do with survival. In most of the world, people don't have the luxury of expending energy on PC gyrations.

For a Westerner, it is a good thing to live for a while in a third world household. It's an abject lesson in fundamental priorities, personal humility, and root systems.

Component Failures and Semi-Enlightenment

For me, one plus one equals two. For you, one plus one also equals two. The natural mechanics of the world are reliable and can be trusted. And human-devised systems will also operate reliably if they are put together properly and then maintained. If they are not put together correctly and/or they are not maintained, they will fail to produce the results we want.

Few people think their problems are a result of system failure. Most see their troubles as isolated events, blaming fate, horoscopes, bad luck, karma, God, the devil, the neighbor, competitor, family member, weather, the President, Congress, liberals, conservatives, global warming, too much

TV, lack of money, too much money, the educational system, or just a world gone bad. And most see problems as overwhelming in number: an onslaught from "out there," only to be fended off by super-human efforts. For many, the excuse/blame list is endless. I had been a life-long resident of that camp, but when the hammer-blow vision engulfed me, things shifted. I would never live in that place again.

I now float through the day in fascination. Instead of wallowing in a hodge-podge of unpredictability and fire-killing, I see everything as part of one structured system or another. This real-time "outside-and-slightly-elevated" perspective has channeled peace and prosperity into my life and in the lives of those who depend on me. OK, call it a semi-enlightenment.

Negatives will sometimes worm their way into my day, most often due to my own failures. It's not often, though—not any more.

This life I lead is a result of actions, actions rooted in my gut-certainty that, *in the systems that compose the world's workings, there is not a cosmic inclination for chaos. Rather, there is a default propensity toward order and efficiency.* Without question, I know inefficiency and its attending pain occur because of rare and isolated component problems within otherwise perfect systems.

The Heart of the Methodology

Now we are at the essence of making things better "on the ground." By fixing a life's individual systems—by identifying them one at a time and then rebuilding them one by one—order, control, and peace accumulate incrementally. However, the improvements in these rebuilt systems must be made permanent or the systems will slip back into dysfunction due to random outside influence. In the workplace, permanence happens first by creating written descriptions of how systems are to operate, and second, by making sure responsible parties follow the steps described in the documentation. We'll get to those details in Part Two.

Once systems are examined and flawed components are exposed and repaired ("tweaked"), systems will produce the desired result. Creating new contributing systems and altogether eliminating dysfunctional systems will do the same. And since this is all mechanical, when the changes are performed and then locked in, improvement is both instant and permanent.

For your personal situation, not only can you count on an overwhelming bias toward efficiency, it's probable you don't have a whole lot of systems to tweak, create, or delete. It won't take long to get things straightened out.

Now, we are at the heart of the Work the System *methodology. These lives we live are composed of countless linear systems, many of which are under our direct control. These systems are the invisible threads that hold the fabric of our lives together. If there is an outcome that doesn't suit us, we can change that outcome by making a component adjustment within a system, adding a system, or eliminating a system. In a life's rejuvenation, it will typically be "all of the above."*

Whether an outcome is to your liking or not, the underlying system is performing exactly as it was constructed. You are not at the mercy of mysterious conspiring forces or of the swirling backwash of chaos. If it is in your power—and so much that affects you *is* in your power—you *can* fix things! What of those systems you can't fix because they are out of your control? Relax. If you can't fix something, don't worry about it. Do what you can, walk away and accept it, or ignore it. But, for sure, don't spend time or energy agonizing over it. If you live in a democracy, vote and then don't complain. If you have a problem with a co-worker, talk to him or her and then don't obsess about the outcome. If you don't like the TV program, change the channel or turn off the set.

Do what you can and/or let it go. Save your energy for efforts that will provide tangible positive results within your circle.

The Objective

Back to my story, and the looming crisis at Centratel.

That night in bed, yet another realization struck: My business needed at least one solid objective. From my new vantage point, I could see we had been operating without any pointed purpose. The closest I could come to a reason for the existence of the business was that I hoped we would "make money and be successful." That is the single mantra of the typical small business owner or corporate middle-manager. It is not concrete and directed, but amorphous and wishy-washy.

Not only had I never considered its individual components, Centratel had no direction! Despite my Jack-of all-trades/fire-killer-extraordinaire comportment, I didn't have a grasp of the "why" of Centratel. To compound the confusion, there was no vision for my personal life, either.

This was the birth of the Strategic Objective document.

The Crux of Control: The Systems-Perspective

Without prodding, nor willing it to happen, I stepped outside my life, rose above it, and looked down, never again to settle back down into the seething morass. There was nothing philosophical about this new vantage point. It was mechanical and logical. And late that night the moles were vivid and stark, their game a silly but exact metaphor for my life. I saw the solution to my business problems did not lie in becoming more proficient at whacking mole heads—the solution was to find a way to eliminate the moles altogether. I had to put aside the hammer, root down into those tunnels to find out exactly where those moles hid. Then, when I found them, I would ruthlessly strangle them right there. Their grinning, furry faces would not distract me. And while I was down there taking care of mole extermination, I would find a way to keep any mole relatives from returning later.

Late that night, my perspective on life permanently shifted. Deep in my gut, I grasped that systems were at play everywhere and all the time. My business—and my whole being, for that matter—were the sum total of the systems that composed them. Confident, I would look down on these systems of my life and isolate them one at a time, viewing each as a separate, autonomous entity. One by one, over whatever period of time it would take, I would disassemble and then rebuild them. In addition to the reconstruction, I would add new systems and discard useless ones.

It seemed logical: Creating efficient sub-systems should cause the primary system to be efficient too. And to take this a step further, it seemed to me if the individual sub-systems of my business and my life could be made *more* than efficient, if they were made potent and powerful, then both my business and my life would become potent and powerful, too. Who could argue with that logic?

I just needed to identify individual sub-systems and then, one by one, optimize them.

I hadn't been looking for a revelation but, in my desperation, I got one. It was a vision that bared the simple mechanics of the world; mechanics that had been cloaked by the dissonance of the day. It was a viewpoint that I would hone, and in the big picture and in the smallest snapshots of my life, I would no longer specialize in killing fires, spinning my wheels in futile attempts to stop chaos.

I would no longer manage the results of inefficient systems. Instead, I would expend my energies on perfecting those systems—*and the results would take care of themselves.*

For a decade and a half, although the simple reality had been floating right there in front of me, the mental turbulence of my fire-killing approach had relegated this simple earth-shaking reality to invisibility: *A life's condition is not the result of luck, or of being good or bad. And it's not about intelligence, karma, education, social class, political stance, religious affiliation, or how hard one works. Life is about simple mechanics—the dispassionate mechanics of the systems that compose it.*

So, now I would optimize the mechanics.

No, this new systems-perspective was not just an interesting new concept; it was an electric, life-changing vision. Once the switch flipped in my head late that night, there was no going back. I was a changed man.

Rebirth of the Business

My thoughts raged on. It was uncanny: Supported by indisputable logic, an entire strategy unfolded as I lay there that night.

I thought, "If Centratel is an organism—like a human body, or a watch or a TV—*smooth and efficient operation will depend on a multitude of simultaneously functioning systems that operate automatically.*"

In other words, the business systems I would fix and/or create would have to function without direct moment-to-moment supervision by me, the majority owner, General Manager, and CEO of the company. To be sure, people would be watching things, but I would not be one of those people. The "watchers" would be system-improvement managers who would supervise the systems of the business without my constant over-the-shoulder intrusion. Centratel would become a self-perpetuating organism.

Further, this organism *would* be the highest quality telephone answering service in the United States. We would accomplish this in three steps.

1. We would permanently define the overall goals and strategies. It would be done on paper by creating the "Strategic Objective," and the "General Operating Principles."

2. We would break down Centratel's workings into sub-systems we could understand: processing calls, staff management, client services, equipment, quality control, the methodology for handling client and customer calls, bookkeeping, purchasing, customer services, etc. Then, each of those sub-systems would be broken down into even smaller contributing sub-sub-systems including receivables software, customer complaints, employee recruitment, equipment maintenance schedules, and so on.

3. Once isolated and exposed, we would refine and perfect those systems—one by one—so each would contribute 100 percent toward overall goals and each would automatically execute every time. As needed, we would create new systems from scratch and we would discard systems that didn't contribute. We would document these systems into "Working Procedures," making them permanent by creating black and white guidelines for execution. Through all of this we would be patient as we improved things incrementally. This wouldn't happen overnight.

From Organic to Mechanical

Why does a car perform the same way every time? Why does a city stay in the same place without spontaneously moving to a new location? Why do we, in our lifetimes, continue to be ourselves? The reason is hard mechanical reality: physicality. With the obvious exceptions of fluids and gasses, physical objects don't morph into other physical objects or dissipate into the ether. They are dependable and predictable.

On the other hand, human communication processes—organic processes—are the antithesis of physical substance. The execution of a given recurring communication protocol not only varies among the individuals performing the process but, for any one person, with the time of day, the weather, or mood. Uncontrolled, they are feathers in the wind.

In the workplace, the challenge and the solution is make these ubiquitous organic human processes as solid and reliable as the mechanical objects that surround us. Boring but true, we do this with documentation.

Strength and Resilience

In the process of rebuilding Centratel system by system, strength and resilience would evolve as byproducts. The outside world would continue to challenge us with unexpected shake-ups, but if we constructed the new systems properly, the business would become rugged and adaptable. The inevitable earthquakes would be reduced to tremors. Until this point, earthquakes had been earthquakes, and there had been too many of them.

If what I saw for the business was true—that it was a primary system composed of component sub-systems, each of which could be brought to high efficiency and strength—then it was logical this would be true for the other primary system that was in immediate crisis: my physical and mental self.

The theory and process for fixing myself would be the same as it would be for fixing Centratel. That's the beauty of the *Work the System* method: It applies to any life situation because it deals with fundamental cause and effect—the basic truth of how the world mechanically operates.

Learning How to Sleep

For any recurring problem, there is a path to sorting things out: Take the inefficient system apart and fix the pieces one by one. This is taking a non-holistic approach in order to produce a holistic result.

Earlier I discussed my problems with getting enough sleep. Sleep intertwines with numerous other biological, social, and relationship processes, but in that broad conception, one can't begin to find a solution to improving it. What did I do via systems methodology to cure this problem? I envisioned sleep as an independent, primary system that is composed of sub-systems.

The vision led me to a doctor who specialized in sleep disorders. The doctor's recommendations had a strong theme: reduction of stress. This led me to the sub-systems of yoga, more sensible exercise, and meditation. I would substantially reduce my intake of caffeine, alcohol, and sugar. There were other systems to modify: changing the layout of my bedroom, removing the clock from the nightstand, refraining from reading in bed, and turning the lights off at the same time every night. In addition, I would adopt a more consistent system routine for preparing for sleep. Another thing: Testing indicated my requirements for sleep were less than average—six hours was enough—and so I should avoid lying awake in bed, expecting to get eight or nine hours. Lying there waiting for sleep to arrive was stressful in itself. Instead, I should get up and read, work, or even exercise.

With the help of my regular doctor, I found my blood chemicals were out of balance. Those chemical imbalances affected my sleep pattern and it was a simple matter to fix those sub-system imbalances with supplements.

I had to reduce my hours at the office and that meant getting the company to run itself without me being there every minute. Of course, that transformation was already underway, using the same *Work the System* thinking.

I got back to a healthy sleeping routine over the course of just a few months, literally doubling each night's sleep duration.

Now, if I find that my sleep is less than what it should be, I can trace the problem back to a violation of one of the dozen or so system guidelines I initially identified in my "sleep system-improvement" project.

I attacked the overall problem by isolating the primary sleep system and then breaking it down into sub-systems that could be manipulated. By taking an outside-and-slightly-elevated vantage point, I was able to tweak my sleep process to more and more efficiency, one piece at a time.

CHAPTER 6

EXECUTION & TRANSFORMATION

Action is a great restorer and builder of confidence. Inaction is not only the result, but the cause, of fear. Perhaps the action you take will be successful; perhaps different action or adjustments will have to follow. But any action is better than no action at all.

Norman Vincent Peale

A New World

Until I woke up, my vision of the business was one of a mass of inter-related and confused events. Because of this presumption of chaotic complexity, unraveling was impossible. Observing the workings of Centratel in a "holistic" way, I could not detect nor isolate the internal inefficiencies that kept pecking away at things.

On a subliminal level, the feel-good precept that "everything is related to everything else so we should consider each of our actions in a global way" encourages paralysis while it masks problems. Any possibility of internal improvement is subverted by the assumption that tampering with things over here will upset things over there. The gibberish notion that a butterfly flapping its wings over the jungles of Brazil has an impact on the weather patterns over New Hampshire, is an interesting concept but it evokes a subtle paranoia. Although the concept illustrates the interrelation of things, taking it literally casts a spell of impotence over an individual's inclination to make changes. In the real world of day-to-day existence, the Brazilian butterfly doesn't make a damn bit of difference.

Now I understand the reason I had felt helpless to fix my business and my personal life was because I had seen them as impenetrable entities. I never contemplated the notion of a process that would dissect them into simple sub-systems that I could optimize one at a time. *Instead of fixing the faulty mechanisms, I had been caught up in attending to the recurring problems those hidden faulty mechanisms had produced.*

So the years had crawled by as I whacked the moles. It seemed there was no other option but to wallow in the middle of it and hope for some kind of magical, holistic solution: a huge loan from the bank, the perfect employee, client, or management consultant. Or maybe the hand of God would reach down and save me....

I could have spent my whole life like that!

But now I had the solution. I would disassemble Centratel, fix the pieces one by one, and put them back together again. If I did that, it seemed sensible that the finished product would be superior.

I would create three sets of documents: first, the Stategic Objective which would define us and set goals; second, the General Operating Principles, our "guidelines for decision-making;" third, our collection of Working Procedures that would exactly define every recurring process of the business.

My insights arrived just days prior to the payroll I was going to miss. We had to find the money to pay staff and keep them working so the repair process could begin. With newfound emotional energy, I convinced my credit card company to raise my credit limit a bit so some cash could be drawn. A friend gave me a loan. Offering a discount, I talked a client into paying for a year of answering service in advance. Several staff members agreed to delay cashing their paychecks.

We made it through the payroll crisis.

I created our Strategic Objective and began our Principles document. Then, to my staff, I explained this new vision, what we would do next, and how they were going to assume new management postures. Tentatively, we began creating our Working Procedures: isolating, fixing, and documenting systems one at a time. For examination and repair, we first selected the most flawed system and then moved on to the next most flawed. From the moment of my late night epiphany, we were on a new path of system-improvement and there was no turning back.

Marching ahead without pause, we began to see results as confusion diminished and cash flow came under control. In the first six months, my workweek dropped from 100 hours to 60. Then, in the next six months, it fell below 40.

Much of our early success had to do with the perfection of our internal communication system. Every moment, each of us knew what was going on in other parts of the business, and each of us could make decisions without stumbling in semantics or bureaucracy. (More on communication in Part Three.)

We made all critical systems, both human and mechanical, redundant. A year passed and we confidently hammered on. Customer and staff complaints steadily declined and chaos dissolved into serenity as we relentlessly performed the work of improving systems while finding more time to spend with clients.

Precisely targeting our efforts through our Strategic Objective and Priciples documents, we tackled the obvious recurring protocols, gobbling up inefficiencies. Everything we did met the criteria of the new systems-thinking. We tackled bookkeeping, operations, HR, vendor relations, customer service, quality control, and marketing. Forging ahead relentlessly, we rebuilt and documented several hundred existing systems, one by one. At the same time we created new systems from scratch and discarded useless ones.

Whew!

Through it all, there was some staff turnover. A couple of staff members wouldn't accept the new systems theory and attending documentation. They were replaced by fresh faces who bought into the systems game plan.

(Today, we attract and keep smart, loyal, goal-oriented people because of how we operate. Also, because of our strict systemized approach, we are expert at sizing up people in job interviews. Of course, another reason for our great staff is because our compensation/benefit package is much higher than other businesses in our region, as well as the TAS industry at large. The high wages we pay are a result of the higher service rates we are able to charge, as well as the super-efficient operation itself.)

As error rates plunged, the quality of our answering service dramatically improved, light years better than industry standards. The growth of the business went into high gear and within two years of instituting our new paradigm, we bought out all three of our local answering service competitors (and we bought five non-local ones, as well). We absorbed both of our voice mail service competitors, too. In that two-year period, our TAS client base grew from 300 to 700.

It was system-improvement at its finest, and to this day, we still spend most of our time "working our systems." But now, most of the system improvement work has to do with staying current with technological advances and market permutations.

In reflecting on those years of rebuilding, it took a long time to straighten things out. But as I look back, that's understandable because we were figuring out the details of the *Work the System* methodology from scratch. We invested (and sometimes inadvertently wasted) time and money as we experimented with new concepts, tried to find the right management people, and stumbled with the system documentation.

Our relationship with a third minor partner was of enormous negative impact. That partnership began in the middle of the rejuvenation and included sending some of our call processing chores overseas, which ultimately resulted in a severe loss of clients. This, in turn, led to full-blown legalities. In the end, we were able to buy the partners out of the company based upon a settlement agreement. But it's my guess the bad partnership and resulting litigation cost us between two and three years of progress.

There was a lot to do because in addition to the rebuilding efforts and the litigation, we had a business to run. But, obviously, there was enough energy to do what we had to do in order to prosper. It was a long five years, but I recall them with nostalgia and satisfaction.

As mentioned, despite the setbacks and the additional work load, my physical involvement with the company's daily operations continued to decline. Today, I spend just a couple of hours a week working on Centratel business. One of those hours is for our weekly staff meeting and the other is for paying bills or attending to miscellaneous CEO/GM tasks.

If we were to do this again with what we know now, how long would it take to reach the lifestyle and income we now enjoy? Fewer than 18 months.

Heart and Mind

In parallel with the business resuscitation, there was no time to delay in regaining my personal health. As with the business, I had to change course right away and it was obvious what I must do. I would handle my physical problems with the same systems methodology.

1) **I changed my viewpoint.** What, exactly, was making me ill? My doctor thought I was "depressed," and after gyrating around that theory for way too long, it suddenly became clear this was not the problem. In fact, my problems stemmed from undergoing too much external stress. I got outside and up, looked down, and saw my body as a collection of interacting systems, many of which could be manipulated. My physical being was not a jumble of random happenings to which I could only react; it was a "system of systems" and some of those systems were not performing adequately. I modified certain stress-inducing systems in order to prevent stress-events from occurring in the first place. (The biggest relief was in cutting back my office hours through the systemizing of Centratel.) Finally, to stop creating stress internally, I took the cognitive approach to eliminate negative thoughts as they emerged spontaneously.

2) **I created a personal written plan,** a simple one-page controlling document describing goals and guidelines—a personal Strategic Objective.

3) **Once things got better, I continued to perform the stress-reducing action items on a regular basis.** Always working

toward the ideal, but not always reaching it, this preventative maintenance is what I have to do to stay healthy.

That's it! The mantra of the *Work the System* method is to isolate-fix-maintain. Again, *it is not enough to know what to do. One must take action.* What good is knowledge unless something changes for the better because of it?

STRESS REDUCTION ACTION ITEMS

It started with a simple list on a piece of paper on which I wrote five or six actions that would reduce stress. I carried the note in my pocket for a few days, jotting down additional ideas as they came to mind. My final list included 15 "action items," each a separate system of its own. These items were not special in any way but most people would agree any one of them would help eliminate stress.

Here's the original raw list: work fewer hours, lose 10 pounds, go to the sleep disorder clinic to find out how to sleep, stop ingesting caffeinated drinks, learn meditation and yoga. Exercise vigorously but not excessively at least four times a week. Eat good food. Drink lots of water. Ingest less sugar and salt. Get a blood test every three months and per those tests, take supplements until my chemicals come into balance. See friends at least once a week. Spend more one-on-one time with my kids. Read a minimum of one hour each day: one book and a half-dozen periodicals per week.

As I compiled the list, my thought was that it would be sensible to choose just some of the items on the list, whichever ones seemed best. However, when the list was complete, I decided to implement all 15 items, leaving nothing out. Why should any of them be dismissed, if each contributed to my well-being?

It was a tough, challenging list, difficult to fully implement, but I gave it my best shot. Today, do I live every minute by these standards? No. But I get close.

I viewed each of my action items as separate sub-systems and incorporated them into the overall system that is my life. Because I had been such a mess, it took two years to get healthy again. Fifty years of stress damage was not unraveled overnight.

Paying the Bills

Here is an example of replacing an old system with a new one.

For years, a nagging problem at Centratel was the time and effort it took to pay the monthly bills. The process did nothing for the bottom line and each month required 10 to 14 hours of my time to process 60-80 payables to various vendors. I wrote the checks, entered the transactions into the check register, stuffed the checks into envelopes and mailed them. Then there was the filing and bookkeeping. As we grew, it became too time-consuming for me, so I hired a part-time bookkeeper. But that created another problem because the expenditures were not being questioned by our bookkeeper in the painstaking way I would question them.

The system solution: Our bank's online Billpayer feature. This system is a perfect illustration of *Work the System* thinking and methodology. Now, writing a hard-copy check seldom happens. Ninety percent of recurring monthly bills are the same amount each month so the system is programmed to pay these bills automatically. QuickBooks® will automatically log these monthly payments, too. For a payable in which the billed amount changes monthly, it's an easy matter for me to review the invoice and then insert the amounts both online and in QuickBooks.

Now, again paying the bills personally, I am able to keep a close eye on every cent of expenditure.

This is a prime example of investing time to set up a new system and then benefiting forever from the effort. Over several weeks, it took 15 hours to work out the bugs and program our vendors into the system—the same amount of time that had been required *each month* to pay bills with the old system. Now I spend maybe two or three hours a month to process these payments, a fraction of the time I spent before.

At home? It's the same process. The homeowner association dues, water, electricity and everything else are paid on time with very little input from me.

Are we "outside-and-slightly-elevated"? Yes! Billpayer is the quintessential illustration of systems methodology, an enormous success for us at work and at home.

I will be bold here: If you are not using it now, you should be.

CHAPTER 7

SYSTEMS REVEALED, SYSTEMS MANAGED

… a person needs new experiences. They jar something deep inside, allowing him to grow. Without change, something sleeps inside us, and seldom awakens. The sleeper must awake!

Duke Leto Atreides (Jürgen Prochnow), from the 1984 movie, *Dune*

Note to the reader: This chapter and the next have a meditative quality. You must ingrain the Work the System *method, so in an attempt to get you there, I present these two chapters in a repetitive, almost hypnotic tone. I thickly describe the core of the mindset, while adding some new elements.*

Converging Chains

Your day can be calm, predictable, and under control. Fire-killing, chronic shortages of time and money, gun-to-the-head decision-making, and dealing with less-than-amusing people can be history. Order and calm can replace anxiety.

Starting with a subtle shift of perspective, elimination of chaos is possible.

This is about a simple mindset change that will cause subsequent modification in how you handle the sub-systems that make up the system-of-systems that is you.

The pathway to control—to eliminating chaos—is to discover, examine, optimize, and then manage your mechanical and biological systems.

The dictionary's definition of a system is "a group of interacting, interrelated, or interdependent elements forming a complex whole." That's perfect.

In every aspect of your being, systems are wall-to-wall. In linear 1-2-3 sequences, they are imbedded everywhere, operating all the time. You wake; you study, read, exercise, and eat. You breathe, walk, and digest. You go to work and then you drive to the store to pick up groceries for dinner. You talk to friends and you put gas in the car. You earn money and put it in the bank, and then later, pay the bills. You switch on the light, wash the dishes, talk to your parents. You get online and buy a book using your credit card, and then go to the restaurant and have dinner. Your cell phone is a system too. So are the workings of your house, your career, your profession, and your passion. Then, of course, there is the ultimate system-of-systems that is your body.

Silent and invisible, your systems work without pause. Sometimes they work alone but often they work together. They support and complement each other—and sometimes they fight each other.

These processes—these systems—are most often recurring; not one-time events. And you can make improvements in many of your systems, manhandling them into efficiency, pointing them in the directions you want them to point, producing the results you want them to produce.

As you examine the systems of your life, investigating your way down through the multiplying, expanding, and intertwining root-like chains, you see the composition of each system is of sub-systems, and for those sub-systems, sub-sub-systems.

Turn things around and work your way back up to the top of the converging chains. As they come together and thicken into a single trunk, see that they add up to the primary system which is *you.* You are a system of systems!

The essence of your work, health, and relationships lies within systems and although veiled behind the buzz of everyday consciousness, there is nothing magical or esoteric about them—or about their management. You will see life for what it is, a collection of individual linear systems;

then, in this clarity, you will extract and perfect these systems one by one before reinserting each back into your life. The huge and wonderful irony of these machinations is that peace and prosperity silently enter through the side door....

Nearing Your Epiphany

Grasp that each of the countless systems of your world are *linear* processes. Like computer program code, they execute their steps in sequence. I'll say it again: More often than not, the systems are recurring: They happen over and over again.

This is important, and notwithstanding a physicist's space/time theoretical objections, a system doesn't execute randomly. It operates in a simple, predictable, 1-2-3, step-by-step progression. Ruthless and relentless, it proceeds the same way every single time unless a component is adjusted, removed, or inserted.

Right now, slow things down for yourself. Find a place where you won't be distracted. Visualize each of the following systems, focusing on their 1-2-3 step sequences.

Start with the closed set of sequential actions for driving a car from point A to point B. (Open the car door, get in, put the seat belt on, insert the key in the ignition, turn the key to start the engine, etc).

Describe the specific linear steps—both mechanical and human—involved in finding a potential customer, making a presentation, and closing a sale. Consider the process of interviewing and hiring a new employee and then keeping this person for the long term while maximizing his or her contribution. Think about nurturing a relationship with a spouse, coping with terminal illness, or giving birth. Then there are the mundane processes of preparing a financial report, writing a paper for a college course, raking the yard, or doing the wash.

Go back to the miraculous human body system that propels you through this world with its countless individual biological and mechanical sub-systems, nearly all of which function without any overt guidance, but many of which are under your control, to enhance or to abuse.

Use your imagination and see uncountable system sequences in motion, most going unnoticed—unless there is this deliberate observation. You see that some don't matter too much, but others have an enormous effect on your happiness and the happiness of those around you.

Again, the systems in your life do not execute randomly. They operate one-step at a time, just like computer code. Invisible and quiet, they slide by without fanfare, repeating themselves over and over.

Yes, systems and sub-systems intertwine and affect each other, yet first they are separate entities.

Although most all of your life-systems are automatic, there are many you perform consciously. Focusing on these systems that are under your conscious direction, you'll see that tweaking each to higher efficiency is nearly always possible. You can add brand new systems, too. Others you'll discard.

THE *WORK THE SYSTEM* SYSTEM

The *Work the System* methodology itself is a system. It's the controlling management tool used to analyze and maintain your personal systems. It's the master control mechanism for organizing yourself into an efficient life: A life of serenity, prosperity, and contribution.

System Management

Without exception, each of your personal systems has direction and thrust. Each is headed somewhere, attempting to accomplish something. Systems and sub-systems are channeled by genetically determined patterns, learned formulas, cultural codes, bias based on race and gender, humanitarian predilections, simple self-interest, and of course the standard physical predispositions for appetite, sleep, sex, and survival. And all of them are propelled by a mysterious force that many of us choose to call God.

So each of us is a system-of-systems. But, here's the rub: Some of our personal systems—each of which, always remember, can be visualized as a distinct entity—are headed in oblique directions, confusing our efforts to reach our conscious goals. At best, a system combines efforts with other systems to help us reach desired targets. At worst, an errant component within a system creates problems that manifest themselves chaotically, chronically, and often subversively, contributing to the feeling that one is not in proper control of one's life. That out-of-control feeling is not rare: Many people are *not* in control of their lives, especially if the definition of control includes the qualifier, "I am getting what I want in my life."

The "system-of-systems" view of things sounds complicated, but *the complexity of life doesn't leave you helpless to gain control of things because, one at a time, you can take action on specific system components that you draw out of the complexity.* This is management in its most elemental form, and the beautiful thing is that neither the sheer complexity of it all, nor your propensity to lean in certain directions, will stop you from improving the mechanical/human systems that turn the wheels of your life.

Examined all at once within a primary system, systems are impossible to get under control, but one by one and over a period of time, separate systems can be seen, understood, and managed. One at a time, you can pluck each system out of your life and then improve and channel each to perfect optimization. Do this over and over and see the results: You'll be getting what you want.

How could it be otherwise?

You will no longer be a captive of the snarling jumble that has stymied you until this moment. Now you will step up and outside of things, look down, and take control. *You* will be in charge of what happens to *you*.

It begins now, one step at a time. Be patient with yourself as you start....

You can list a multitude of individual systems that are necessary for just getting through the day, not to mention running a business, holding a job, coping with college, raising children, making retirement vibrant and meaningful—or just staying level-headed while balancing a household, negotiating with family members, and providing an income. (I was a single parent for 15 years and—don't argue with me—this role is the supreme test of a human's ability to simultaneously kill fires, build something for the future, and stay sane.)

In our culture it is common to call the management of the day's myriad of events "multi-tasking." Here's another: "poly-phasic activity." These are flawed expressions because they suggest the performance of multiple simultaneous tasks is some kind of heroic accomplishment.

Per the *Work the System* method, the term "system management" is what we're after, the term to replace multi-tasking. System management describes a thought-out orchestration, a demonstration of moment-to-moment control in which one has a firm grip on details and is not living at the edge of crisis, floating along on hope, fingers crossed, prayers recited, and obsessions indulged.

Here it is: The focus must be on the proactive management of systems, not on coping with random system results. If the majority of time is spent examining and tweaking systems to perfection, great results will materialize. Conversely, think about "holistic" solutions that cover life's complexity like a blanket: Another market for the product, a better manager for the company, a larger house, a new boss...a new spouse. These are attempts to straighten things out in one fell swoop and, although applicable in certain situations, are opposite of what I am proposing here.

The way to find control—to get what you want—is to stop looking for a sudden hand-of-God solution to problems, drop the idea that life is convoluted and mysterious, strip away the complexity, and get to work repairing the underlying inefficient mechanisms one by one. Trying to find peace and personal control through drugs, food, work, money, esoteric psycho-babble, fanatical adherence to religious/political dogma, running away, or excessive preoccupation with the external—obsession—is an abomination of the simplicity of it all. These blanket applications falsely promise to soothe life's complexities in one fell swoop. Instead, the *Work the System* methodology goes inside and fixes building-block components one at a time. It's about making small, mechanical system improvements rather than being swallowed up by the promise of some cure-all that only masks chronic internal inefficiency.

Let's set aside the complexity and find a way to manage the mechanics of the systems that are right in front of us. The first steps you'll take include setting direction and deciding on strategy (you will begin this process by creating the Strategic Objective and the General Operation Procedures. More about these documents soon).

THE SUBVERSIVE HOLISTIC THOUGHT PROCESS

According to the American Heritage dictionary, there are two definitions of "holistic." First, "emphasizing the importance of the whole and the interdependence of its parts." And second, "concerned with wholes rather than analysis or separation into parts." Clearly, the *Work the System* methodology is the antithesis of the second definition. Yet, the *results* of the methodology are in exact accordance with the first definition.

In the last 30 years, the terms "holistic" and "global" have inserted themselves into the fabric of our culture, supposing, "We're all in this together," and "if we do this over here, it will have consequences over there, so let's be careful," etc. These generalizations create a paralysis in which we identify a problematic primary system, assume the entire primary system is faulty, and then try to force an overall solution—without examining the sub-system components.

For instance, if someone is unhappy, they visit a psychologist, are diagnosed in the first session as "depressed," and are prescribed an antidepressant that will affect their entire mental and physical being. If a nine-year-old boy is rambunctious in school, the child psychologist wants him to take a "prescription stimulant." These drugs are a shock to the child's entire physiology.

Another example of generalization is the "all war is bad" mantra. Is it that simple? Does everyone agree this is true? Look dispassionately at the world, and its history: If it weren't for wars, wouldn't our societal choices be nazism, fascism, communism, and/or slavery? In the long term, for the overall good of humanity, would *that* be better than a limited-time war that challenges and then stops tyranny? Or, "religion is the world's greatest cause of conflict and suffering." Really? That conclusion ignores billions who quietly find personal solace and strength in their faiths, causing no harm.

Others: "Deport all illegal aliens!" And, "there should be open borders!" In the real world, either of these actions would be tramatic.

Too often we go after a holistic, bumper-sticker solution when it would be more sensible to simply examine the primary system's context and fix a faulty component. From the start, the overall primary system is probably better than OK, working well in most situations. Could we apply a minor internal adjustment to bring things closer to perfection instead of disrupting or replacing the entire system?

In any case, it is difficult to dictate an overall solution to a problematic primary system and expect great results all around. We can't take a fix-it pill, legislate social mores, or repair the car by washing and waxing it. If there is a problem with a primary system, we must go inside to root out and fix one or more faulty sub-systems. Do that, and because of the increased efficiency of the contributing component parts, the end result is a cleaner working and entirely "holistic" primary system. Of course, sometimes solutions include adding a new sub-system or discarding an old one.

System-Improvement and Working Procedures

If you are like most people, you do not *consciously* consider the involvement of systems in your daily life. Therefore, you have not *consciously* thought in terms of adjusting systems in order to eliminate problems from occurring in the first place. For most people, an emerging mole is to be whacked, and burrowing inside the mole-hole for some serious mole extermination is not an option that's considered. The recurring process is to wait for a mole, whack it, and then wait for the next mole to appear. Thus, endless mole whacking.

The little moles are cute-faced, but they are decoys that distract us from the critical moves we should be making. I say, let's burrow deep inside their tunnels and kill them all. And then, before we leave, let's do some system adjusting—let's do what we have to do—so no more moles show up later. Then, confident moles will never distract us again, we'll climb back above ground and start fixing the other systems of our lives that need fixing.

Yes, the systems methodology that I recommend is quite pointed in its approach.

Here is a mechanical truth of how the world works, an absurdly simple fact: *One can compensate for the negative outcome of a recurring problem, but without repairing the errant system that caused the problem, the problem will undoubtedly occur again.*

Few people understand the systems-management approach of successful leaders who intuitively grasp that a seemingly isolated problem is not isolated at all. These leaders see problems as the result of a flaw in an errant system—an errant system they can fix. For these pacesetters (corporate usually; governmental, not so often), a problem is not a disappointment just to be corrected and then written off. It's a wake-up call. This means that once the manager corrects the immediate negative effects, there is a second step. It is this second step that is key: The problem's cause is traced to the errant sub-system which is modified so the problem doesn't happen again.

Through the astute leader's observation, a problem calls for a sub-system modification. The leader makes the permanent improvement causing the entire system to be incrementally more robust and reliable than before the problem occurred. Addressing the problem and then taking this second step to fix the cause of the problem, distinguishes the people who are in control from the people who are not in control—the successful from the unsuccessful.

So, the improvement of a system is a system improvement and the documentation of that improved system is called a Working Procedure.

By focusing on repairing problems in this way, the primary system becomes ever more efficient. Over time, rough edges dissolve. It's a beautiful thing, this system-improvement process, because as time passes things improve. *Imagine a system that improves with time, rather than wears out.*

At the start, these one-by-one system-improvements can seem daunting. You work at them for awhile and then ask, "When will the problems cease, and when can I stop fixing and documenting things?" But you carry on despite the demanding work ahead. After plugging along for awhile, you notice the pace and quantity of incoming problems decreases. You see the fire-killings aren't coming so fast and *this* is the point where a powerful belief takes hold. With fervor, you accelerate the System-Improvement/Working Procedure process so even fewer errors occur, and your organization and personal life become smooth and efficient. The bottom line improves while personal vitality increases. Things come under control!

You'll never go back.

PERMANENCE

As the *Work the System* methodology is applied, your focus is on fixing one system after another, not careening through the day randomly taking care of whatever problems erupt. *Your job is not to be a fire-killer. Your job is to prevent fires.* Of course, in daily life you will always encounter fire-killing, but the idea is to minimize it. The documentation of each improved system is critical. Making a system-improvement without it guarantees the improved system will revert to an inefficient unpredictability borne of short-cuts, outdated but comfortable methodologies, the pressures of the day, and/or confusion infused by assorted personalities and talents.

Documentation gives permanence to your system-improvements. It has to happen.

Ripples and Heavy Seas

System repair, creation, and ongoing maintenance, along with providing the requisite documentation, are the system manager's primary roles. The failure to focus on permanent system-improvement is the main reason 80 percent of small businesses fail within five years. (Do a Google search on the above statement and find any number of studies that support this statistic). This is lack of management; a failure to self-discipline.

For Centratel, the system-improvement process continues, eight years after the implementation of the *Work the System* method. Now, problems are so few that when one surfaces, my staff pounces on it with a vengeance. It is hard to describe the satisfaction of leading a company that operates this way. Like the business, my personal life still has its occasional unexpected ups and downs (that's life!), but now it is enormously more resilient and I am well-prepared to absorb unexpected blows. For the apple vendor, an overturned apple cart is a disaster—but an apple falling off the side of the cart now and then is a small, easily managed occurrence.

Is random human error a system problem? Many times, yes, because random errors are often the result of inattention to important physical and mental systems (lack of written protocol, not enough sleep, intake of harmful substances, overwork, etc.). However, assuming proper maintenance of physical and mental systems, we must accept that random human missteps are just part of things. There is no getting around being human.

So, no matter the precision and strength of a systems-based business or personal life, overt human miscalculation will occur. The good news is that in organizations and in personal lives, outright mistakes account for only a small percentage of total errors. Most problems stem from non-existent system management and show themselves as "errors of omission." The further good news is that the *Work the System* method dramatically reduces this form of inefficiency (We'll cover errors of omission in Part Three.)

What about the unexpected heavy seas of a debilitating injury or the loss of a loved one? Here it is again: Strength and resilience are by-products of the *Work the System* method. A life that is stronger and more resilient will be better able to navigate the inevitable dark waters.

Tweaking

Once the one-time repair of errant systems is complete, the system manager focuses on routine reviews of the entire collection of systems. Per the *Work the System* method, an important aspect of everyday life is to examine established systems on a regular basis and to make system-improvements as required. This ongoing review process keeps life smooth over the long term.

With the *Work the System* method, the percentage of time and effort expended fixing systems decreases with time, while the percentage of time and effort expended on improving systems, what I call "tweaking," increases with time.

MORE TIME AND ENERGY

The idea is to correct and refine sub-systems one by one, thereby reducing future problems. Then, without so many fires to kill (being on the defense), more time and energy will be available to expend elsewhere. Much of this additional time and energy is reinvested in refining even more sub-systems (being on the offense) so the primary system becomes ever more efficient and powerful. This is the "cycle of increasing returns."

Noticing Poor System Management

When you get a feel for system management in your daily life, you will notice when it isn't happening around you. As you interact with the world, you'll find yourself critiquing what works and what doesn't, aware of not only your personal systems and their quality of execution, but in the systems others manage. This new posture as an informal "service quality observer" will go with you everywhere.

Once you get the systems-perspective, you will see fire-killing all around you. You will understand the real reasons why people who promise to call, don't call; why there is lousy service in certain restaurants, retail stores, and hotels; why there is haphazard communication with a service provider. You will develop a knack for instantly recognizing shoddy workmanship, missed deadlines, promises not kept, bad attitudes, and sloppy execution. These dysfunctional human performances are the logical end result of poor system management, both organizational and personal. Human dysfunction is pervasive. You can't miss it. The better you get at system management, the more you will notice these inefficiencies. But when you encounter efficiency and calm in a business, organization, or another individual, you will notice that, too, and you will recognize it as the beautiful thing it is.

When you're at the receiving end of poor service, you will understand the ultimate problem is not with the person who is facing you, who may indeed be rude or uncaring, but with the individual at the top of the organization who is not managing properly. Even so, be sympathetic with the absent leader. Most people don't understand the system-improvement process, or even that there is such a thing. With best intentions, and working hard, they muddle along, batting off the fastballs as they come hurtling in from all directions. I was like that.

What about selfish people? Yes, some are ready to circumvent the rules as they ignore common expectations and don't consider others. But, be careful here, too. Don't confuse someone's personality flaw with their mechanical problem, which is a simple lack of attention to the details of personal relationship systems. *How one goes about cultivating good relationships is also a system, and the methodology must be set up with care and executed with consistency.* For thoughtless people, the base problem is not a personality flaw, but the lack of a functional "relationship maintenance system." This is a vicious circle. These people do not return calls, remember birthdays, send thank-you notes, extend invitations, and don't show the least interest in the vicissitudes of the people around them. The consequence is they receive little positive attention in return. These lonely people feel rejected and alienated and they reflect that rejection and alienation, digging themselves deeper and deeper into loneliness.

Is it their fault? Well, yes it is.

But it's not about a "bad" person. It's about the absence of system management. It sounds antiseptic but it's the reality: Some people don't apply the system fundamentals necessary to make and keep friends. Maybe they don't care enough or, more probably, they just don't get it....

Despite the near perfection of our mechanical world, look around you right now and notice the human qualities of dependability and consistency are in short supply. And because they are in short supply, people accept that condition as normal—and people SHOULD accept it as normal: It IS normal, and happily for you, that means standing out from the crowd won't take much effort.

Once *Work the System* protocols are functional in your life, the people around you will start to notice your quick execution of detail, your consistent reliability, and the congruency between what you say and what you do and, especially, your calm, confident comportment. New customers, great employees, and reliable friends will be attracted to you because you doggedly adhere to the simple system management tenets for cultivating great personal and business relationships. People can depend on you.

Your Life: Problematic or Orderly?

So, bottom line, how do you perceive your life? Do you see it as problematic—unfair, unpredictable, and inhospitable? Or do you view it as orderly and in control, ready to do your bidding?

Yet again, this isn't a matter of having a positive or negative attitude or adopting some philosophical stance based on esoteric theory. This is about simplicity, mechanics, and logic.

How do you see things?

A Certain Billionaire

We were on vacation in Siena, Italy. We'd been there just a few days and at night the jet lag had me either entertaining strange dreams, or was keeping me awake. This particular night, it was both. An interesting midnight dream inspired this 2 a.m. writing session.

In the vivid dream, a well-known multi-billionaire asked me to take the equivalent of the Chief Operations Officer position for his conglomeration of international corporations.

Upon receiving the offer in this tycoon's ad hoc board room located on the tarmac of an airport somewhere, my central dream-thought as I faced him was *I would succeed.* I would succeed despite my small-town heritage, my lack of advanced educational degrees, and the shortage of other seemingly necessary background requisites. My challenges would be prosaic, limited to dealing with frequent travel, the certain inevitable corporate personality clashes, and whether or not being a part of the enterprise would cause me to feel trapped in a cage (my current world is much smaller but at least I call the shots).

In my dream, why was I confident? It was because my position would entail dealing with the same simple mechanical realities of cause and effect that I deal with now, just on a larger scale. I would work my systems in this enormous corporate structure where, metaphorically speaking, one plus one would continue to equal two, just like everywhere else. Other than the scale of the endeavor, my tasks would be no different from the tasks I accomplish now.

CHAPTER 8

GETTING IT

I'm trying to free your mind but I can only show you the door.
You're the one who has to walk through it.

Morpheus (Laurence Fishburne), from the 1999 movie, *The Matrix*

A Room Full of Boxes

There have been problems. There is a department that has been a source of frustration to the owner of the organization. In fact, just today the owner terminated the department manager's employment. It had become clear that this manager had neglected his department and it showed in the lack of output, the number of problems, and the general chaos.

You feel badly for the department manager who lost his job but you understand why it happened. You remember, "that's the deal," and that each member of the organization is paid very well to perform at maximum capacity.

You are a troubleshooter for your organization and your assignment is to straighten things out. You have been sent to the department which resides within a single room in your building. Repairing things is what you do and you relish the challenge. You gather your tools and the necessary background documentation and make your way to the job site.

You walk through a door into a large, well-lit room, one that you have been in many times before. Surrounding you are dozens of wooden boxes varying in size from one to four feet square. The closed-but-not-locked boxes,

88

each with a hinged wooden lid, are scattered around the room.

You are there for a single reason—to fix things. It is a substantial undertaking because of your predecessor's long-term neglect of these boxes and their contents. So you begin by pushing the boxes around so they are in order, taking the time to organize them so you can work in a logical, efficient way.

You've brought your tool box and, of course, you have written technical instructions should there be questions. The repair and maintenance procedures are understandable and well thought-out.

Because of the previous neglect of the contents of these boxes, you knew before you came here that completing this job would require a long day. You hunker down and get to work.

You open the lid of the first box and inside is a single system. The system is a physical, mechanical apparatus. It's made up of gears, wires, and levers, and because you are a technician trained in understanding the construction of such devices, what you see makes sense. It's a simple thing, really. It is clear to you what this device does and how it is put together. Peering into the box, examining the system, it is apparent that mechanical adjustments are necessary. You reach into the box with steady hands. You make the adjustments. In the course of your work, you notice an obsolete component. You replace it with an updated version (you always carry spares). This upgrade will make the device more efficient and reliable.

Then, you oil all the moving parts and finish by cleaning up the mechanism, wiping it off. You test the system to make sure it's working perfectly. It is.

On the inside of the lid you write the date and your initials, along with a brief summary of what you did so when someone else does maintenance work later on, they will know what you've done, and when.

You close the lid and move on to the next box. You go through the same process with the system within that box. One by one you move through all the boxes, making each of the unique systems within them perfect, closing the lids afterwards.

It indeed takes the entire day to complete your work.

It's late, and you gather your tools to leave. You stand just inside the door and turn around to take a last look. The boxes are in neat rows, their lids closed, and you are confident the systems within each box are working perfectly. You leave. You know the department's output will now be very, very good because each of its systems is working flawlessly. How could it be otherwise? You also know the new department manager will be system improvement-oriented, watching over things, not allowing the systems to fall back into disarray. There will be routine maintenance.

As you walk away, you feel intensely satisfied with your work and with yourself.

———

There it is, the *Work the System* process of seeing the world as a collection of systems that are, one by one, isolated and made perfect, and once perfected, routinely managed for maintenance and upgrading.

Here's the no-brainer that eludes most people: In the course of a day and in the course of a life, each movement we make is a single step in a linear sequence of steps intending to accomplish something. *Each thing we do is a component of a system.*

My intention in these first chapters is to present illustrations and evidence from a variety of angles so you will see the systems of your own life on a visceral level. I'm being repetitive, hammering things home. Are you "there" yet? If not, be patient as I belabor the elements of the new perspective while slowly introducing the how-tos.

If you don't experience the "ah-ha" soon, it's OK. The fake-it-'til-you-make-it routine can get you there.

Your First Step: Make Your Systems Visible

You know this by now. First, make the various systems consciously visible. Second, one at a time, bring them to the foreground for examination. Third, adjust them. Fourth, document them. Fifth, maintain them.

By plucking individual systems out of the amorphous mass of your real-time existence—that intense, swirling fracas of sights, sounds, and events that is your life—you can examine and then precisely manipulate the workings of those systems.

But, first you must see them.

Reaching the point where you *see* the systems around you is the first and most significant step. It's a mini-enlightenment. When the epiphany occurs, you will have internalized that *systems make up your life* and you will know that asserting control of them is management at the most fundamental level. You will view the world with new clarity. Details will be sharper, more vivid; the colors more vibrant.

Moment by moment, real-time, you will proceed through your day seeing everything around you as part of a system. No more will you perceive your world as a random conglomeration of people, objects and situations. You'll see life as a logical collection of individual processes.

What seemed complex will suddenly appear elementary.

With confidence in your new vision, you will change your strategy from fire-killing to system improvement because it is obvious this is the most sensible thing to do.

You Must Stand Outside of It

If you want to see where you fit in the machine that is your life, you must observe it from an external vantage point. *You must stand outside of it if you are to see how you are a part of it.*

There is nothing shadowy in this. This is simply about seeing things in a different way. But let's be clear, and pay close attention here to something I've already mentioned: *This mindset is different from the mental posture most people pack around. Instead of seeing oneself as an internal component of circumstances, enmeshed within the day's swirling events, the* Work the System *vantage point is outside-and-slightly-elevated from those events.*

You are an observer from above as you watch yourself down there in the middle of it all. You see things clearly and reach down to take action, almost like a child with a tiny toy action figure, firm hands deftly controlling the toy's every movement.

You are the child and the toy is your life.

There is no need for me to list a one-through-ten-step process for making the *Work the System* method produce results in your life: You must simply "get" the new perspective—"get" the perspective of seeing the systems in your life with the same clarity with which you see the rest of the physical world around you. Once that happens, the rest will be fill-in-the-blanks sensibility.

Again, here's how you will see your world: The day's happenings are visible as individual elements, arranged in logical sequences. It's borderline metaphysical as you hover above your world. You are the "watcher," the observer of your life.

Your day is spent working on your systems. These are "one-time" tasks as you make each system perfect, one by one. Over time, self-confidence replaces confusion. Your systems—business, personal, mechanical—hum along. Not often is there confusion. You gaze down at your handiwork and feel an intense self-respect. You are proud of what you have accomplished.

Considering your new mindset, you think, "Why couldn't I see this before?" You look back on your previous life and observe that, embroiled in minutia, you were blind to the systems that lay beneath your comings and goings. You remember the day when the shroud lifted, when sequential life systems became visible and your perception of the world's workings shifted. You also remember the first inklings of the potency of systems methodology and how soon it proved itself in action: Tangible rewards came quickly.

You remember that removing the shroud didn't take a whole lot of faith or hard work, just some quiet observation.

Acquiring the *Work the System* posture is a transformation. You can look forward with anticipation because the moment of shift is an intuitive leap. It will be the consummate insight; the singular event that changes everything. The day you "get it" is a day you will remember. My prediction is that this will happen soon, possibly before you finish this book. Maybe it grips you now.

Your Day Will Never Be the Same

It is incredibly satisfying to have control, to have things make sense, and to determine your own destiny. And you'll become tenacious about this new direction because the improvements come fast and strong.

I belabor this point because it is key: *Once the* Work the System *methodology is internalized and applied, your day will never be the same. You will be a different person.* No more feeling anxious in the morning, your head filling with encroaching worries even before you get out of bed. During the day, no more long hours spent killing fires. No more evenings spent buried in paperwork or sitting exhausted, zombie-like in front of the TV, with no hope of relief for tomorrow.

Instead, at the end of the day you look back and see that you spent your time immersed in one-time creative projects and productive conversations with staff, customers, friends, and family. You feel gratification that the past day's efforts were further incremental steps toward even more freedom and prosperity. You don't pine for the "big break" because it's clear the big break is already occurring piece by piece, step by step. In control from dawn to dusk, you know you are building your destiny in a solid and honorable way.

Your circle of influence is growing.

Despite the solid progress toward your goals, it was an easy, relaxed day that gave you plenty of additional time to do the things you enjoy. You not only made incremental progress toward your most important goals, you spent time with the people who matter most to you and you did the things that gave you pleasure.

There's plenty enough money now, too.

You are happy with yourself. You know why your life has improved, why you feel in control. It's because of you: *You did that to you!*

The *Work the System* process is not magical. It's logical. You can see the cause-and-effect of your own actions.

You will know; then you will act. Consider these points:

First, *it's what one DOES that counts.* Good intentions and a positive attitude are not enough. What matters is the action one takes, right here in the tangible world.

Second, getting things right most of the time is good enough. The part that doesn't come out well is just part of the overhead—the cost of doing business, of taking risks, of external confusion, of coping with a changing world that is often one step ahead of your best efforts—of being alive. You could say this is part of the imbedded numbers game that comes along with having a life. So, as by-products of advancing forward, accept that less-than-perfect events are going to happen. Three steps forward. One step back. It's the way it goes.

Third, remember that most people don't fail by making overt mistakes. They fail because they don't take action. If this is you, prepare to change your ways. We'll talk more about this soon.

Yet again: System-Improvements

The *Work the System* treatise is about the mechanics of the world's workings; the linear processing of things. It's about the physics of it all, the cause-and-effect, real-world reality that is *right there*, visible to anyone who will open the door and look inside. With a bias toward lean-and-mean simplicity, the *Work the System* method examines, reorganizes, and prepares for what comes next.

It's nuts and bolts: *For a given primary system, in order to ensure the best results occur over and over again, the task is to adjust that primary system's sub-systems so the correct components are being used and they are sequenced properly. This is the goal of any manager, the work of "system-improvement."*

So, the *Work the System* process is about preparation. *If you spend your time attending to the mechanical details of your world, making strategic adjustments to key systems—in other words, making system-improvement the main focus—you will construct a life that flows.* It will be a life unencumbered with fire-killing, one seldom absorbed with urgency. You will be flexible, strong, and resilient; negotiating smooth, calm days that have lots of room for thinking and planning, for friends and family, for just being you.

In its forward motion, it's a life that encounters road bumps instead of earthquakes.

THE BIG DIFFERENCE

What is the most important difference between the manager of a large successful business and the manager of a small struggling business? The first manages systems; the second copes with bad results.

Violating a Social System

We're in Italy, in a small guest house in the tiny coastal town of Monterosso. It's 9 a.m. I sit alone at a breakfast table in the corner of the dining room. Other tourists surround me, quietly enjoying their cappuccinos, pastries, and cereal. I work on my laptop, putting the final touches on this book, my breakfast dishes pushed aside.

The manager of the guest house approaches me, and in halting English, asks, "Are you finished with your breakfast?" I answer, "Si."

She says, "Please. To work, take your computer to the lobby downstairs. *This is a place of breakfast.*"

That odd phrasing—*"this is a place of breakfast"*—is perfect. In her wonderful, nuanced English, my host gets directly to the point and I instantly understand. There is no quibbling with the logic. I am working in "a place of breakfast" and working here is wrong. Italians consider eating to be an encapsulated system, a semi-sacred process one should not sully with work. My incursion is callous; I am not respecting a system that has been operating for hundreds of generations.

I move downstairs to the lobby, a location more appropriate for a man obsessed with finishing his work. This is a place where many things—including too-busy Americans with laptops—are allowed.

I understand how Europeans can sometimes consider Americans crass and overbearing. It is a humbling, outside-and-slightly-elevated reminder that I must respect the systems of others.

CHAPTER 9

Swallowing
the Horse Pill

Why aren't you going to step up to do something about it?
Don't you feel there are enough live people passing off
as dead people already?

Anonymous

The Unassuming Work That Must Be Done

At Centratel, I spent 15 years in the trenches working long, hard hours. Nonetheless, I was always on the brink of failure. Borderline clueless, failure was evaded only by my ridiculous persistence. I was Atlas, scrunched over with the weight of the excruciating load, the entire enormous bulk of a contorted business on my shoulders as I killed one fire after another while attempting to convince my worn-out employees to stretch their own limits even further. It seemed, *we're just not working hard enough!* I look back at those years and think, my God, it was just a small business! How could it have ever become such a burden? And, beyond Centratel, how could my personal life have become such a living-on-the-edge epic?

One day not long after the systems-perspective light bulb switched on in my head, an additional insight arrived. It dawned on me that creating the necessary Working Procedures would not be flashy. It would be tedious, and it was clear that documenting all of our systems would take time. The Working Procedures would not fall into place as easily as the first two controlling documents, the Strategic Objective and the General Operating Principles. Nevertheless, it would be a mandatory undertaking.

First hand, I saw that within my own TAS industry, few owners/managers perceive their businesses from an outside-and-slightly-elevated perspective. Instead, they thrash within the inner workings, smacking those moles. Still fewer document their direction or create written procedures, and of the few who do, it's hit or miss.

So, why is that? I thought, if this systems methodology is so simple and so potent, why aren't more small business owners doing it? Could it be because the system-improvement work is too much of a challenge or that it's not sexy? Or, is it...*too hard?*

I thought, it's all of those things! *And, the sheer unassuming nature of what must be done, combined with the fact that other small business owners don't do it, is smoking-gun evidence of its viability!* In itself, this revelation gave me a surge of excitement about the documentation chores that lay ahead.

In any case, if I was to hone a process to perfection, and then expect that process to continue to be perfect in the future, it was logical the steps would have to be written down. There was no getting away from it. And after a system's documentation was complete, the next prosaic task would be to ensure my staff precisely followed the written procedure.

My next moves were obvious, but creating the documentation would take time away from the ongoing efforts of keeping the business afloat from day to day. Business demands would not step aside while we improved systems and wrote up the attending documentation. Could we find the time to write everything down? This was a moot question. Accomplishing the work was mandatory because if we didn't do it the company would fail—and my guess was if we *did* do it, the company would flourish.

So I swallowed the gigantic horse pill that there was some serious work to do—unexciting documentation work—and plunged ahead full steam.

To get off the mark, remember there will never be an "easy button" you can push to make everything instantly better. Documenting systems takes time and focus. But you are already working hard, so what's the big deal? Now you must continue to work hard for just a bit longer.

Preparation Leads to Better Control

Yes, the system-improvement documentation, the one-time heavy lifting, will be intensive at first, but once it's in place the ongoing work will dramatically decrease (i.e., in my case, I transformed 100-hour workweeks into 2-hour workweeks).

A primary thrust of the *Work the System* method is to generate extra time so one can better prepare. This is a beautiful and simple reality of the *Work the System* method: *Proper preparation leads to better control of future events, which leads to higher efficiency. Higher efficiency produces more available time—and some of that available time is reinvested in additional preparation.*

This is the opposite of a diminishing returns cycle. It's a cycle of *increasing* returns, a circular system, building upon itself to ever higher positive results.

What is the largest obstacle to better preparation? It is the reluctance to invest the necessary time to be better prepared! At the beginning, even if you have experienced the gut insight that systems make up everything in your life, you must be patient and self-disciplined. You must keep your head down and grind out those Working Procedures until prosperity and free time begin to arrive, thus confirming deep down in your belly that *Work the System* preparation is a smart thing to do. When the results begin to materialize—and again, it won't take long—you will become a fanatic for documentation.

Note that some documentation will be useful in your personal life, but it will be informal and less intensive.

Here is a summary of what you will put together:

Work the System Documentation

1. The one-page **Strategic Objective** document will provide overall direction for your business and your personal life. You will create this document yourself. It won't take more than six to eight hours total to complete. (Caution: this is not a job for a committee. It's a job for you, the leader). Once completed, you will get feedback from your staff and, over time, you will tweak it as necessary. As the years pass, it won't change much. In Chapter 13 you will find Centratel's Strategic Objective.

2. Upon completion of the Strategic Objective, you will begin to put together a collection of written **General Operating Principles**. Just two or three pages long, you will complete this condensed, "guidelines for decision making" document in maybe ten to twenty hours, but these hours will be spread over a period of a month or two. (Again, the composition of this document is a job for *you*, although you will want to get other's input.) You will extract these principles from your everyday experience while formulating them from under the umbrella of your new systems mindset. *These Principles are what you believe,* and they will crawl out of their hiding places unannounced. Avoid rushing the list. Be thoughtful and patient with yourself, and when complete, your written Principles will change little over the years. For business, this document is thorough. For personal life, informal. Centratel's 30 Principles document is in Chapter 14.

3. Instead of killing fires, you will spend time creating a fireproof environment. Your **Working Procedures** will be the nitty-gritty, blue-collar fundamentals of your work. This documentation is your specific collection of protocols that outline how the systems of your business or your job will operate. (Working Procedures are not necessary for your personal life although the concept should travel with you everywhere.) Brief, concise, and authored by you and your key staff people, 95 percent of your procedures will follow the same 1-2-3 step format. The other 5 percent will follow an open, "narrative" format. (Note that we have developed

special software to channel and simplify the process. Called the *Work the System Easy-Template* product, see information at **workthesystem.com/easy**). Every system-improvement you make will have its own written Working Procedure. As you did with the General Operating Principles, you will begin creating your procedures just after you complete your Strategic Objective. You will start with the most critical systems and then work through dozens if not hundreds of additional systems, depending on the complexity of your business, job, or profession. But, over this period, it won't be a full-time job. If you have staff, use your best people to do the majority of this legwork. Foundational to your everyday business experience and adjusted with evolving circumstances, Working Procedures are the fluid part of the *Work the System* method. An example is provided in Chapter 15.

LIFESTYLE REQUIREMENTS

If we choose to live a certain lifestyle, that lifestyle has certain requirements. There are tasks that *must* be accomplished. These are task *requirements*, not "when-I-get-around-to-it tasks," or "if-I-feel-like-it tasks." To achieve your desired lifestyle, you must accomplish these tasks no matter your disposition at the moment. The ability to get the job done—no matter the current frame of mind—is necessary for success. No matter how onerous the job, or how little you want to do what is required, the payoff *will* arrive as long as you take the steps. *You do not have to like the steps you must take. You just have to take them.* Nine out of 10 people don't understand this. Rather, they think, "If I don't enjoy what I am doing, that indicates what I am doing is incorrect."

Bad presumption.

The documents that you will create are mechanical aids. However, something else is important about them. They are tangible. It makes what you are doing and where you are going, *real*. With written documentation, you can put your hands on your work and your future. Every day you will *see* your methodology and goals and this will be a reminder to stay on the path. Always remember that surging thoughts, desires, and hopes are intangibles but they can divert you. *Documentation is real and it will keep you straight.* Once you begin to get things down on paper, this will become obvious.

The Giant Machine

Deep in the hills of Northern Italy, the world's largest computer printer manufacturer keeps a factory running 24/7/365. The mechanical and electronic workers labor 24 hours a day, don't take breaks, and work their entire lives in a fixed location. A daily line of semi-trucks delivers new raw materials and picks up fully packaged products. If not for the presence of these trucks, the casual observer would assume the facility is abandoned.

A few cars in the tiny parking lot indicates there is a small contingent of human workers. A single security guard minds the gate. Inside, the plant is nearly devoid of humans yet activities rarely cease. Standing at one end of this "system of systems," one can barely make out the other end. It's a huge *machine*, as wide as it is long.

Given the proper security clearances, a brave person can walk through the center of this machine. Doing so, one quickly learns that even human visitors are under the system's control. Approaching a well-defined walkway, red flashing lights warn the human visitor to hold his or her place while a part of the mechanical line physically retracts in order to allow passage. Once the visitor passes, the track closes and the machine continues at a somewhat accelerated pace to make up for the time lost due to the human intruder's incursion.

In the middle of the night, standing in the center of this giant machine, it's an eerie feeling watching the frenzied activity all around: It's not the place for the faint of heart or the claustrophobic, as there are no escape routes. Should the machine fail to detect your presence, there are no humans readily available to intervene on your behalf. Yes, you are free to leave but only at the mercy of the system and only at a pace that doesn't interfere with system requirements.

The giant machine is made up of sub-assemblies, and those sub-assemblies cooperate with each other until complete products are rolling off the end of the line. The fully tested printers are packaged and shipped to a local store near you, and in all likelihood the first human hands to touch the printers are those of retail purchasers.

This is a system of systems with a clear goal—the production of things of value. And where are the human masters? Outside-and-slightly-elevated, of course, monitoring, adjusting, and maintaining.

Submitted by J. CORNELIUS

CHAPTER 10

CALMING THE STORMS

You better live your best and act your best and think your best today, for today is the sure preparation for tomorrow and all the other tomorrows that follow.

Harriet Martineau, 19th century English economist and novelist

Emotional Fluctuations

Your controlling documents do not have to be perfect in the first drafts. They can be grammatically incorrect, the sentence structure can be less than perfect, and they can be brief. What *is* important is that you begin to create and use your documentation. Just begin! You can clean it up later. It is critically important to be self-disciplined from the beginning—and this self-discipline will be evident in just getting started.

Like bedrock, your three controlling documents will stand against the storms that blow across your world. And what storms create the most havoc, slowing, halting or reversing forward progress? Your own emotions.

Documentation lays out everything that is important for getting you to a place of control in your life: your goals and how you will achieve them, your beliefs about how things work, what is most important to you, and how you will operate. Because of it, your forward progress will ebb only slightly as you encounter the unpredictable and inevitable emotional surges that are part of the human condition. *With the* Work the System *methodology in place, you will minimize the impact of your negative emotional fluctuations.* It may be slower progress in those times, but it *will* be progress.

Then there are the hammer-blows: No matter what, there will be times when you think you are sinking. Nonetheless, when those times happen, your documentation will reach down and yank you to the surface before you drown.

THE HIDDEN BENEFIT OF DOCUMENTATION

The potency of documentation is it is tangible. If you can garner the self-discipline to create your Strategic Objective, you will find new strength as you hold the single-sheet document in your hand. You have direction! And once you have tangible representation of who you are, where you are going, and how you will get there, you will find it uncanny how the physical world aligns itself with what you have written.

When you get past the words in this book and take mechanical, physical steps in your real world—the first of which is the creation of your Strategic Objective—you will see for yourself.

The Down Times: Get Outside Yourself

The Strategic Objective, General Operating Principles, and Working Procedures are your self-created guiding lights. In the tough times, they remind you that you are a system-of-systems and that tweaking certain external and internal sub-systems is what you must do. When you are not feeling strong and your emotions are negative, your guidelines are right there, ready to get you back on track, or at least keep you from straying too far. As Mick Jagger said, "It's alright to let yourself go as long as you can get yourself back."

Create your controlling documents in moments of lucidity when your thinking is clear and you have a firm grip on the unadulterated truths of your life.

The self-discipline of today will pay off later when you are not so strong. *When you realize you are watching your temporary depression from the outside, you will know you have reached a higher level of control.* This is cognitive self-management, the ability to examine and adjust your thoughts from an external vantage point. You see your thoughts as independent of *you*, an endless film clip; a system to itself—a singular entity, just like any of the other systems under your control.

Your systems-perspective will remind you the reasons for the down times are most often due to simple things: too little sleep, low-blood sugar, excessive work or TV, negative people, a depressing environment, the payback for ingesting a mood-altering substance, and so on. Get outside these influences and see them for what they are. Minimize them and they will no longer eat away at self-control and progress. They will no longer drain your energy or create depression.

In my own life, being tired drives me downhill faster than anything else. Like clockwork, every day between 1 p.m. and 2 p.m., I go into a physical and mental downturn and I either nap it off, or I crawl through the afternoon understanding that my physical body—and my thinking process—is at low ebb. Either way, by 4 p.m. I am fine again. Discover your own cycles, document them, and work with them. (I go into detail about this in Chapter 23).

THE STORMS OF THE CRIMINAL MIND

The criminal mind has a certain grasp of the mechanics of the world, sometimes more so than the average law-abiding citizen. In the classic, colloquial sense, the criminal "works the system," as he or she strips away the niceties, examines the raw mechanisms of the world's workings, and without concern for others, manipulates those mechanisms to selfish benefit. Yes, the criminal approaches things with a malefic bent, but one can't deny the viewpoint is outside-and-slightly-elevated.

Nevertheless, criminality is a losing game because it violates overarching societal systems. If we consider society as a primary system, criminality is nothing less than a flaw; a flaw the primary system works hard to eliminate one way or the other.

Consider the plight of the chronic law-breaker who gyrates

outside of things, bucking accepted notions of how one should act. For selfish reasons, the law-breaker directs energy toward personal gain without regard for the accepted rules of the primary system—society—taking shortcuts, exploiting system elements, and making small-time gains. As the system is bucked and manipulated without regard for fairness and compassion—the bulwarks of a just society—personal pain arrives in an overt way, jail time for instance, or in a more covert lack of personal peace. The criminal is afloat in a stormy sea. The TV series *The Sopranos* was a perfect illustration of the paranoia of "fighting the system." The characters were diabolical and tormented, ultimately doomed.

The law-breaker gums the works of the established smooth-working societal system. The society, which is much more powerful, will work hard to either bring the lawbreaker into conformity or it will do what it needs to do to protect itself. If you are a criminal, the force is *not* with you.

If one is working "outside the system," what is the solution? It is to make the decision to accept the general human process as it is; to play the game as it's laid out—to follow the rules. Things are just smoother that way. In the free world there is a lot of latitude to fit into things and to get ahead: career, social, personal.... One has unlimited options to succeed without breaking the rules.

The universe welcomes manipulation if it results in a better, more efficient system, but it will fight manipulation that is disruptive.

How It Works

Look forward to this: In the midst of a less than perfect day, you will watch yourself drag your emotions out of a black hole rather than allowing them to swallow you up. You will see yourself do this from your outside-and-slightly-elevated vantage point. Later, you will see it happen again, and then later, again. These self-rescues incrementally strengthen control and after a while you expect this even-keeled response. Soon you will find you won't be so inclined to resort to the old antidotes of avoidance and no longer will you bludgeon your way through the down-times with over-work, alcohol, coffee, sugar, or drugs, the things that rescue your mood in the moment but guarantee more intense down-times in the future.

The learning cycle will continue upward until you have a solid grip on your world and you realize your Strategic Objective, General Operating Principles, and Working Procedures have pushed you to become one of those rare individuals whose backbone is made of steel. It seems odd that dispassionate documentation could have this kind of effect, but as you can see, there is much more to this than the written word.

Losing Key Employees

At Centratel, each of our half-dozen key management people has had several years of on-the-job experience. Training managers to operate a telephone answering service is a long, drawn-out affair because it is necessary to understand a myriad of technical details and random facts. The introduction of documentation speeds up this training process, but the new manager must understand the subtleties, and that takes time.

So, in the past, when one of our managers left, it was a large step backwards. Getting a new person up to speed could take months, if not years. Who suffered? Our staff, our clients, and the bottom line. In short, losing a manager was among the worst set-backs that could happen to Centratel.

How did we solve this problem?

We developed and then documented a simple principle. This principle, important enough for us to mention in our Strategic Objective, states, "we have backup personnel for all management and staff positions."

We developed this principle through our vision of the business: The primary system is Centratel and we see each manager's role as a sub-system.

Note: The *role* is the system, not the person.

The company's stated policy of having two people who can perform a role stems from a vantage point outside-and-slightly-elevated from the primary system. We look down on an individual role and mandate "for this sub-system, we shall have a duplicate."

The everyday effect of this policy? Each manager mentors their understudy to ensure he or she can perform all of the manager's tasks should the manager, heaven forbid, "get run over by a truck." The added benefit of this policy is that if a manager is temporarily out of the office, or is occasionally overwhelmed with tasks, the understudy can assist without hesitation.

It sounds like a simple solution, and it is.

In the past two years, we lost two managers (who left on good terms, for personal reasons). When it happened, there was not a ripple in our customer service quality or our internal workings because each of the people who left had been mentors to individuals who were able to slip effortlessly into their former superior's larger shoes.

Is this a new approach? Of course not, but the truth of the real world is few small business owners/managers give enough attention to potential problems, even ones so obvious as the unexpected loss of key people. These leaders wait until problems move from potential to kinetic, and then they panic. Not instituting a system for training replacement managers and staff is a classic leadership "error of omission."

CHAPTER 11

WE ARE
PROJECT ENGINEERS

Management works in the system;
Leadership works on the system.

Stephen R. Covey

A Quick Summary of the Method

As an ad-hoc synopsis—by now you know how much I like to review things, to drill them home—the essence of the *Work the System* method is to:

1. Internalize the fundamental outside-and-slightly-elevated, system-improvement perspective.

2. Pinpoint and describe goals for your business, job, and life. Briefly define the general methods you will use to achieve those goals. This is your Strategic Objective.

3. Create your personal collection of General Operating Principles. Use them to control decision-making.

4. Define specific systems for improvement, including the ones that exist and the ones you must create. Be ready to discard others.

5. Dissect each system into its most fundamental components. For your business or your job, describe each system on paper in a 1-2-3 step format.

6. One system at a time, and leaning hard toward stark simplicity, improve the efficiency of the component steps. Change sequences and add or delete steps as necessary. Make each of your systems perfect.

7. For your business or your job, to ensure continuity of your systems, document each system into a Working Procedure. (Working Procedures are not necessary for your non-work life).

8. Put the new Working Procedures into play and tend to them on a regular basis, inspecting and tweaking as necessary.

Your Personal Analogy

In step one above, *internalizing the system-improvement perspective is mandatory.* Without this visceral grasp, subsequent steps two through eight just won't happen in your real, mechanical world. *The strength to take a new direction comes more from a belief lodged in the belly than from something new learned in the head.*

To really grasp the system-improvement perspective, it is useful to create a personal system analogy, a "systems template," that you find personally meaningful. Your analogy will illustrate systems methodology to *you.* In your day-to-day existence, you will keep this analogy in mind in order to keep your systems-perspective front and center, and as a reminder of the characteristics that all systems share. The analogy will keep you on target.

A vivid personal system analogy is the antidote to a too-busy day; a day that ruthlessly attempts to divert your attention from the system-improvement process to the wasteful act of fire-killing.

You want your analogy to be personally believable. Its mechanical basis must be something you don't question. Also, it is essential to find one that is easy to visualize as separate from its surroundings, one that can stand on its own.

If you are in medicine, bodily systems offer a myriad of possibilities. You can draw examples from organ function, skeletal structure, or recovery from injury.

If you sell cars, consider the conveyor belt of an auto plant, or a car itself with all of its sub-systems and how they must be monitored and tweaked to stay at peak efficiency.

As a firefighter, think about the equipment and procedures that must function efficiently no matter what.

A pilot has the pre-flight checklist which is a terrific example of examining an existing system for flaws while insuring that all sub-systems are at peak efficiency. The airplane itself is a great system analogy, or even a single flight as the aircraft automatically conducts directional micro-adjustments, confirms sub-systems are functional, and warns of system dysfunction.

Your analogy will keep your energies channeled toward system management as it reminds you that a jumbled morass of fire-killing will drag you down. It will be a steady reminder that you are a project engineer who creates and maintains efficient systems, not a troubleshooter who responds to crisis after crisis.

The analogy will help you enormously at the beginning. Later, it will be an occasional pleasant reflection of who you are, where you stand, and how you get through the day.

As an illustration, here is the analogy I use. As you read, start to think of one that fits your own world. No, you don't have to put it down on paper.

The New-Service Facilitator

My personal analogy is about electricity: how it reaches people in their homes and businesses, and my past role as an electric utility project engineer.

Power line circuits perfectly illustrate the mechanics of the *Work the System* methodology *to me*, so this is *my* analogy of a closed system. It is easy for me to visualize an electricity distribution system as a separate, unique entity and not one in which surrounding complexities of the world infringe. It's my personal, perfect illustration of the mechanics of linear systems everywhere.

When I was 28, and before I went into business for myself, I took a job in the engineering department of a rural electric utility near my home in Central Oregon. The utility is one of the largest REA (Rural Electrification Administration) Co-Ops in the United States, with thousands of miles of power lines branching throughout the Central Oregon region and serving tens of thousands of residential, commercial, and agricultural customers.

Of all Co-Ops in the U.S., its operations and engineering personnel face the most extreme environmental, meteorological and socioeconomical challenges: On the same day, linemen can face both mountain snowstorms and one hundred degree desert heat; vertical mountain pitches and long river crossings; high density city construction and remote rural trouble-shooting.

For the first half of my seven-year stint with the Co-Op, my job title was "new-service facilitator."

As one of the Co-op's four new-service facilitators, I met with contractors and landowners who were about to build homes. My task was to arrange for our construction crews to "tap" into the nearest existing power line in order to extend new electric service to the customer's construction site. Usually, the distance from the power line to the site was fewer than 100 yards.

I examined the new home site, located the closest power pole, and wrote up instructions and a list of materials for the construction crews so they could get the electricity delivered to the customer.

My job had little to do with the primary electrical system. My area of responsibility was outside the massive power-generating dams that created the electricity far to the north on the Columbia River, and the thousands of miles of high-voltage power lines and associated complex equipment that distributes electricity in bulk throughout the region. My task was to establish small power line extensions to individual new customers by designing small sub-systems. These sub-systems were simple additions to my utility's massive "electricity distribution network," the primary system.

I filled this position as new-service facilitator for three years. Then I got a promotion. The promotion moved me from the periphery of the system to the heart of it, where I would have a much greater impact on the primary system itself, and on the many customers it served.

My new job title was "project engineer," a perfect description of my new role (and in *your* new role, it will be your title too, so pay attention here). I would be responsible for designing and supervising the construction of large "distribution feeders" into whole subdivisions, as well as working on complex "system-improvement" projects that affected thousands of customers at a time. It was also my job to keep an eye on large segments of the primary electrical system in order to spot problems and to recommend improvements. There was the necessary overall maintenance, too. System components aged and the environment changed, and it was my job to monitor these variables and recommend repairs.

In summary, my job was to analyze portions of the main electrical distribution system, design improvements, and then pass those designs on to the construction crews.

My designs were put down on paper using a precise format. The goal was to be thorough yet concise; to give the construction crews what they needed—no more and no less—so they could proceed quickly through the construction work.

Note how the analogy describes my transition from handling small and isolated add-on tasks, to large internal system-improvement projects. Also note there were strict design and documentation protocols.

Flirting With the New Perspective

My previous position and my new position had an important commonality. In each case, when I went to work, from the beginning of the day to the end of the day, I was focused on the Co-Op's electrical system. *While I was on the job, the system stood separate from the rest of the world.* Sure I took breaks, had lunch, and made a personal phone call now and then, but all-in-all, the electricity distribution system—the network of poles and wire—was paramount in my consciousness, standing out in my mind as its own entity, separate and distinct from my children, my finances, my politics. When I was on the job, the electricity distribution system had my focused attention as if nothing else existed. *And it was not just separate in my mind, it was that way in reality*, a primary system inserted into the world as an independent entity, spreading its tentacles as it fulfilled its singular purpose of delivering electricity to lots of people.

At the end of the day, as I returned home to pay attention to the other systems of my life, I changed my perspective as if I had flipped a switch. I didn't consciously notice this daily transition (and little did I know that I was toying with the outside-and-slightly-elevated perspective that would form the basis of this book, which I write 20 years later).

If you are like most people you are in that same place, with an unconscious tendency for dissecting complexities so the exposed elements can be dealt with one at a time. *The* Work the System *method will turn that soft, ephemeral tendency into an assertive, structured quest—an everyday pilgrimage to "work" the systems that compose your world.*

System Management

With the promotion at the Co-op, my role morphed from designing small sub-systems for individual customers, to making system improvements in the primary electrical system that served thousands of customers. Instead of adding to the primary electrical system in bits and pieces, I was managing large segments to ensure it continued to provide an uninterrupted supply of electricity to large numbers of customers. I tweaked and coddled the primary system to keep it strong and efficient.

Notice I was not climbing the poles or stringing wire. My job was to devise system improvements that would make the primary electrical system more robust, and then to oversee the implementation of those system improvements by other people. This is a crucial point of the analogy.

All of this was "system management." I was unconciously "working the system," and this management process would later insert itself into all parts of my life as I came to understand the logic of it. Today, my former role serves me well as an analogy—a template—for how I want to visualize all aspects of my life. Like my position as project engineer with the electric utility years ago, today I examine, tweak, maintain, and upgrade all the systems of my existence, while I avoid getting caught up in minor add-ons.

I no longer "major in minors." Your own analogy will remind you to avoid that, too.

Maintenance and 99.9 Percent Reliability

I was one of 60 employees at the electric company. Whatever our various roles—engineering, construction, administration—each of us either consciously or unconsciously viewed the electrical system as a separate entity, an entity that required consistent attention. It was its own being, an organism with a life of its own.

In any part of life, in order to avoid system failures and to ensure top efficiency, the performance of regular system maintenance is mandatory. Now that you understand that systems are everywhere, it will make sense to you that maintenance of *all* human systems is necessary: changing the car's oil, staff meetings, watering the house plants, dinner out with a spouse, ball games with the kids, bonuses for the best employees, routine visits with customers, record keeping, physical fitness, etc. However, for many people in the midst of chaos-control, skipping these important "wheel greasing" chores is the first casualty. *In so many life situations that include people, homes, careers, marriages, mechanical devices, friendships, play, personal health—all of it—the necessary routine maintenance is skipped because of fire-killing, simple laziness, and especially, ignorance of the way linear systems proceed in the real, mechanical world.*

Electricity originates from a generating facility and then power lines carry it to the end user. For the electricity, it's a long, hazard-wrought trip through multiple electrical sub-systems and tough terrain. Weather extremes, vandalism, and the incessant ravages of time imperil the electricity's delivery. But this is interesting: In checking official statistics at the utility where I used to work, I found that over the last seven years, the average customer's power failed an average of just 73 minutes per year. Wow! Think about that: There are 525,600 minutes in a year, which means the average electric utility customer had steady electric power more than 99.9 percent of the time. Does that percentage sound familiar?

In considering a power line's path through hundreds of miles of hostile environment, combined with the volatile high-voltage electricity itself which is so anxious to escape its confining wires and transformers, how does the management and staff of an electric utility accomplish this astonishing degree of reliability? They do it by viewing their electrical network as a *system* that must be assertively and relentlessly maintained, not just a conglomeration of poles, wire, and equipment that receives attention only when things go wrong. The people employed by the electric company start by designing and installing a robust electrical system, and then they coddle it.

The Heart of the Analogy

In summary, my role as project engineer on a large electrical system was to isolate the electrical system and then look down on it from an outside-and-slightly-elevated vantage point in order to:

1. Design system improvements.

2. Create new sub-systems from scratch while eliminating ones that are obsolete.

3. Monitor existing systems to make sure they function reliably in a changing, demanding environment.

What's your analogy? A car, human body, airplane, or ship? Use it to remind yourself to view your world with the system perspective. See the perfection of your encapsulated system analogy and apply it to whatever situation you find yourself in. You can do this because, for practical purposes, *all the systems of the world operate in exactly the same way. This is not theory and there is no mystery. This is mechanical reality.*

Let's take a breather to discuss a point of clarification regarding the terms "system," and "sub-system."

These are arbitrary name tags. For instance, the utility I have described is just one of hundreds of electric utilities across the country, each of them connected to surrounding utilities and each capable of transferring electric "load" back and forth. Therefore, one could dispute my previous statement that the utility where I worked is a primary system. True enough: My utility can also be identified as a sub-system because of its relationship to the other utilities with which it connects—the conglomeration of utilities that makes up the overall electric grid of North America. In this perspective, the primary system is the entire electric grid that covers the continent.

But, the choice to use "system" or "sub-system" is a matter of individual perspective. Decide for yourself what is a primary system and what is a sub-system, but be sure you do it in a way that works in the real world—and that means you must bring things close to home, breaking your life down into separate entities that can be easily visualized, described, and manipulated.

In your own *Work the System* world, you may choose to visualize the following as primary systems (each of which, needless to say, is composed of subsystems): your business or job, body, car, house, computer, office, city, country, and relationships with the people who are important to you. The commonality—indeed, the definition—of these, or any other primary systems, is that each has a singular, over-arching purpose.

You Must be a Project Engineer

As I visualize an electrical power system as a metaphor for my life, it is a reminder to avoid being a worker and, rather, be a project engineer. As you apply your own analogy to your business or supervisory job, you will find yourself deflecting hands-on work to others. You, on the other hand, will be creating new systems, designing improvements on existing systems, and supervising the people who do the actual work. (Of course, if you are an artist or other creator, or work for someone else, this will not be entirely true. However, whatever your life's role, there is room for movement in the *Work the System* direction—a direction that can only improve your situation, whatever it is. More on the "Job and Work" aspect in Chapter 23).

In considering your new analogy, and from your new posture as a project engineer, you will begin to watch things from a distance, from that place that is outside-and-slightly-elevated. The more time you spend seeing your world with this bird's-eye view, the faster you will attain your goals—and the more time you will have to spend on that outside-and-slightly-elevated perch. If you are not at the head of your organization, no problem, the systems-perspective will quickly propel you upward through the ranks.

It really is this simple: *Your job is to avoid becoming caught up in the work. Instead, you step outside, look down, and isolate individual systems on paper in a 1-2-3 format. Then, deciding overall what you want the systems to accomplish, you identify defects as well as outside changing situations. Then you improve the systems, always documenting. Because you have designed these systems to operate without your constant involvement, you can back off and then occasionally (but routinely) monitor and direct things.*

I approach all my personal systems with the project engineer's viewpoint: systems to stay fit, keep in touch with extended family, invest money, maintain computers, and even climbing mountains. An especially satisfying one is the daily half hour I spend at home working my "reorganizing system." This is perhaps my simplest system, nothing more than an allocated daily time period dedicated to a narrow purpose: 30 minutes spent reorganizing. It's free-form time used to clean things up, to straighten things out in my office, in my closet, in the garage. Sometimes it's going outside and pruning the shrubs. It's about putting things in order, and it is an antidote to insidious, looming clutter, both physical and mental.

Half a dozen years ago, in the beginning of my new systems-oriented lifestyle, I would constantly visualize my personal electric system analogy and its dictate that I be a project engineer. Now it's just an occasional pleasant reflection. I don't think about it too often because the systems mindset is visceral, hard-wired inside my being.

So, the analogy you choose matters. Match your world to your analogy and your everyday actions will become efficient and productive. Not too far down the line, bit by bit, freedom and power will materialize.

Toilet Paper

This illustration borders on nonsensical, but makes two points. First, that the systems-perspective is not common. And second, the perspective will become permanently in-grained once the logic of it is understood.

As an example of systems-thinking, and at the risk of an awful pun, reaching for a piece of toilet paper is the bottom line.

Toilet paper is a mandatory accessory. It may be the one thing that all of us have used daily for all our lives. As an illustration of a system that is ubiquitous, it's perfect.

The act of loading toilet paper on a toilet paper roll is a system—a system that proceeds in a linear fashion until the goal is accomplished. Step one: In the bathroom, approach the sink. Step two: Open the cabinet door underneath the sink. Step three: Reach under the sink and grasp a roll of toilet paper. Step four: Take the protective wrap off the roll. Step five: Approach the toilet paper dispenser with the roll, etc.

Ask yourself the following question. Right now, in your own house or apartment, is the paper roll loaded on the dispenser with the free end of the paper off the top of the roll where it can be easily grasped? Or, is the leading edge off the bottom, against the wall, where one must awkwardly reach underneath the roll to retrieve it?

For the fun of it, over the years I've kept an informal tally. Not counting hotels and motels where professional housecleaners have been instructed on the most efficient positioning, it is a nearly 50-50 split with a slight advantage going to those who chose "top." This means most people don't think one way or the other about the insertion of the roll in the dispenser. (Or, implausibly, one half the population is adamant the roll be inserted one way and the other half of the population, the other way.)

So, not many people think of this triviality. Is it important? Of course not—but that is not what matters here. The important point is the illustration of the lack of systems-thinking by the vast majority of people.

Since having the retrieving end of the paper on the top of the roll makes grasping the paper easier, why don't all people load the paper that way every time? Is the task of inserting the roll one way more difficult than inserting it the other way? Not at all. But deciding to always do it this way would require a one-time analysis of the goal and the process—in this case just a few seconds of time—and we Westerners don't often consider underlying processes, even ones so innocuous as this one. *Most of us are not naturally predisposed to see life with the systems-perspective.*

Yes, this is a silly illustration, but try to get past that. See that in considering loading the paper in a different way, you are putting yourself outside-and-above the act of loading toilet paper. *You are deliberately managing the process in order to produce an incrementally better result every single time the process executes in the future.*

There is another, more visceral lesson here, and maybe it's a bit unnerving. Because you have considered this toilet paper question, it may cause you to choose to load your rolls in a more deliberate way, or the contrarian in you may consciously decide *not* to. Whatever your choice, my prediction is that from now on you will think about the process every time you replace a toilet paper roll. Like it or not, due to this end-of-chapter illustration, there is a small slice of systems methodology that has been permanently imbedded in your thinking process.

Welcome to my world.

For the record, when I polled my management staff in a staff meeting on how they load their toilet paper at home, I got a 100 percent "Pleeeze! Off the top, of course!" response. Even in the most mundane tasks, the Centratel staff reflexively takes a posture of outside-and-slightly-elevated.

CHAPTER 12

NOW, THIS IS HOW IT IS

First you work your systems.
Then your systems do the work.

SC

Outside-and-Slightly-Elevated

At Centratel, when we took action from our new external stance, turmoil evaporated and was replaced by order. Once we began the new methodology, it was easy to continue because positive results accumulated quickly. The more we invested in system-improvement—working the system—the more positive results we experienced.

Centratel is highly profitable now, and I spend little time managing it because the business is self-propelling. As project engineer, I watch over things from a distance, nudging here and there to keep the business traveling in a straight line and at full speed. Centratel is not under control because of my presence as a detail chaser. It's under control because of my insistence on perfecting the systems that compose it. Of course, another critical element of our success is my staff's enthusiasm for the method they helped put into place. They are project engineers, too.

Centratel is a pleasant place to work. Calm efficiency pervades every aspect of the company.

Concurrent with the enormous improvements at my business, the systems-perspective flows through my personal life and I have the same levels of control and freedom there, too. I regained my health years ago and today consider myself more than robust.

One might think my adoption of the new systems perspective came about because I was courageous. But that wasn't the case. It was fear and exhaustion. It took impending doom to see life was not going to conform to my wishes just because I thought it should.

Why weren't the answers obvious to me *before* there was a gun to my head? Part of the reason was although the year-to-year struggle was killing me, it was more comfortable—more convenient—to acquiesce to predictable day-to-day pain than to question my overall vision and methodology. And, there was also arrogance: *It was easier to posture myself as a hero, facing and then overcoming incredible external odds, doggedly marching on, rather than question my presumption the world would someday get a clue and adjust to my personal requirements. When catastrophe was finally upon me, everything distilled down to the raw indisputable fact that I was not managing the systems of my life.*

Am I happy the insight came as the end-result of trauma? If that was what was required, yes. Do you have to have a gun-to-the-head experience to get to the same place? No!

Late that night, eight years ago when the light bulb in my head finally flicked on, it struck me that although there was some work to do, it would be maddeningly simple to repair my business and my life: *All I had to do was identify systems, isolate them, and then fix them one at a time!* Does this make sense now? Do you see there is no need to undergo a cataclysm in order to change your perspective and then fix things?

In retrospect, the almost humorous aspect of my outside-and-slightly-elevated enlightenment was the realization this was not some kind of divine blessing, bestowed upon me alone. Despite the glaring exception of most small businesses, the systems-perspective is already permanently etched into the minds of those who manage large, successful organizations everywhere. But, it's an interesting thing. The systems-perspective is such a simple concept, many of the people who innately embrace it can't describe it, much less identify it as the critical factor of their success.

SYSTEM QUESTIONS

Maybe there are ghosts all around, waiting to communicate good tidings. Maybe horoscopes and tarot cards predict the future, and maybe you are somehow special enough to win a multi-million dollar lottery. But don't hold your breath. By dispassionately dealing with hard reality, the odds of getting what you want are infinitely higher. *Be mechanical.* Can you imagine how you will feel as you watch yourself get a grip on life and create what you want due to your own actions, not because of improbable fate, magic, dumb luck, or someone else's benevolence?

So, are there system questions—system filters—you can pose in a given situation that will enable you to really see the hard and cold reality of any given situation? Yes. Ask, *"Without regard for my personal preference, what exactly is going on here?"* Carry that question around with you everywhere, and when the necessary action is obvious but you hesitate, ask this: *"Is not wanting to take action in this moment enough of a reason to NOT take action?"*

Flow

I watch in fascination as the endless myriad of the world's systems ripple on. It is nothing less than flow, and I like seeing it, being part of it. I view my personal existence from this nearly metaphysical systems-perspective that is a step away and a-little-bit-above events. In my business and my personal life, my job is to tweak my systems, gently goading each to more and more efficiency. (Regarding systems out of my control, I make no attempts at adjustment because it is a waste of time and energy.)

This world operates at 99.9 percent efficiency because there are unalterable physical laws that are powered by an unfathomable strength—a strength that hungers for order and efficiency. In the systems that make up our lives, results occur in a cold-blooded way; outcomes don't mysteriously conform to our personal desires just because we want them to. But it's a beautiful thing, really, because this mechanical reality is predictable; something we can depend upon and therefore confidently use to our own benefit. Think about that shovel in the garage. Do you ever question it won't dig a hole? And that rope? There is no question it will secure something, if that is your need. Conversely, will you ever attempt to dig a hole with the rope? The certainty you feel answering these questions are the same certainties you will feel for the larger mechanics of the world, of the machinations that are predictable and reliable, once you "get" the systems mindset.

When you understand the relentless dependability of reality's mechanics, and then carefully "work" those mechanics, you will get what you want.

THE PRICE TO BE PAID

In a personal sense, working outside the system too often means introducing medications into the miraculous near-perfect system that is the body. Perceiving themselves to be unhappy, people complicate their already flawed thinking process by contaminating themselves. The ice-cold reality? One plus one always equals two, and with the same utter reliability, a drunken night out on the town equals days of sub-par physical and mental performance as the human body works overtime to repair itself from the chemical assault. Too often, we make things worse in the long term by violating systems in the short term, as we ignore the simple truth that disruption of an efficient system always has its price. One could say that substance abuse is a criminal attack against one's self.

Three Large Steps Ahead

In the middle of my business and health rejuvenation, I was pounded hard by two unexpected, earth-shaking blows. One was the nasty legal battle mentioned earlier. The other was a bone-crushing personal family loss. The nightmares arrived at the same time, with the first lasting two years, and the second continuing until recently. Those were dark times, but I was able to roll through those days with sanity and effectiveness, watching the goings-on from my outside-and-slightly-elevated vantage point.

In Chapter One there were two paragraphs I will repeat here:

The Work the System mindset is different from the mental posture most people pack around from day to day. Instead of seeing yourself as an internal component of circumstances, enmeshed within the day's swirling events, your Work the System vantage point is "outside-and-slightly-elevated" from those events. The day's happenings are visible as separate and individual elements, arranged in logical sequences. You are an observer looking down on things, examining the comings and goings of the day as if they are tangible, physical objects. Things are simple and understandable. Wherever you look, the machinations of the world make sense: Step-by-step, one thing leads to another as the systems around you continuously execute.

You constantly work on those systems. You make them better, one by one. Over time, complexity and confusion decrease to be replaced by order, calm, and rock-solid self-confidence. There is little fire-killing, little confusion, and as you continue to peer down at your handiwork, you feel an intense self-respect and you are proud of what you've accomplished.

Does this make more sense now?

Once you "get it," the *Work the System* mindset is natural and unforced. Here is how it will be: You wake up in the morning with an immediate focus on what is most important for the day ahead. The tasks you will accomplish this day will be one-time, creative efforts, each aimed at carrying you closer to the objectives outlined in your two Strategic Objective documents. (One for your business, one for your personal life.) Although you will minimize stepping backwards, there is no avoiding it because that is what getting through the day includes. You accept those imperfect movements as part of the overhead that comes with the much more significant forward movement—three large steps ahead for every one small step back. And the inevitable earthquakes? You'll be ready.

And at the end of the day, you feel satisfied because there has been tangible advancement toward your prime personal objectives.

Working or relaxing, you don't float or obsess anymore. You direct, build, watch, and enjoy. It flows.

The Cardiovascular Equipment Sign-Up System

Here's a remove-the-system-altogether scenario. It's the ultimate in simplifying things, per Sir Ockham. My staff and I take delight in chucking unnecessary Centratel protocols. System-elimination is great to see in personal life, too.

The cardio room at the gym where I work out is equipped with dozens of treadmills, step climbers, and stationary bikes. It's a busy place, so queuing up to use any of these machines was done by noting one's initials, the desired start-up time, and the machine number on a sign-up board. It seemed sensible to use this procedure in order to promote efficiency and prevent conflict.

All club members knew the logic of the system and in the course of any given day, hundreds of us took the time to sign up for the various machines we wanted.

Then one day the sign-up board disappeared without explanation. Why did the new club manager remove this logical, order-inducing system without so much as a warning? Probably because the sign-up board was a classic Rube Goldberg creation that attempted to cure a problem that didn't exist.

The sign-up board had been duplicating—and therefore complicating—a system that was already in place: the system known as common courtesy.

The system of common courtesy is a mutual agreement regarding actions between people. The fundamental rule is person A will have consideration for person B, and fairness rules. If people abide by the common courtesy system, seldom will conflict or confusion occur. Step out of the system, and there will be trouble. The common courtesy rule in the cardio room is if person A is using a machine, it will be available to person B only after Person A is finished. For human interaction in neutral situations, this is the familiar "first come, first served" principle. "One takes second position to the one who is already there." If it is important to use a certain machine, one will wait until it is available. That is the absurdly simple rule. That is the system.

Obviously, "common courtesy" is a system that lies outside-and-slightly-elevated from minute-to-minute goings-on. It's a collection of unwritten rules—a system—that supersedes immediate personal ambitions. *Common courtesy is the most fundamental and rigid social system in our culture.* Today's common courtesy system is a beautiful thing, much improved over Neanderthal days when the lack of it caused strangers to be killed. Things have improved!

PART TWO

CRITICAL
DOCUMENTATION

Here are the fundamentals of *Work the System* documentation. They are presented here as we use them at Centratel. Copy and customize at will. Plagiarism is not a problem. (To make the creation of these documents fill-in-the-blanks simple and fast, use our *Work the System Easy-Template*™ software package. Go to **workthesystem.com/easy** for details).

Note that having your protocols written down is at least as important as what you say.

Linda came up with an analogy. It's perfect, and I can't resist adding it. Here it is: The Strategic Objective is your Declaration of Independence, your mandate for a better future. The General Operating Principles document is your Constitution, a set of guidelines for future decision-making. Working Procedures are your laws, the rules of your game.

Can you imagine the basis for our government not being in written form? Why would it be any different for your business or your job—or your life?

Here are the raw essentials. Now is the time to start.

CHAPTER 13

AT THE HEART
OF THE MATTER:
THE STRATEGIC OBJECTIVE

People with goals succeed because they know where they are
going. It's as simple as that.

Earl Nightingale

To review: The systems insight arrived because I was under enormous
mental and physical pressure. Until that late-night revelation, my strategy
was to approach life with a bulldog, damn-the-torpedoes, pound-the-moles,
I'm-so-damn-clever persona. It was a toxic brew of arrogance and ignorance—perhaps the most noxious combination of negative human traits.

The seething chaos had reared up and was about to crush me for good.
Instead, with a flash of insight, it released me. I dropped the bulldog
routine, adopted a new outside-and-slightly-elevated perspective, and
found new confidence. I knew what moves to make and charged out of
my self-imposed prison.

As I mentioned in the beginning of the book, when I bought the ailing
answering service business my goal had been to make the company the
best in the industry. I described how that mission had quickly evaporated
as my staff and I coped with serial fire-killing. For 15 years we thrashed.

But in year 16, as we began to plow through the systemizing process and witnessed immediate quality improvement, the "Best in the U.S." goal crawled out from its hiding place and took center stage. We would not just survive: Per verifiable statistics, we would become the best in our industry, an industry of 2,000+ competitors.

THE FOCUS IS ON THE MECHANISM

The successful leader keeps the wheels of the mechanism turning at full speed, and with enormous efficiency.

Creating the Strategic Objective

More questions jumped out as I saw the business for the first time from my new, outside vantage point. *Did Centratel have objectives and a plan for reaching them?* I dug in and laid out our goals and strategy in the pragmatic, one-page written document.

The Strategic Objective is the first and most important of the three documents used to manage Centratel. It gives us direction and prevents us from flailing away in a hodgepodge. It is also the foundation for the General Operating Principles and Working Procedures documents, so it *must* come first.

With the Strategic Objective at the forefront, no longer do we squander time and energy heading down roads that don't contribute to the overall objectives of the business.

For Centratel, the ultimate purpose of the Strategic Objective is straightforward, as noted in present tense in the first line: "We are the highest quality answering service in the United States."

All decisions follow from that statement. Large decisions, small decisions—it doesn't matter. Every ounce of energy is laser-beam focused on the primary objective. The Strategic Objective publicizes goals in a mechanized, non-wishful thinking way, and ours came together with a gut-level practicality.

The Strategic Objective is not a feel-good "Mission Statement" based on self-aggrandized hope; something designed to make the Board of Directors feel good about themselves, and intended to impress stockholders and staff. Instead, it's a concise, one-page blueprint in which we acknowledge the day-to-day real world. Without syrupy excess, it includes a brief narration of what the company does, where things are headed, and how management and staff will get there. (The interesting thing is that most business owners already know *what* they have to do to succeed, but because they hamstring themselves with fire-killing, they don't have time to even think about establishing goals or developing strategy—they don't know *how* to succeed.)

I'll repeat myself here: To ensure congruency among the three controlling documents, *it is critical to tackle the Strategic Objective first. This gives solid direction for creating the General Operating Principles and the Working Procedures.*

Following is Centratel's Strategic Objective.

CENTRATEL'S STRATEGIC OBJECTIVE

Note to Staff: The Centratel Strategic Objective is the basis for all corporate and individual decision making.

Trite mission statements that declare, "We want to be the best and we want our customers to be happy," don't provide meaningful direction and do little more than make company stockholders feel good for the moment. And voluminous multi-year work plans can't account for the day-by-day changes of the telecommunications world.

Instead, the Strategic Objective gives us an overview of general strategy, describes our direction, who we are, and how we function. By following its guidelines, growth and success will take care of themselves. In the spirit of simplicity, we limit the length of the Strategic Objective to one page. We've modified it through the years, but the fundamentals have never changed.

—SC (slightly updated, 7/7/2008)

Centratel Strategic Objective

We are the highest-quality telephone answering service in the United States.

Our fundamental strategy is to relentlessly "work" the systems of the busines to perfection.

Our guiding documents are the Strategic Objective, 30 Principles, and the collection of Working Procedures.

Centratel's primary offering is 24/7/365 telephone answering service for business and professional offices throughout the United States. Peripheral services are voice mail and paging for the Central Oregon region only.

Through intense commitment to our employees, we are dedicated to the success of our clients. The consequence of having loyal, smart, hardworking, long-term and well-compensated employees is superb quality service to customers.

Our business is complex, with many human, mechanical, and computer systems in simultaneous motion. Success depends on refined communication and organizational systems, dedicated staff, documented point-of-sale procedures, first-class office space and equipment, rigorous quality control with continuous measurement, assertive innovation, intense system maintenance/system improvement, assertive and measured marketing, and relentless attention to detail in every nook and cranny.

Competitive advantages include a near-flawless level of message processing accuracy, products designed around the unique needs of the customer, assertive yet thoughtful customer service that is immediate and consistent, the latest high-tech equipment, rigorous marketing, and personal/corporate integrity.

To grow, we proceed with an "if we build it, they will come" philosophy, juxtaposed with assertive marketing efforts.

Although we tightly control Centratel's operation through guiding documentation, we will modify that documentation immediately if an improvement can be made: "Our operational framework is constructed of rigid steel, but that framework can be modified instantly."

We segment responsibilities into specialized "expert compartments" with appropriate cross-training among departments. We have backup personnel for all management and staff positions. We use extraordinarily efficient communication tools and protocols. We constantly refine and improve all internal systems.

Primary vertical markets include medical, veterinary, home health/hospice, funeral home, HVAC, hi-tech, 24/7 on-call, front office/receptionist, and utility.

Frank Zappa's
System Improvement Strategy

If you think your business or work situation is "different" and therefore some of these principles won't necessarily apply, consider this:

Frank Zappa (*1940-1993*), was one of the most brilliant avant-garde rock artists of the '70s and '80s. He scored each note of every song and required 100 percent performance accuracy from his band members. After a concert, when most of his contemporaries would likely be attending a post-performance party, Frank would be conducting a mandatory-attendance, post-mortem with his backup band.

During these performance autopsies, individual players were assessed a $50 fine for each and every note missed. New band members were quick to challenge Zappa's recollection of the score and their individual performances; more experienced members knew better. Frank's perfect recall of the performance was easy enough to verify: The evening's audio recordings would confirm what Frank already knew, and the fines would stand. Band members who were fined were not likely to forget to rehearse their parts before the next performance. Frank set the bar high and his success is rock music history.

By the way, Frank Zappa never used drugs and was quite the family man.

CHAPTER 14

GUIDELINES FOR DECISION MAKING: GENERAL OPERATING PRINCIPLES

...Keep your eyes on the road, your hands upon the wheel...

From the song *Roadhouse Blues* written and performed
by the Doors (vocal by Jim Morrison)

After I completed the first draft of the Strategic Objective, I began creating the second critical document, the General Operating Principles. Congruent with the spirit and the specifics of the Strategic Objective, this would be a collection of root guidelines for making decisions. In the end, it included 30 separate operating principles, so we called it, "30 Principles."

Centratel's 30 Principles document is, of course, a system in itself. (Note it is a non-linear system—a set of parameters that are not necessarily directly related, but each of which must be considered across a wide spectrum of decision-making possibilities). The 30 Principles are tried-and-true, sensible, and easy to understand and remember. Do they change with evolving circumstances? Not much. Over time they have been tweaked, but their overall intractability is evidence of their soundness.

Listed here are Centratel's 30 Principles. You will have your own, and of course, they may number more or less than 30. Think of your General Operating Principles as your guidelines-for-decision-making for your business or your job.

It's helpful to make up a set for your personal life, too. You will find your personal principles resemble the set you put together for your work because they reflect your character and your preferred way of approaching the workings of the world. Business or not, these Principles will remain constant in all aspects of your life.

Most of the Principles lie quietly underneath the things we do every day. They are not flashy. For an illustration of how they can work, consider Centratel's Principle number 8, where we state that we provide "just a few services implemented in superb fashion." Seven years ago, this tenet mandated that we stop selling cellular telephones as an add-on service. Because we could not depend on the quality of customer service provided by the cellular company for which we were a reseller, this decision kept things simple, gave us better control, and insured *all* of our products are high quality. Had we not written down this principle in tangible form and then abided by it, we would still be selling cellular phones at a considerable detriment to our overall operation.

The General Operating Principles tenets, like the elements of the Strategic Objective, keep us moving in a focused direction no matter any tendency toward non-action on one hand, or momentary burst of impetuousness on the other. We are dogmatic about following our principles.

Another example is principle number 30: "This can't be legislated, but we strive for a social climate that is serious and quiet, yet pleasant, serene, light, and friendly." Because of this principle, our office *is* like that because the principle is a hoop through which all decisions must pass. Due to the live decorative plants, immaculate restrooms, special lighting, pleasant physical lay-out of the office, clear-cut policies and guidelines, and so on, Centratel is a nice place to work.

As with the Strategic Objective, all individual and corporate decisions are laser-beam focused on the 30 Principle's objectives.

Don't expect your Principles document to be finished in one sitting. Although it was two minutes here and five minutes there, it took me over a month to create the rough list, select the proper wording, and polish it. Begin by writing down several principles you already have in mind. Then, take notes as additional principles pop into your head. Be sure to seek other's input as you put it together.

CENTRATEL'S 30 PRINCIPLES

1. Company decisions must conform to the Strategic Objective, 30 Principles, and Working Procedure documents.

2. We are the highest-quality answering service in the United States. We do whatever it takes to ensure the quality of service to our clients is unmatched anywhere.

3. We draw solid lines, thus providing an exact status of where things stand. Documented procedures are the main defense against gray-area problems.

4. "Get the job done." Can the employee *do* his or her job, or is there always a complication of one kind or another? This ability to "get the job done quickly and accurately without excuses or complications," is the most valuable trait an employee can possess.

5. Employees come first. We employ people who have an innate desire to perform at 100 percent. We reward them accordingly. The natural outcome is we serve our clients well.

6. We are not fire-killers. We are fire prevention specialists. We don't manage problems; we work on system-improvements and system-maintenance in order to prevent problems from happening in the first place.

7. Problems are gifts that inspire us to action. A problem prompts the act of creating or improving a system or procedure. We don't want setbacks, but when one occurs, we think, "thank you for this wake-up call," and take system-improvement action to prevent the setback from happening again.

8. We focus on just a few manageable services. Although we watch for new opportunities, in the end we provide "just a few services implemented in superb fashion," rather than a complex array of average-quality offerings.

9. We find the simplest solution. Ockham's Law, also called the Law of Economy, states, "Entities are not to be multiplied beyond necessity…the simplest solution is invariably the correct solution."

10. The money we save or waste is not Monopoly money. We are careful not to devalue the worth of a dollar just because it has to do with the business.

11. We operate the company via documented procedures and systems. "Any recurring problem can be solved with a system." We take the necessary time to create and implement systems and procedures, and in the end, it is well worth it. If there is a recurring problem, a written procedure is adjusted in order to prevent the problem from happening again. On the other hand, we don't bog down the organization with systems and procedures that target once-in-awhile situations. Sometimes we elect to *not* create a procedure.

12. "Just *don't* do it." Eliminate the unnecessary. Think simplicity. Automate. Refine to the smallest amount of steps or discard altogether. Would a simple "no" save time, energy, and/or money? Many times, elimination of a system, protocol, or potential project is a good thing.

13. Our documented systems, procedures, and functions are "off the street." This means anyone with normal intelligence can perform procedures unassisted. The real-world evidence of this is we can hire an individual "off the street" who has good typing skills, and have him or her processing calls within three days. (Before

we implemented our systemized training protocol, it would take six weeks to train a TSR). For this result, systems have to be efficient, simple, and thoroughly documented.

14. Do it NOW. All actions build on "point-of-sale" theory. We don't delay an action if it can be done immediately. Just like any major retail outlet, we "update inventories and databases at the exact time the transaction takes place." There is no paperwork floating around the office after a physical transaction. We ask, "How can we perform the task NOW without creating lingering details that we must clean up later?"

15. We glean the Centratel mindset from Steven Covey's books including *The 7 Habits of Highly Successful People, First Things First,* and *The Eighth Habit.* As well, we consider *From Good to Great* by Jim Collins; *The E-Myth Revisited* by Michael Gerber, and *Release the Giant Within* by Tony Robbins.

16. We pattern personal organization upon Franklin Covey theory. We use personal organizing systems that are always at hand. We prioritize, schedule, and document. The system is always up-to-date and we use it all the time. (For Centratel, this system is Microsoft Outlook).

17. Sequence is critical. We work on the most important tasks first. We spend maximum time on "non-urgent/important" tasks via Steven Covey's time-matrix philosophy.

18. We double-check everything before its release. If a penchant for double-checking is not an innate personal habit, then it must be cultivated. Double-checking is a conscious step in every task, performed either by the individual managing the task, or someone else.

19. Our environment is spotless: clean and ordered, simple, efficient, functional. No "rat's nests," literally or figuratively.

20. Employee training is structured, scheduled, and thorough. Assertive client contact is also structured, scheduled, and thorough.

21. We are deadline-obsessed. If someone in the organization says he or she will be finished with a task or project by a certain date and time, then he or she commits to finishing by that deadline (or, if legitimate delays intrude, advises their co-workers well in advance the deadline is impossible).

22. We maintain equipment and keep it 100 percent functional at all times. If something is not working as it should, fix it now—fix it now even if it's not necessary to fix it now. It's a matter of good housekeeping and of maintaining good habits. This is just the way we do things.

23. Mastery of the English language is critical. We are aware of how we sound and what we write. We do whatever we can to improve. We are patient as a co-worker corrects us.

24. We study to increase our skills. A steady diet of reading and contemplation is vital to personal development. It is a matter of self-discipline.

25. As opposed to "doing the work," the department manager's job is to create, monitor, and document systems (which consist of people, equipment, procedures, and maintenance schedules).

26. The CEO/General Manager oversees department heads and systems. It is the CEO/GM's job to direct, coordinate, and monitor the entire operation.

27. We avoid multi-tasking activities. For example, when communicating with someone else, we are 100 percent present. We give full attention to the person in front of us. We focus on listening and understanding. Read the classic *Treating Type A Behavior and Your Heart* by Meyer Friedman. "Mindfulness" is paying complete attention to one thing at a time: Read *Full Catastrophe Living* by Jon Kabat-Zinn.

28. When in the office, we work hard on Centratel business. We keep our heads down; we focus, and in turn the company pays very well. That's "the deal." The workweek rarely exceeds 40 hours.

29. "Complete" means *complete*. "Almost" or "tomorrow" is not "complete." In particular, this is germane to administration staff's use of Outlook task functions.

30. This can't be legislated, but we strive for a social climate that is serious and quiet, yet pleasant, serene, light, and friendly. Centratel is a nice place to work.

IQ Tests for Employees?

System thinking sometimes points out the status-quo is in error; that common assumptions are questionable.

A TSR must have the sharp-witted ability to process multiple, unrelated snippets of information and make hundreds of decisions within the course of a single eight-hour shift. Some of these decisions are matters of life-and-death, so hiring the right people is critical. Because the job requires individuals with solid reasoning ability and mental agility, would it make sense to use an IQ test as part of the application process? After all, an IQ test measures a person's ability to reason—and, more prosaic to the position—how well a person can quickly and accurately process information. But, it just seems *so 1984...* and maybe a violation of personal rights, or discrimination of some kind. What to do?

We checked with an outside employment specialist and the Oregon Employment Department and found that as long as we didn't violate anyone's rights, we could test job applicants in this way. So now, every job applicant takes the "Aptitude Test." If the applicant achieves the minimum score we require, they are considered for a position.

We administer the test early in the application process because without adequate reasoning ability, no matter their other attributes, the new employee would not be able to master the position. By disqualifying a job applicant for an inadequate aptitude test score, we evade weeks of expensive, frustrating training followed by inevitable dismissal. And, to any employee, job termination because of inability to perform is a psychological blow far worse than not receiving the job in the first place. (Note that we *never* give the job applicant his or her test score. If applicants want to know their IQ, they must take the test on their own. There are plenty of online tests available.)

But the aptitude test is just one sub-system of the primary hiring system. Every job applicant goes through the identical interview/testing routine. Covering all bases in identical methodical sequence, the hiring system is fair, simple to administer, and potently effective. We seldom hire an individual who doesn't succeed.

With our aptitude test, are we outside-and-slightly-elevated? Yes, especially in the sense that we apply our hiring process in exactly the same way for every applicant. Hiring is no longer a gut-feeling decision; we don't reinvent it with every new job applicant, and the applicant's success or failure does not depend on variables such as the interviewing manager's momentary state of mind.

CHAPTER 15

THE STODGY CURE FOR WORKPLACE CHAOS: WORKING PROCEDURES

I don't want to be a product of my environment. I want my environment to be a product of me.

Frank Costello (Jack Nicholson), from the movie, *The Departed*

It's boring but true: The cure to workplace chaos is to get things down on paper.

First, put together the Strategic Objective. It will require a few hours to develop a draft, and a few more hours over another couple of days to get it right. Creating it is pretty much a one-time event, but allow for minor future revisions as the environment changes.

Next, after you write the Strategic Objective's first draft, you will begin work on the General Operating Principles, the contents of which will be accumulated bit-by-bit and then perfected over a few weeks' time. Still, the total time invested isn't much. Once completed, this document will also remain relatively static over the years.

Third, for your business or your job, you will create a collection of Working Procedures.

A Working Procedure is in itself the archetypical system. Products of system improvement, each is an exact guideline for executing the process it describes.

Over the long-term, you and your staff will spend the majority of documentation time creating new Working Procedures and tweaking existing ones.

Although the Strategic Objective and the General Operating Principles will get little mechanical adjustment later on, their fundamentals are key to the creation of your Working Procedures (or, in your personal life, in just navigating the day). In any case, at work, all three documents will remain front and center in your mind.

For every unit of effort and time you expend on the three documents, the return in personal time and financial freedom will be at least one hundredfold. *I am not exaggerating.*

There is no need for written Working Procedures in your personal life, but you will carry the concept with you everywhere you go. To understand the Working Procedure concept for life outside of work, read between the lines in the following for-business discussion.

The Small Packages That Are Working Procedures

At Centratel, the same inefficiencies kept cropping up over and over. It was "death by a thousand cuts." These recurring problems were the natural result of undocumented, uncontrolled processes. Now, Working Procedures, products of the system improvement process, prevent these serial headaches by providing exact direction for flawless operation and for solving unexpected, one-time, wild-card challenges.

From the chaos, we break things down into small "system package units" by extracting inefficient systems from the daily operation and outlining them on paper in a simple 1-2-3 step linear, chronological format. (First, this happens; second that happens; third…etc.). Yes, we have a number of non-linear Working Procedures that are better explained in either a narrative or bullet-point format. But note that a non-linear procedure can be listed in a non-sequential, numerical format. (As previously mentioned, Centratel's 30 Principles document, a working procedure in itself, is presented in this way).

In a nutshell, here's the system improvement process: After documenting a given protocol as it is, we analyze the mechanical process on paper, and from that, develop a streamlined finished product with attending final documentation.

Then we implement it. Everyone follows the new procedure exactly as it is written. Over time, we tweak it to perfection.

We follow this system improvement routine over and over again, making every individual system perfect.

The finished products are our "Working Procedures," or simply, "Procedures." At Centratel, we have approximately 300 of them. Depending on the task, they can range from the utter simplicity of two short sentences, to line after line of detail encompassing a half-dozen pages.

FEATHERS IN THE WIND

Remember that *a set of instructions for a process is not a Working Procedure until it is written down. Instructions that are not written down are feathers in the wind.* Think of it this way: One can't represent being a college graduate unless the parchment is in hand. No parchment. No degree. No exceptions. You are either a college graduate or you are not. Think of your Working Procedures in the same way: If they are not tangible, they don't exist.

Two Key Points in Creating Working Procedures

Here is key point number one for designing, producing, and executing procedures: For a recurring problem or process, if there is a "best solution," it is optimal to use that best solution every single time the problem or process surfaces. At Centratel, we collectively decide what works best in the majority of circumstances, we "cast the procedure in concrete" in written form, and then apply the procedure exactly as written every single time. No matter who applies the protocol, the same "best solution" will always be applied and therefore, "best results" will almost always occur.

Will the Working Procedure provide the perfect solution for every situation? No, but it will be perfect *most* of the time and that is far better than haphazard solutions that are applied on a whim. So, over time, incremental "best results" add up to a "big best result" for the primary system.

Key point number two: Procedure documentation is not limited to fixing obvious problems. It applies to all internal processes. Documenting a seemingly flawless process will often reveal small imperfections. It will take a while to turn every process into a Working Procedure, but the efficiency increases earned from this effort will accumulate. If a sub-system is 90 percent effective, and it can be boosted to 98 percent effectiveness, that's a good thing. *What could be better for a primary system than to spend time improving all of its sub-systems?*

These days, little goes wrong at Centratel, and the things that do go wrong are fixed immediately. As fire-killing is reduced and more and more processes are automated and delegated, more free time becomes available. This is the main reason our managers' workweek is seldom more than forty hours and why mine, as company CEO and GM, is rarely more than two hours. This overall efficiency is also the reason I now earn more in a month than what I used to earn in a year.

LARGE AND SUCCESSFUL, OR SMALL AND FAILING?

Without exception, the businesses that are large and successful are "working their systems." And the ones without stuctured, sensible protocols and logical direction—many small businesses, governmental agencies, and non-profit organizations—are struggling. Very simple.

Our First Working Procedure

Again, this is mandatory: *A system improvement requires a written Working Procedure. The Working Procedure makes the system tangible—something to be seen, grasped, understood, perfected, shared, and then applied exactly the same way every time.*

Know this: A this-will-happen-every-single-time protocol won't materialize via mind reading, a one-time conversation, or when it is discussed in a meeting. *An effective process must be set in concrete and that means creating it hard and/or soft copy, distributing it, and then insuring it is implemented.*

Our first Working Procedure was the "Deposit Procedure" which provided our management staff with exact directions for processing the dozens of client payments that come in the mail each day. This process involves more than the actual bank deposit. It also includes receiving incoming checks, crediting them to clients' accounts in the receivables software, and cross-checking totals. Eight years ago, when we created this first Working Procedure, three management people, including me, were authorized to make a deposit. No written instructions existed.

The reason we focused on the Deposit Procedure first was because it was a critical system and it had deep flaws. Without any set-in-writing protocol, and with each of us performing the task in our own unique way, we too often made random mistakes, seldom in Centratel's favor (and if they *were* in our favor, a client was short-changed). Sometimes we applied payments to the wrong accounts, and too many times deposit sums were incorrect. One time, a three thousand dollar deposit was lost by one of our managers, to be found weeks later under her car seat. Of course, any wasted money was subtracted dollar-for-dollar from the bottom line. As we describe in Operating Principle number 10, "the money we save or waste is *not* Monopoly money!"

And with all the gyrations and outright errors, the process was taking far too much time and *that* was a waste.

So, the three of us put our heads together. After thoroughly interviewing my managers, this first system improvement/Working Procedure took me four hours to compose. Then, to tweak it to perfection, it took maybe three more hours spread over a couple more days.

This first Deposit Procedure contained 53 individual steps. Here is how they went: Step one: "Put the envelopes in a stack in front of you on the desk and open all the envelopes. (Do not take the contents out of the envelopes.)" Step two: "Open the receivables software and go to the deposit module." Step three, etc., until step 50, which was "take the deposit to the bank and make the deposit." Then, step 51: "At the bank, get a deposit slip and check the amount deposited to make sure it matches the amount on the deposit slip." Then, step 52: "Back in the office, staple the bank deposit slip to the upper left hand corner of the receivables batch printout," and finally, step 53: "place the printout in the daily deposit file in the receivables file cabinet in the CFO's office."

We agreed that if one of us saw room for improvement in a working procedure, we would collaborate on the spot. If we all agreed the change would be good, we would instantly update the procedure's documentation—and just as quickly implement the procedure in its revised form. *The published procedure itself was inflexible yet we would immediately change the construction of the procedure if a change would improve it.* (This "change it immediately" parameter was per our do-it-now Operating Principle #14.)

We put the Deposit Procedure into play. From then on, no matter who performed it, the deposit process proceeded the same way every single time. Over time, we tweaked it and the procedure got better and better. We built double-checks into it so we knew for sure the payments were tallied correctly, and we built in steps to ensure deposits made it to the bank.

Because we put the procedure together in a simple 1-2-3 step format, anyone within the company could make a deposit. As a result, I didn't do deposits anymore as we delegated my portion of the task to another staff member. Neither did I have to take the time to train someone else to do the job. Completing that first Working Procedure reduced my personal workload by a couple of hours each week. My one-hundred hour workweek was now ninety-eight hours. That's two hours per week over eight years. Do the math.

In its own way, that first procedure was a tiny masterpiece, and yet we continued to polish it to even more effectiveness. Since we started using it, there has been only one small, easily-corrected error. Of course, repairing that particular error meant yet another small improvement in the written procedure (per General Operating Principle #7).

Even though we put the first procedure together eight years ago, I remember this: It was satisfying beyond words to know the deposit processing was finally stable and efficient. And, it was no small satisfaction to realize I would never have to personally do another deposit.

A Working Procedure, a mandatory element of the system improvement process, is not theory or feel-good fluff. Rather, it is something that is down-and-dirty *useful* in the real-time world. Raymond Carver, now deceased, wrote a short story titled, *A Small Good Thing*. That's what a solid Working Procedure is…"a small good thing." *The idea is to make your business and your life a huge accumulation of small good things.*

We were energized by this first success. Would a complete collection of Working Procedures add up to a profitable business and personal freedom? How could it be otherwise? This point in time—just after we instituted the first procedure—was when I became convinced beyond any doubt we were on the right path. Deep inside, I knew we would succeed. My motivation was red hot.

It was back in those first post "ah-ha" days that I coined the term "Working Procedure." I've always liked that term as it reflects the simple, primal nature of it.

THE TEST OF TIME

Regarding the Strategic Objective and the Operating Principles, know that a confirmation of their viability is the test of time. If you are truly using them and they change little over the months and years, this is confirmation they are sound. On the other hand, Working Procedures should constantly evolve, and that evolution is confirmation *they* are valid.

Revisiting the Deposit Procedure

Today, after an eight-year hiatus, I decided to personally make the day's deposit. Since we created it, I had not seen the Deposit Procedure until this morning when Andi cheerfully dropped it on my desk and then walked away. She knew she didn't have to review it with me even though it had seen massive changes through the years.

It was not the procedure I remembered. With a big stack of checks in front of me, the evolved process was slow-going at first, but I followed it line by line. I picked up speed, finished, and on the way to the bank to make the deposit, I realized the procedure was flawless—still a beautiful thing. And sitting here this evening, writing these words, I am feeling as fulfilled as eight years ago when I wallowed in the satisfaction of completing the original 53-step procedure. It was original folk art then—and is a refined masterpiece today. (I thank Andi, our Chief Operations Officer, for that; for following the systems strategy exactly.) The Deposit Procedure is 23 steps now, due to better software and my staff's learned ability to simplify, streamline, and economize. Per Sir Ockham, simplicity is evidence a solution is sound.

What was our second Working Procedure? We analyzed, dissected, and set in stone the methodology the TSRs use to process incoming calls. Our TSRs have executed this Working Procedure thousands of times *every day* since we put it into place over eight years ago.

In the months after we instituted the Deposit and TSR Answering Procedures, we analyzed and streamlined scores of other recurring processes including how to put together the staffing schedule, how to streamline collections, and how to pay the bills. We created procedures for performing the monthly customer invoicing, ensuring the various housekeeping tasks were done on a regular basis, making the most effective sales presentation, etc.

For some undocumented processes that were in place, our system improvement analysis suggested creating a Working Procedure wasn't necessary, and in fact we had been wasting our time performing the process at all! Discarding paper records of customer contacts is a good example of this purging action. In analyzing the process, we discovered that after years of accumulating hard-copy evidence of every client interaction, no staff member had *ever* gone back to those files for information!

When these obsolete processes occasionally appeared, we dumped them with a flourish, a collective grin on our faces. For other less-than-efficient tasks, we found ourselves devising radically altered protocols, with final versions unrecognizable from the originals. It was a cleansing process. The assertive effort to root out and improve every single system led us to these unexpected deletions and substitutions.

Centratel was becoming dramatically more efficient.

We worked hard, improving and documenting system after system. Interestingly, there were rarely relationships among the procedures we created or revised. *The sore spots we tackled were unrelated but we had a methodology for setting priorities: We straightened out the weightiest problems first.*

As we worked up the new procedures and "released" them as official, I found myself delegating more and more tasks that had been my responsibility. I simply handed a completed Working Procedure over to the appropriate manager and walked away. I was steadily gaining additional personal time to reinvest in tackling more problem areas. It was the same situation for my managers as they delegated processes down the chain of command while the rate of incoming problems continued to decrease.

Although the original, one-time heavy lifting—the documentation of all of our procedures in one gigantic effort—ended years ago, we continue to apply the system improvement methodology on a moment-to-moment basis. *No longer do we fire-kill. Instead, we "work our systems."*

ARE YOU WILLING?

Today, are you willing to invest X hours of your time in order to save 100X hours down the line?

IN A NUTSHELL:
CREATING WORKING PROCEDURES

> We analyze a system individually, document it as it is, find the cause of the recurring problem or inefficiency, devise a system improvement to fix the problem or cure the inefficiency, and then create a prototype written Working Procedure. We then test the procedure in the real world, tweaking it into a final procedure that precisely explains the desired execution of the process. The new Working Procedure is released and the Centratel staff follows it exactly as written. That's it!

A Procedure to Create Procedures

As we first began creating Working Procedures at Centratel, I felt compelled to do much of the documentation myself. It took me months to see this was unnecessary, and I caution you not to fall into the same trap.

There is a system for everything so certainly there is one that will oversee the creation of procedures by people other than you—a "Procedure for Procedures." This master document lays out the format and tone you wish to be used in creating everyday Working Procedures. Once complete, you will train your managers to use it exactly.

The core of the training is the Procedure for Procedures itself. And when I say train, I mean *train*. Each manager must "get it." Set aside group classes that will be uninterrupted. You will be the teacher and your managers will be the students. Consider having your staff study this book. (Note there is a quiz for testing comprehension at **www.workthesystem.com/quiz**.)

An added benefit of having your staff create Working Procedures is the process will encourage them to buy into the methodology. They will see the beauty of it first-hand, from the bottom up. However, be ruthless in examining every single procedure they create. You want to know what's happening: It's your responsibility to ensure your people are following directions exactly.

CENTRATEL'S PROCEDURE
FOR PROCEDURES

Following is our master Procedure for Procedures, which contains precise instructions for creating a Working Procedure. It is the "Mother of All Procedures," the master instructions for creating the several hundred that are necessary for our operation. This document ensures each will share the same tone and format.

Don't be discouraged by the length and complexity of it, and don't get bogged down in what it says. Of all the procedures at Centratel, it's the longest and most intricate. Simply consider its essence and then apply it to your own situation. It begins with a narration.

Procedure for Procedures

Overview to staff: We base Centratel's mechanical functioning on Working Procedures (or simply, "Procedures"). With hundreds of human and mechanical operating processes in action at any one time, keeping things organized in any other way would be impossible. Working Procedures guide everything from an emergency relay for a TAS account, to how we deposit payments in the bank, to job descriptions for staff members, to greeting customers at the door.

Strict adherence to written procedure is critical, but we counterbalance this strictness with our eagerness to make instant adjustments should the environment change or should someone come up with a better idea. Whatever your job description, if you have a suggestion for improvement, pass it on. If it's good, we'll change the written procedure and implement it now!

Strict yet easy-to-modify procedures provide a huge degree of freedom to the individual staff member because the guidelines eliminate guesswork. Answers and instructions are right there. This is the heart of Centratel's operational model: "freedom and responsibility within a structured yet flexible business system."

Specifics:

- Is there a recurring problem or task? Then a Working Procedure is necessary. Or, if there is already a procedure and a problem arises, we will modify the existing procedure to eliminate the problem. If there is no problem, let's streamline the procedure to make it as efficient as possible.

- In the earliest stage of creating a procedure, get feedback from those people affected. It is mandatory the creator of the procedure and the relevant department manager be advised of any changes before they are made. In fact, they must be intimately involved with the revision, and each must give final approval to changes.

- Per point-of-sale strategy, we will change a procedure instantly. *Improvement of a procedure by modification, addition, deletion, or outright elimination is quick and without hesitation.* We operate within a strict framework but that framework can be quickly changed by group consent.

- Post all new or modified procedures on the procedures drive. In the modified procedure, date the change, and show the new information in blue type. Hard copies are immediately printed, and placed in alphabetical order in either the Administrative Procedures Folder or the Operations Procedures Folder.

- Each affected staff member will review the new procedure. Upon understanding it, the staff member initials and dates the hard copy.

- The staff member directs questions and suggestions back to the person who created the procedure. (If there *is* a question, it is evidence the procedure itself should be further modified so questions will not have to be asked in the future). Before release, all new or significantly modified procedures must be OK'd by the General Manager.

- The staff member follows the new procedure exactly. HEAR THIS: IF A PROBLEM ARISES WITH A PROCEDURE, WE INSTANTLY ADJUST THE PROCEDURE. WE DO NOT CIRCUMVENT IT!

Design:*

- Use template on P: drive entitled "Procedures Template" and in the Template folder.

- Create the procedure with an "off the street" simplicity. Be simple, concise, and thorough.

- Remember the overall goal: "Freedom and responsibility within a highly developed system."

- How much information should be included?

  - *For narrative procedures:* Add as much information as possible, but do it in a way that the information is easily found. Use alphabetical listings, logical subheadings, numbering and bullet formats, simple and concise sentence structure, etc.

  - *For charts and graph procedures*: Design it to be simple, concise, and fast to read. Often it will be necessary to leave out information in order to make it more readable. Limit the typefaces and sizes, special formats, etc.

- Start with the title, in the Heading 1 style (Verdana bold size 12).

- Follow the title with the date, in the Procedure Date style (Verdana regular 10).

- For subheadings, use the Heading 2 style (Verdana bold size 10) and for further subdivision within those subheadings, use the Heading 3 style (Verdana italics size 10).

- For the body text, use the Normal style (Verdana regular size 10).

- For any bullets or numbering, use the default bullets and numbering styles.

- Procedures are addressed at the bottom of the last page in this way:

  - Select View, Headers, and Footers.

  - Click in Footer.

  - 1st line: Choose Insert AutoText "Filename and Path."

- 2nd line: Choose Insert AutoText "Created By." Add your name. You may have to do this manually, depending on what computer you are using and how it is set up.

- 3rd line: Choose Insert AutoText "created on." Add date and time.

- Use the Footer style.

- Use italics and bold sparingly.

- Use the 1-2-3 step format when applicable.

- Use bullets or numbers when applicable.

- If a relay is involved, use numbering and the same acronyms and methodology used in TAS relays.

- Do not assume anything. Every step must be obvious and logical. Especially do not assume the user of the procedure will be knowledgeable regarding the subject or can read your mind: remember the "off the street" methodology!

- General layout: After the title, if necessary, start the procedure with a concise narrative that provides a quick overall description of the what, why, how, who, and when of the procedure. Follow this, if applicable to the particular procedure, with bulleted or numbered instructions.

- Never title a procedure "Procedure for..." The title must be concise yet descriptive and make sense to an "off the street" staff member. The title must be logical so the subject can be found quickly. Start the title with the subject. For example: Sales Call Procedure," not, "Procedure for Sales Calls." Then start with a brief narrative of what the procedure accomplishes.

- Critical: Test the procedure before release! Use an "off the street" subject (a staff member who is *not* involved with the subject).

Note: Easy Template Software eliminates these complex details. See appendix C or go to **workthesystem.com/easy**.

Is the above procedure long and complicated? Yes and no. The "Specifics" portion is simple. The "Design" portion is necessarily long because the details are complex—it's the actual mechanical guideline for creating a procedure. But, its detail is clear and concise, and therefore not at all complicated. You will note, like the 30 Principles document, it is non-linear.

As leader of the company, *it is my job to make sure employees have exact guidelines for each task they do.* Then, it is the employee's job to follow those instructions precisely. On this point, I am adamant and can't harp on it enough: It is the staff member's first responsibility to implement a procedure *exactly* as written. There is no latitude here. There must be strict adherence. Does my staff comply? Yes, for four reasons: First, simple logic. Because the written procedure methodology works, they buy into it one-hundred percent. Second, they are involved with the creation and the approval of nearly all procedures, so they are fully vested in them. (In fact, Centratel's staff writes ninety-eight percent of all procedures and has a heavy hand in the other two percent that I create.) Third, if an employee has a good idea for improving a procedure, we will make an instant modification—with no bureaucratic hang-ups. No one wades through the system improvement/Working Procedure process grumbling about how dysfunctional it is. Instead, he or she assertively works to make it better. Fourth, if a procedure is followed and something goes wrong, the staff member is held harmless. It is the procedure that is in error.

Ruthlessness and Flexibility

This is also important enough to belabor: Yes, be ruthless in insisting your staff follows procedures exactly, but balance this strict rule with the understanding that if a procedure must be changed in order to remain effective, with proper consensus, it will be changed instantly. *The procedure itself is rock-solid and inflexible until the moment your management staff agrees changes are necessary.* At Centratel, we make the decision to modify a procedure *right now*, in an ad hoc meeting any time, any place. We modify the procedure in that moment and in the next moment, the adjusted procedure will be distributed to all parties affected.

We insist on adherence to procedure protocol while being open to changing it on a moment's notice. Unwieldy bureaucracy is the enemy, and each time one of us witnesses slow-moving decision-making in other businesses, it's smug confirmation that our own operation is flexible, efficient, and potent.

The perfect example of bureaucratic paralysis is, of course, government—the quintessential non-profit organization that is in business to spend other people's money. Government has given written procedures a bad name. If there is a ubiquitous generalization about "the nightmare of paperwork and bureaucracy" one can say thank you to the overabundance of governmental organizations that surround and engulf us.

Your Competitors Don't Do This

I used to be involved with answering service trade groups. I've served as president of two national associations and was a board member for a couple of others. I became knowledgeable about the politics of my industry and enjoyed communicating with my peers.

At the tail end of my involvement with these groups, I gave a presentation to 60 answering service owners in Las Vegas. The topic was "Procedures and Their Importance." At the beginning of the one-hour session, I asked the group "How many of you have written procedures for your operation?" *No one raised a hand!* I am still shocked to think of that day: Of five dozen answering services, not one owner had written guidelines! That is the way it is for most small businesses.

To compound the wide-scale problem, not only do 98 percent of small business managers fail to write down the intricacies and processes of their businesses, even fewer have written goals. How about you?

Most small business owners are looking for answers in the wrong places because they have not gone through the dissection process that thorough documentation demands. They don't have goals and they don't see the internal inefficiencies of their systems, so they seek spur-of-the-moment "global" solutions: some quick fix—a magic pill—that in one fell swoop will make everything better. Often, the magic pill they seek is a God-like new employee, a mind reader and fortuneteller, an extraordinary individual who will flawlessly manage the business and, with little guidance, take it take it to its deserved success.

Here is the curious fact that most small business owner/managers don't get: Terrific employees *are* out there, but in a non-documented business none will function anywhere near their potential *because mind reading and fortune telling is not something humans can do, no matter their IQ and/or educational pedigree.*

And so it is: After 15 years, less than one out of a hundred small businesses survive.

At the risk of audaciousness, is it no wonder Centratel operates and advertises itself as "the highest quality telephone answering service in the United States"? My staff knows exactly what to do and exactly how to do it. Errors seldom occur because actions are the most efficient possible as the staff relentlessly tweaks systems to perfection. And when there is an error, that error spurs us to devise an even better mechanical system for the future. *We don't spend our time coping with bad results that are the products of neglected systems. We work our systems so bad results don't happen!*

It's elementary: *If each component of an organization is near-flawless, the organization as a whole will be near-flawless,* as evidenced by profitability, net worth, customer reported-error rate, client longevity, staff longevity, reputation, etc.

Centratel's five managers are tenacious in applying the *Work the System* strategy. They assertively search for system inefficiencies, revel in devising system improvements, and enthusiastically create Working Procedures to make those systems permanently efficient. Their individual reward includes reasonable-length workweeks, personal freedom with lots of room for creativity, and intense pride in what they do and where they work. Also, they are highly paid.

Systems, systems, systems!

It all adds up to supreme satisfaction for the staff, superb quality for customers, and solid profits for my partner and me. Further tangible evidence of our efficiency: In our TSR quality statistics for the 12 months prior to publication of this book, we averaged one client-reported error for every 9,990 messages processed. (In that time-period, one TSR, Kathleen, had but a single error in the more than sixty thousand messages she personally processed).

Our service rates? They are higher than the competition—but not by much—because our systems methodology has, while creating unmatched quality, eliminated waste and generated tremendous cost-savings efficiency. Our customers? Successful in their own businesses, they are happy with the arrangement with Centratel as illustrated by our average client tenure which exceeds seven years (remember, the average new business has an eighty percent chance of failing in the first five years).

And, for you and your small business or management position? Attain the systems-perspective epiphany and then buckle down to start the documentation. The day you begin you will be in select company, way out in front of 98 percent of your small business competitors (or, if you work for someone else, your coworkers).

Again, written Working Procedures are not necessary for your personal life. Why? First (and forgive my firm grasp of the obvious), it's just silly to write down how you will maintain the car, work on the details of your marriage, stay in shape, pay bills, or develop a system for staying in touch with friends. With your new vision ingrained, you'll handle these processes systematically without having to write up documentation. And second: A primary reason for creating Working Procedures is to make sure the people you supervise are handling details just as you would handle them. Since *you* are the only one operating your personal life, it is good enough to hard-wire your personal Working Procedures in your head without documentation. The exceptions? Lists for travel or shopping, travel itineraries, to-do lists, and intricate technical instructions that are easy to forget.

A primary mandate at Centratel is that "Procedures will be followed exactly." For our TSRs, who make hundreds and even thousands of decisions daily, precisely following procedures is a ticket to relax and enjoy the work. For example, if there is an error in delivering a message, the TSR holds no blame as long as he or she followed the message delivery procedure exactly. As it turns out, nearly all message relay problems are due to system error, not TSR error. Because our TSRs follow written procedures exactly, nearly all errors are traced back to clients who have not informed us of changes—changes that invalidate the previous, on-record Working Procedure for that client. The procedure was at fault, not the employee. The cure is to make an immediate mechanical update in that client's Message-Relay Working Procedure, not chew someone out.

Maybe the best part of all this is that very seldom does a Centratel employee come under scrutiny for making an error. This lack of finger-pointing contributes much to the serenity of the office.

Just Write it Down

At first, it will seem you don't have the "spare" time to work through the system improvement/Working Procedures process. That's a mistaken premise because if you think creating procedures is a spare time task, the process will take a back seat to the crisis du jour. Procedure documentation must go to the top of your priority list or the process won't start, or will be derailed in a week or two. You will fail. For your business or job, raise the importance level of writing procedures to the number one position, above even some of the fire-killing of the day. So, forget about "finding spare time" to do this work. Don't waste your efforts by starting on that premise. Anyway, *there is no such thing as "spare" time*.

Although it might take an hour or two a day to write up and then institute a new procedure—do it anyway. Personal time savings will begin immediately upon implementation. Soon, you will crave spending time on your quest to document your entire operation, while the time you spend doing non-procedure work will be frustrating.

As noted earlier, for your new linear Working Procedures you will usually use a simple 1-2-3 step format. Remember that the litmus test for simplicity is that anyone from outside the company, "off the street," could perform the procedure. Of course, depending on your business or job, this simplicity might have to be more specific. For example, writing an electrical engineering procedure for an "off the street layperson" is not going to work. But writing an electrical engineering procedure for an "off the street electrical engineer" is reasonable. You get the idea.

With Working Procedures, you will save enormous time in training people to full effectiveness. An employee who doesn't know the ropes of a particular task will simply read the procedure and then get the job done without assistance from other staff members. There will be no error-prone and belabored, "learning by osmosis."

And of course, for yourself and for your managers, the extra time saved is used for improving the systemization even more: The "cycle of increasing returns."

Here's another large plus: With written Working Procedures in place, your operation's comportment becomes more professional. Your people will recognize this and raise expectations of themselves and for their company. Your staff's pride and enthusiasm will shine brightly for your customers.

A Summary of Procedure Documentation:

1. Every recurring process requires a Working Procedure. The procedure will precisely define the best method of performing the action, handling the situation, or answering the question.

2. A problem is a good thing when your staff takes it as a cue for the creation or modification of a Working Procedure. However, be reasonable. Do not create an unwieldy bureaucracy by writing up procedures for problems that are random or seldom;

problems that have little chance of resurfacing. There is a danger of being inundated with a massive conglomeration of rarely used procedures, thus creating complexity due to the sheer volume of information. Solving infrequent problems requires just a bit of common sense based on the guidelines provided by the Strategic Objective and Operating Principles documents.

3. Be sure your staff is involved in creating the new procedures. In fact, relentlessly delegate.

4. Most of your procedures will be in a linear, step-by-step format (made simple with the *Work the System Easy-Template* product—for details, go to **workthesystem.com/easy**). By making procedures identical in presentation, their individual instructions will come through loud and clear without becoming confused by various style or tone variations. This is where you as the leader come in. It's up to you to keep things on track.

5. Without exception, test every new procedure. Before releasing, give it to a staff member who will carefully go through the steps to spot glitches. Take this stance: In a new or revamped procedure, glitches will *always* occur.

6. As the leader, sign off on procedures yourself. Make sure they are consistent with your overall vision. *Keep things in order, always in line with your Strategic Objective. As the leader, that's your job.*

DO THE RIGHT THING

Consider it your ethical responsibility—not just an efficient way to operate—to provide Working Procedures for your staff. I occasionally remind our managers that it is my personal obligation to provide them with the tools to do their jobs. Expecting an employee to be able to read the boss's mind is not just an absurd expectation, it's unfair. I tell them that.

Jim Morrison and Mick Jagger

Morrison and Jagger are arguably the best lead singers rock has ever produced: Morrison's voice and lyrics; Jagger's voice and flair.

Jim Morrison's short, wild ride was fueled by his brilliant observations and brazen thought-images, built around a mystique of chaos. He wallowed in the haunting darkness, and wondered at the great unknown beyond death. He lived that way, too, awash in alcohol and drugs, abusing his physical and mental systems. He died at the age of 27 after just four years of performing and recording. His too-short life was the antithesis of systemization and order.

Mick Jagger, however, has been hammering away for over 40 years, ten times longer than did Morrison. Essentially, Jagger is general manager and CEO of the Rolling Stones, personally attending to the operation of the enormously complex Rolling Stones touring and recording machine. He is as fit as any 25 year old, eschewing drugs and alcohol. Whether it's creating music, performing, recording, or managing the enormous complexity that is his world, system improvement is clearly his primary aim. Enormously talented, healthy, and wealthy, a connoisseur of antiques and art, he is a master of systemizing, tweaking, and maintaining.

PART THREE

FURTHER CONSIDERATIONS

HERE IS A NON-LINEAR collection of how-tos that complement the methodology presented in Parts One and Two. You will find hard and fast techniques as well as subjective "positioning principles."

As usual, as I write of a business matter, read between the lines for application to personal life.

CHAPTER 16

Good Enough

*A good plan violently executed right now is far better
than a perfect plan executed next week.*

George S. Patton

That's Why It's Called *Work*

To preface this discussion, understand this is about *work*, not about relaxing or some combination of the two. If you own a business, the mission is to work hard but not long, to reduce the workweek by 95 percent, and to make more money than you require. If you have a job, the goal is to use your forty hour workweek to produce large quantities of superior work in order to quickly ascend the management ranks until you can call your own shots.

This needs to be said and it's a good time to say it: No matter what your situation, if you are going to work, then *work*! Turn the radio off, get your feet off the desk, stop the pointless babbling with co-workers, and put your head down.

Get in, do the work, and get out.

Smell the flowers later when it's time to give those flowers all your attention. Multi-tasking between working and relaxing will result in frustration in both areas: in your work, long hours spent in a mish-mash of unsatisfying mediocrity, and in your leisure, an unsettled persona.

Less Than Perfect Performance Is an OK Thing

For the *Work the System* method, here is a qualifier: *Getting things too perfect is counterproductive and shortsighted.*

In my background as a land surveyor, there is a story that illustrates the good-enough concept. In vocational school, back when I was 24 years old, our surveying instructor told the class a fictitious story at the beginning of the year, prepping us for the rest of the technical lessons that would follow. The story setting was the early '70s when the typical survey crew consisted of a party chief (the crew leader, responsible for supervising the actual in-the-field survey work), and three additional crew members.

The party chief is given a project and it is up to him (in those days, it was almost always a "him") to take the crew into the field, do the job, and report back to the owner of the surveying company with accurate and usable notes so a map of the surveyed land can be created. With the notes and the map, the land owner's questions of property size, boundary lines, and future development possibilities can be answered.

A survey project is a linear, encapsulated process—yes, a system—and a project begins when the survey company owner tells the party chief, in not so many words, "here's the job. I presume you can handle it. Be quick and accurate according to the specifications I give you, then come back and give me your field notes so the draftsman can make a map of the property. Then I can get paid by the land owner."

Ben and John

This scenario is about a small surveying company and two of the half dozen survey crews it employs. The party chiefs and their respective crews are to survey the boundaries of a landowner's two parcels of land.

The owner of the survey firm assigns the first parcel to one crew (with Ben as the party chief), and the other parcel to another crew (John is the party chief). The owner of the land wants the surveys performed in order to get a general feel for where the property lines and property corners are located.

The survey company owner provides Ben and John with brief yet detailed verbal instructions about what is required. As in any survey project, the crews must measure the distances and angles of the property boundaries quickly, efficiently, and accurately. The degree of accuracy depends on the reason for the survey, and of course, higher degrees of accuracy require more crew time and therefore are more expensive. In survey work, it's a balancing act between speed and accuracy, as the crew moves along, physically marking property corners and providing distance and angle statistics to the party chief, who takes notes.

Time is always of the essence to the survey company owner because he pays his crews by the hour but receives a flat fee from the client upon completion of the project. In this story, time is even more critical because the property owner has a deadline to meet. The crews must get to work immediately and finish the two surveys promptly.

The surveying will be challenging. Each parcel is wooded, undulating, and has irregular perimeters. Each is similar in size—several miles in circumference. Based on the survey company owner's verbal briefing, each party chief makes a determination of how much accuracy is required to survey his particular parcel.

The next day, the two crews separately gather the necessary materials and equipment and head off to their projects. The two crews go to work, each surveying their respective properties.

Ben decides his survey requires measurement to the nearest one-hundredth of a foot—a high level of accuracy. Using a theodolite (a sophisticated tripod-mounted instrument for measuring precise angles), and a "steel chain" for measuring near-exact distances, his crew slowly and methodically works through their project, carefully marking the physical property corners, exactly measuring distances and angles, checking and double-checking their work. Ben takes careful notes in his field book, as the notes will be the on-paper representation of what the crew accomplishes. The four are focused and fastidious; their work exact.

It takes the crew three days to complete the survey at a total cost of $800 to their boss, the owner of the survey company. Their work is perfect; the submitted survey notes neat and concise, with Ben taking an additional day to review them to make sure they are superbly understandable.

In the meantime, John had determined his crew would survey their parcel with less accuracy, measuring only to the nearest whole foot. They would finish the job quickly that way. The crew moves at a blistering pace, using the same equipment as Ben's crew but not taking time to measure distances and angles as precisely. John takes quick notes, double-checking them as he goes. The crew moves at full-tilt, marking property corners while rapidly taking angle and distance measurements.

They complete the survey in just one day and John immediately submits his work, telling the survey company owner that the measured distances and angles are not precise. The submitted notes are smudged and wrinkled, evidence of a quick moving crew that is not concerned with appearances. The total cost for John's one-day survey is $200.

Three days after John turned in his notes, Ben turns in his. His crew's measurement of the distances and angles of the property are exact, with property corners set within one-hundredth of a foot of absolute accuracy. Ben has worked diligently, producing a remarkably beautiful piece of work. He is proud of what he has done. His notes are elegant, standing in stark contrast to the smudged notes John submitted three days before. Ben's notes inspire confidence that his field work was precise.

The owner of the survey company reviews both party chief's notes, and...*he fires Ben.*

The party chief who took so much care and produced such accurate work, is *fired?* Why?

Because Ben did not pay close attention to his boss's original instructions indicating a rough survey was all that was required, and time was critical! Ben's extra efforts at accuracy were not just a waste of time—they were a waste of money.

In land surveyor parlance, Ben committed a "blunder." The survey didn't require measurements to one-hundredth of a foot, so the additional time expended to provide that level of accuracy was an utter waste. In his original briefing to each party chief, the survey company owner had explained the property owner wanted only a general idea of where the property lines and property corners were located. Ben had not listened carefully, self-enamored with his ability to produce tremendous accuracy. In his zeal for precision, he wasted three days and $600 by providing a huge amount of useless information.

It was a blunder based on arrogance and narrow vision. Precision that is not required is often just that.

This story illustrates the importance of "good enough." *Better than good enough is a waste of time and money.*

SOCIAL SYSTEMS THEN AND NOW

This monologue, "Congratulations," written by an unknown author and addressed to early baby boomers, appears in various forms on the Internet. You may have seen it. Whatever your age, avoid being judgmental here. The point of including this piece is to inspire you to begin to dispassionately consider various system structures and to think about the lack of systems in day's past, compared to the abundance of systems today. Be mechanical in your analysis. Were there too few systems in the '60s? Are there too many today? Were children tougher back then? Is there a price to be paid for over-systemizing?

Congratulations!

"You lived as a child in the '60s or the '70s. Looking back, it's hard to believe we have managed to live as long as we have. As children, we would ride in cars with no seat belts or air bags. Riding in the back of a pickup truck on a warm day was always a special treat. Our baby cribs were covered with bright colored lead-based paint.

We had no childproof lids on medicine bottles, doors, or cabinets, and when we rode our bikes, we had no helmets. (Not to mention hitchhiking to town as a young kid!) We drank water from the garden hose and not from a bottle. Horrors! We would spend hours building our go-carts out of scraps and then ride down the hill, only to find we forgot the brakes. After running into the bushes a few times, we learned to solve the problem.

We would leave home in the morning and play all day, as long as we were back when the streetlights came on. No one was able to reach us all day. No cell phones. Unthinkable. We played dodge ball and sometimes the ball would really hurt. We got cut and broke bones and broke teeth and there were no lawsuits from these accidents. They were accidents. No one was to blame but us.

We had fights and punched each other and got black and blue and learned to get over it. We ate cupcakes, bread and butter, and drank sugar soda but we were seldom overweight because we were always outside playing. We shared one grape soda with four friends, from one bottle, and no one died. We did not have PlayStations, Nintendo 64, X Boxes, video games, 99 channels on cable, DVD movies, surround sound, personal cellular phones, personal computers, or internet chat rooms. We had friends next door.

We went outside and found them. We rode bikes, or walked to a friend's home and knocked on the door, or rung the bell or just walked in and talked to them. Imagine such a thing. Without asking a parent! By ourselves! Out there in the cold cruel world! Without a guardian. How did we do it? How did we survive? We made up games with sticks and tennis balls and ate worms and although we were told it would happen, we did not put out eyes, nor did the worms live inside us forever.

Little League had tryouts and not everyone made the team. Those who didn't had to learn to deal with disappointment. Some students weren't as smart as others so they failed a grade and were held back to repeat the same grade. Horrors! Tests were not adjusted for any reason. Our actions were our own. Consequences were expected. No one to hide behind. The idea of a parent bailing us out if we broke a law was unheard of. They actually sided with the law. Imagine that!

The generation of people who were kids during the '60s and '70s has produced some of the best risk-takers and problem solvers and inventors, ever. The past 50 years has been an explosion of innovation and new ideas. We had freedom, failure, success and responsibility, and we learned how to survive and prosper with what we had. And you're one of them, so congratulations."

98 Percent Perfection

Time and money wasted is time and money gone forever. And a waste of time and money means some other positive thing that could have happened, didn't.

The "Good Enough" rule is especially applicable to Working Procedures. A 100 percent perfect document that took forever to create carries an unintended imperfection: The extra time spent creating the masterpiece is lost forever, therefore the finished product carries an imbedded taint and—catch 22—can never be called "perfect."

So, make your procedures detailed but don't make them *too* detailed. They should be good enough so the desired results are consistently produced, and so someone "off the street" can execute them, but no more. See it this way: *In putting your procedures together quickly, you are reaching a kind of perfection—the perfection of a useful product created without waste.*

Throughout this book I have asserted that you must "tweak your procedures to perfection." Now you better understand why my definition of perfection is 98 percent, not 100 percent.

Regarding the *Work the System* process, are there exceptions to the rule? Yes, there are two. Both your Strategic Objective and Operating Principles should be as close to 100 percent perfect as possible, despite the additional time it takes to get there. These documents are the heart of your efforts—the guiding lights for today and tomorrow. They are short, and you and your people will read them repeatedly. Imperfections will stand out, overshadowing the message. The Strategic Objective and the Operating Principles documents are the brief summations of everything you are and how you will proceed so, yes, spend good time on them.

BEWARE USELESS INFORMATION & WHINING

Guard your consciousness and your focus. Don't waste time on useless information or complain about what you can't effect.

With the people and things around you, be militant about relegating unimportant media and advertisement-driven trivia to the trash pile of useless information that resides on the periphery of your consciousness. Don't let zero-value details poison what is important to your life, no matter how dogged the encroachment.

Do you get caught up with what is not fair in the world? That's an utter waste of time if you can't accomplish something tangible to fix the unfairness (and whining and complaining doesn't count as accomplishment...)

Choose your battles.

This is Not a (expletive) Clock

For a while, I was a free-lance construction inspector working with power line crews who build overhead transmission lines. Following written construction designs, the crews use massive crane trucks to insert enormous 70 to 80 foot wood poles in the ground. Then they go back to string heavy gauge conductor (wire) between them.

These crews are made up of weather-beaten, hard-living, all-American linemen. Straight out of the union hall, good men, they have the surly countenance of loggers and roustabouts and are not apt to "suffer fools gladly."

I was working with such a crew in the hot, wind-swept backcountry of eastern Oregon when I found fault with the work they had just completed. In sighting down a half mile-long line stretch of six poles, one pole was clearly two to three feet out of alignment with the others.

I pointed out the problem to the crusty foreman. To correct the error, he would have to order his men to go back with the heavy equipment, remove the poorly placed pole from the ground, fill in the old hole, re-drill a new hole, and then reset the pole in the proper location. The foreman was not pleased. Nobody likes to do the same job twice, especially when there is an attached degree of humiliation.

I will never forget his grizzled scowl and clear disdain for college boy inspectors like me, as he growled, "*We're building a (expletive) power line, not a (expletive) clock!*"

Well, the pole *was* out of alignment and his crew *did* go back to reset it properly, but his power line/clock metaphor has stuck with me through the years. That cut-to-the-bone comment, however off-target in that particular circumstance, is an enduring reminder the quality of work must not exceed the required result.

CHAPTER 17

ERRORS OF OMISSION

We do not so much look at things as overlook them.

Zen proverb

What Are Your Life's Five Largest Mistakes?

It's an interesting exercise to look back and ask, "In descending order of impact, what have been the top five mistakes of my life?" When I propose this question to friends, they chide me about dwelling on the past and focusing on the negative. Yes, I understand all that, but if one spends some time summarizing, an interesting commonality will surface, one that will be useful for future decision-making.

It is important to approach the task with an objective and detached persona. Take time to think it out, get it down on paper with objectivity, and the list will stand the test of time. That's how it has been for me, with my top-five list cast in concrete, unchanged for 16 years.

In my list—and I'll bet yours, too—a primary thread reveals the largest errors were not the result of overt mistakes, but were the outcome of failing to take steps that should have been taken. These are "errors of omission." The large errors of omission are bad enough, but the small ones can add up to "death by a thousand cuts."

Is there a primary cause for errors of omission? Yes, it's too often procrastination, what I call a lack of "quiet courage." We'll discuss quiet courage in the next chapter.

Chronic, Covert, and Insidious

A list of a life's five largest mistakes could include not finishing college, not heeding that stop sign just before the traffic accident, or not starting that savings account way back in the teen years. What about not keeping one's mouth shut at a crucial moment, or not doing the little things which could have saved a marriage? Or maybe declining to apologize when it was the perfect time to do so? Other errors of omission: failing to get enough sleep, forgetting to lock the door of the car, and not submitting taxes by April 15th.

"Not taking action" is the physical manifestation of any error of omission.

What Haven't You Done?

The error of omission principle is a simple enough concept but it lies hidden, buried beneath the jumble of life's demands. As usual, recognition is 90 percent of the solution. And just as the outside-and-slightly-elevated perspective provides a better vantage point for observation of life's mechanics, understanding the errors-of-omission principle gives one a better stance from which to view the hard, cold reality of human nature.

Following are more errors of omission. Think of examples in your own life.

Failure to:

- exercise leads to a lethargic energy level and an unhealthy mind/body.
- recognize birthdays, anniversaries, and holidays contributes to the transformation of a passionate relationship to one of mutual complacency.
- pay a bill leads to late charges.
- get enough sleep leads to a less-than-productive next day.

- make the phone call, close the sale, smooth out the misunderstanding, or ask for help, contributes to less-than-desirable outcomes.

- clean the house contributes to an underlying sense of confusion.

- write up a Working Procedure for staff leads to repeated mistakes.

- apologize or admit a mistake leads to the end of a relationship.

- create a daily schedule that includes time to build the business, the relationship, or the new idea leads to no change, no improvement, and continued general malaise.

The errors-of-omission principle works hand-in-hand with the axiom: *"What you say or think is irrelevant; it's what you DO that counts."* The simplicity of that adage conforms perfectly to Ockham's law.

Another great saying is Nike's *"Just Do It"* credo, which is as metaphysical and profound as a maxim can be. (Maybe the most recognizable three word sequence in modern day language, it reconfirms Ockham's principle of "parsimony in scientific explanation.")

INACTION IS ACTION

In any context, an omission is something left out, something not done. Here's the rub: It is a *choice* not to do something that should be done. So, laziness and procrastination are choices. *Not taking action is a choice!* No matter what we do or don't do, we are always making choices.

Sitting on a couch and not moving a muscle is a *choice*. In this life, at a minimum, we take up physical space, absorb resouces and create waste. Even if we do nothing, we continue to make an impact on the world around us. So it makes sense to get off the couch, take that body that is using up space anyway, and do something constructive with it.

It boils down to the usual utter simplicity: *Since you are making choices all the time anyway, focus on making more active choices, and fewer inactive choices.*

Is your physical condition a system that needs attention? Then segregate it into manageable sub-systems and take first steps to improve those sub-systems. Does a disorganized home system require attention? Acknowledge the disorder and begin to organize it, one room at a time.

Don't just sit there!

What Am I Not Doing Right Now?

How can you begin to use this action principle in your daily life, business, or job? By watching the events of your day as they occur, and while they are occurring, ask, "What am I *not* doing right now that is holding me back?" Should I stop and buy a small gift for the person I love? Should I find a way to exercise for an hour? Should I have a chat with a certain employee who seems a bit disconsolate lately? Shall I start, right this minute, to read that book I bought two months ago? Today, will I make an active effort to get control of things by writing a first draft of my Strategic Objective?

The Power Is Out

Here is an example of placing a new sub-system between two dependent sub-systems in order to gain a more reliable primary system. The story also illustrates how one can use a problem as a wake-up call for improvement.

Late in the afternoon on July 3, 2006, the electricity in Bend, Oregon failed. A lightning strike had disabled a main transformer at the electric company substation on the edge of town. Linda and I were 160 miles to the north, in Portland, at a family Fourth of July celebration when Andi called to say that half of Bend was without electricity, including Centratel.

A rare event, the power outage did not present an immediate problem because Centratel's internal battery backup system automatically took over, keeping all TAS computer systems operational.

The backup system has a three hour capacity so while the electricity was out, we held our breaths, hoping the power company crews would fix the problem quickly. They did, replacing the main transformer in just over two hours.

Over the years, it had been my experience that the occasional and infrequent power outages had been brief, and in this case, although the outage lasted longer than usual, our backup system yet again covered things perfectly. Without a hitch, our TSRs continued to process emergency calls during the outage.

But because of an aspect of our documented systems methodology, this was not the end of the story. Consider principle number 7 of our 30 Principles document: *"Problems are gifts that inspire us to action. A problem prompts the act of creating or improving a system or procedure. We don't want setbacks, but when one occurs, we think—thank you for this wake-up call—and take system-improvement action to prevent the setback from happening again."*

Yes, our internal backup system worked flawlessly, but per principle number 7, we didn't breathe a sigh of relief and move on. Instead, we asked this question: "If we have only three hours of battery backup, what would happen in a worst-case scenario? What if the electricity was out for more than that, maybe an entire day, or longer?" That condition had not occurred for over 40 years because we reside in a region of the country where devastating storms are rare. But, nonetheless, *what if?*

The answer to that hypothetical question is the emergency phone lines of 1,000 answering service accounts, scattered all across the United States, would go unanswered, while our TSRs would sit idle.

We concluded the possibility of a long-term outage was real, and for the welfare of our clients and the viability of the company itself, we had to consider the worst-case scenario. We were relying on an outside electric company in a part of the United States that is not prone to meteorological heavy-handedness, but we also knew we inhabited a world where unexpected catastrophes happen.

So, we took the July 3rd incident as a warning shot and decided we could not rely on the electric company anymore. We had to be able to process calls without interruption, with or without externally supplied electricity.

The system solution: We installed an on-site generator. It was a long, drawn-out, and expensive process with numerous complications including structural challenges, permits and approvals from the city government, and finding the right people to do the installation. But, the new generator, which operates on either natural gas or propane, ensures that should a catastrophic power outage occur, we will be able to continue to process calls indefinitely. (Power outages don't typically cause telephone service to fail because telephone companies have their own sophisticated backup generators.)

Without exception, one of our managers tests the generator once a month. Our staff has documented every single step of the generator activation process with "off the street" simplicity, and we always use that documentation in our testing exercises. (It's interesting that with each monthly test, invariably there are incremental improvements made in the lengthy written procedure. The Power Outage Working Procedure is a living thing, conforming to a changing environment and the tester's additional ideas for improvement).

And how does this installation conform to the Work the System *dictate of posturing oneself outside-and-slightly-elevated? Perfectly: We inserted a generator between the power company and Centratel, creating the option of having independence from the outside power grid—now, we are "outside-and-slightly-elevated" from it and no longer must we rely on a critical system that is not in our control.*

CHAPTER 18

Quiet Courage

Faith is knowledge within the heart, beyond the reach of proof.
Kahil Gibran

Although there are many possible technical excuses for failure, it is a lack of what I call "quiet courage" that often precedes downfall.

What is quiet courage? *Quiet courage is unadorned action. It is the opposite of procrastination. It resides deep in the gut and causes one to buck up to do what needs to be done whether one wants to do it or not. Founded on internal fortitude, it is made real by self-discipline.*

The classic sequence: A lack of quiet courage incites an error of omission. Understanding the quiet courage concept is, as usual, just a matter of digging a little deeper. Here are some demonstrations of quiet courage:

- In the evening, a tired parent faces a misbehaving child with the same fairness and respect as was delivered to the child in the morning when the parent was fresh.

- Going to work on a day when one doesn't want to go to work.

- Facing up to a dead-end situation and taking action to end it once and for all.

- Exercising on a regular basis.

- Taking on a long-term, frustrating project, finding it even more draining than what was expected, but carrying on to finish anyway.

- Quiet and unruffled, walking away from an argument with someone who is unreasonable.

- Living up to an agreement when it is more convenient to make excuses not to.

- Taking extra time to train an employee when things are busy.

- Making an organizational change when sitting still would be more acceptable to everyone else around you.

- And you knew this was coming: Taking the time to create a Strategic Objective and a set of General Operating Principles, not to mention starting to put together a collection of Working Procedures.

The quiet-courage scenarios that escape notice are in contrast to the occasional overt courageous acts that earn instant recognition, such as challenging the boss with a delicate subject, approaching a neighbor with a legitimate but inflammatory complaint, or removing the delinquent young adult from the house.

Don't get me wrong: I'm a big fan of overt courageous acts; the more the better. But never underestimate the damage caused by chronic, under-the-radar avoidance and procrastination.

Steady doses of quiet, unassuming courage, combined with the step-by-step system-improvement methodology, will take you where you want to go.

ONE CAN'T MEASURE
NEGATIVE EVENTS THAT NEVER HAPPEN

Problems that will never happen can't sap your time and energy; can't hold you back. Therefore, problems that will never occur have tangible value. But, how can we measure future problems that won't happen—problems one can prevent before they can become reality? The answer is it can't be done.

Measurement and stark objectivity are beautiful things, but an inability to measure should not stymie efforts to invest resources. This is where one must summon courage *and* common sense.

Here is an example of action based on—and in spite of—an immeasurable. At Centratel, the staff wage scale is close to 100 percent higher than competitors. How do we measure if this elevated pay scale is a smart thing to do? The answer is we *don't* measure it because we *can't* measure it. Too many variables and too much subjectivity preclude analysis. Instead, *we pay high wages because we have enough courage and common sense to know it is worth the extra cost.*

It was tough to take this expensive subjective stance when a hard objective statistic screamed for *lower* wages: the total payroll dollars we paid out every two weeks. An escalating payroll is easy to measure, but the benefits of the additional expenditure are impossible to pin down in hard numbers.

For instance, our high wages engender low staff turnover which means less hiring and training. In dollars and cents, how does one measure the savings of the training costs that *won't* happen? Additionally, because of our superior quality staff, some quantity of error won't ever happen. How do we measure that?

And how does one gauge the value of customers not lost due to the poor quality that didn't occur? How many customers remain with us today who otherwise would have gone elsewhere?

So we invest time and money to prevent immeasurable negative events that won't happen, and to foster equally immeasurable posi-

tive events that will happen. This is quiet courage.

Yes, when it is possible and appropriate, we should measure, but just because a future condition is immeasurable doesn't mean action should not be taken.

Procrastination is the Evil One

At Centratel and at home, the quiet courage posture is easy for me because it aligns with the rest of the *Work the System* philosophy. It's a learned habit, ingrained by simple Pavlovian positive reinforcement.

It works, so I do it.

When Centratel was just moments away from collapse, finding the resources to summon up quiet and not-so-quiet courage was not a problem because there was a gun to my head. The loss of everything was a vision just in front of my face, and I exhibited the same visceral protective reaction I would display if someone were pushing me toward a cliff's edge. (And of course, desperation can be an effective self-motivator. Henry Ford said, "The greatest inspiration is often born of desperation.")

But without a gun-to-the-head motivator, and when excuses entice, I can see that quiet courage's number one nemesis, procrastination, is at work once again. The antidote is the point-of-sale action posture—the "that's just how we do things" principle. (More on point-of-sale in the next chapter.)

Here are two cognitive strategies for when the internal battle rages.

First, rise above it and *visualize laziness as an object, something tangible that is outside of you.* Once the mechanical laziness is observed—most often it is temporary indolence cloaked by some lame excuse such as "I'm too busy right now," or "I'm too tired"—just ignore the seduction and get moving without a second thought.

Here's the second ploy when you "lean toward loiter." As the excuses line themselves up, ask, "Why am I lacking courage at this moment? *Why am I being a sissy?*" It's a bit of twisted psychology that rattles the cage and causes a passionate reaction. *Of all human failures, perhaps cowardice is the most abhorred.*

Procrastination—the lack of quiet courage—will ruin your life if you let it.

You Will Begin Now

Here is a real-time, outside-and-slightly-elevated exercise. This end-of-chapter example is about you, and it's about what is happening right NOW. Here, you are the story....

Anyone can read a book, but it's a courageous act to shift in a new direction. Clearly, because you have read this far, implementing the *Work the System* methodology is a new life-trajectory that you are considering.

How do you get to the point of actually beginning the process without relegating it to a future date when "spare time" is available? Here's how: Right now—this second—put this book down—*Yes, right now, this sec-ond*—find a blank piece of paper and write "Strategic Objective" at the top. Do it.

Now, place the paper in a location where you will easily find it later.

Congratulations! Your pilgrimage has begun!

My bet is you will get back to your titled paper sooner rather than later. Why? Because you have begun, and beginning is the hard part.

CHAPTER 19

POINT-OF-SALE
THINKING

Why? Because I'm the mommy and I said so.

Anonymous mommy

D*o it now and let's get on with whatever is next!*

Point-of-sale is a phrase taken from the cash register industry. It describes action "where the purchase takes place."

Consider the latest generation of cash register which instantly updates inventory and orders new product. Before the customer walks out of the store, a replacement for the purchased item is in the works. The concept is a key component of the *Work the System* method as described in our 30 Principles document, item number 14: *Do it NOW. All actions build on "point-of-sale" theory. We don't delay an action if it can be done immediately. Just like any major retail outlet, we "update inventories and databases at the exact time the transaction takes place." There is no paperwork floating around the office after a physical transaction. We ask, "How can we perform the task NOW without creating lingering details that we must clean up later?"*

The concept of point-of-sale, with its various subtleties, has the single purpose of gobbling up details and tasks as they arise. Accomplishing this is the antithesis of fire-killing. *Point-of-sale means being in the offense, eyes open, ready to handle whatever comes up, instead of defensively looking backward, burning up precious time sorting through piles of old details.*

For business and personal life, the point-of-sale posture allows you to focus on the path ahead while your other systems-strategies take care of the details that arise behind. Wear the point-of-sale banner on your sleeve and you will experience robust confidence, the opposite of overwhelm. The excuses "I don't have enough time" and "I've been too busy" will disappear from your life.

In a nutshell, here are two point-of-sale strategies that will make your life simple and clean:

The first is to reject procrastination. Get tasks out of the way *now* by immediately doing them, delegating them, or discarding them. Make it your quest to *knock off tasks as they appear!* The second strategy is to eliminate the requirement for personal action by automating and system-izing tasks. By making things happen automatically, the "do it now" goal is achieved without any effort at all.

Here's an additional benefit of the point-of-sale stance: You will be in an alert, assertive posture, prepared to handle the inevitable body-slams that are part of having a life.

YOUR CONGA LINE DANCE LEADERSHIP

Embracing the point-of-sale stance makes you the first person in the conga line, the line's trajectory and speed determined by you alone. The dozens of followers, each with hands firmly attached to the hips of the preceding dancer, just shadow along. The conga line goes where you want it to go despite the disparity in shape, size, and finesse of the following dancers. You are at the front, the leader, forging the path ahead while the gyrations that emerge behind take care of themselves. (And, what are the "system prin-ciples" for the members of the conga line following behind? There are just two: Each must keep his or her hands on the hips of the preceding dancer, and each must keep in step.)

It's Just the Way We Do Things Around Here

When the "Shall I do it now or later?" question comes up for a new Centratel staff member, their not-yet-disciplined internal dialogue goes something like this: "What's the difference if I do this task now or later? I just don't *feel* like doing it right now. I'll do it later because my guess is I will feel more like doing it then." A variation is, "I function better under pressure. I need an imminent deadline to force me to take action, so I'll do this task next week when that condition will exist (or, maybe, the task will miraculously disappear by then)." Sound familiar?

During job orientation, we ask the new staff member to change that internal self-talk to "I'll do it *now* because that is how things are done at Centratel."

Our experienced managers embrace the "Do it now" credo because it is so potently effective, not just because it's our policy, but because it just works! No need for self-explanation; no time for inane back-and-forth internal dialogue. The rule is, *"just do it NOW and let's get on with things!"*

Yes, this "because I said so" dictate may grate a bit, especially with the independence and freedom we Westerners take for granted. We don't like arbitrary rules imposed by others, but in a business an employee has the freedom to quit if the rules don't seem reasonable. In the free world, anyone can leave a job to go to work for someone else, start a new business, or sit on the couch and do nothing.

But, for the new Centratel employee, once a concept is tested and the workability of it proven, it's a no-brainer. It's just logic: Consistently superior end-results are justification for cast-in-concrete methodology.

MULTI-TASKING IS FOR MACHINES

The goal of the point-of-sale strategy is to create super-efficient primary systems. However, it is important to remember that in a point-of-sale cash register, the all-at-the-same-time tasks are *automated:* a computer does the multi-tasking, not a human. In fact, a tenet of Centratel's philosophy is that our staff members do *not* multi-task, but pay full attention to the detail at hand. (#27 of Centratel's 30 Principles). This means proceeding in a linear format. Multi-tasking, or "many systems functioning at one time," is a perfect application for a computer, not a human.

The Workweek is 40 Hours Long

The *Work the System* methodology produces many system strategies that save time, and there is no question point-of-sale thinking has much to do with keeping our salaried management staff's workweek to a reasonable length. My partner Sam and I say to our employees, "Here's the deal: If you give us 100 percent, we will compensate you well." Yes, it's a generalized promise but nonetheless it is our personal guarantee to staff that when they work hard *and* produce, we will provide them a healthy wage, great benefits, and a workweek of reasonable length.

Because of our procedure-driven, point-of-sale methodology, and "the deal," our people do not see the 50- to 60-hour (or more) workweeks that are common in small to medium-sized service businesses like ours. They also earn double what they would make elsewhere. (Why do my partner and I require that well-paid, salaried employees work a limited number of hours? First, we want them to have a life outside the business. And second, when they have time to unwind, they are fresh and spunky when they return to work, able to give the required 100 percent that is part of "the deal.").

The point-of-sale concept also folds over into personal life decisions. Here's an over-simplification, but it captures the point: "I'm shopping. While I'm out, should I make one more stop to buy groceries for tomorrow?" The answer is, of course, "Yes!"

Communications and Point-of-Sale

Our internal operations hinge on Microsoft Outlook which keeps us organized with the standard calendar, task list, and contact information sections. It's an electronic version of the Franklin Day Planner I carried around for 12 years. For a manager, the most important part of the software is the tasking feature. In a moment's notice the leader can issue instructions to a staff member that include precise direction of what must be accomplished, as well as when it must be completed. The job doesn't disappear from that manager's task list until the job is finished per the written-in-stone Outlook task. In the process of job completion, Outlook prompts the staff member to provide regular updates. The task won't fall through the cracks and no error of omission will occur. The feature is also perfect for keeping track of personal tasks.

Point-of-sale methodology is at the heart of our personal communications strategy, too. For anyone, fine ideas can flow quickly through the thought process without being captured. One might be driving, talking to a colleague, lying in bed, riding a bicycle, or traveling cross-country when a great idea arrives out of nowhere only to depart in the next instant. To solve this problem, a digital voice recorder is perfect. I carry mine everywhere.

AGAIN: HOW MUCH REALLY MATTERS?

In your business or job, or in your personal life, how much of what you do *really* matters? This is not a loaded question but one of enormous pragmatic consideration. Be cold-blooded in examining your situation and eliminating the thoughts, data, and preoccupations that don't have value. Also, look hard at the information that is of *some* value. See if it serves *enough* value to make its existence worthwhile. If any information you receive is not used, or is of marginal use, categorize it for what it is—a waste of time, energy, and/or money—and then dismiss it from your life.

What will you do with the time you save? You'll expend it on things that *do* matter.

Strengthening the Habit

Procrastination appears in the low times, the times when personal willpower is weak because of stress, fatigue, problems and distractions. Failing to carry through with the point-of-sale philosophy is often the first casualty. You think, "OK, I can understand, in the long run, point-of-sale is a good concept, but this afternoon I'm tired, and there is always tomorrow...."

You are probably right. More often than not, a task probably *can* happen tomorrow. The danger is when one compromises a habit, the habit becomes weaker. So, take the "it's just the way we do things around here" stance and know when an excuse arrives and you perform the task anyway, the do-it-now habit becomes incrementally stronger. In everything you do, think beyond immediate temptation and stick with the plan as outlined in your critical documents. Your documentation will keep you from sinking as it relentlessly moves you toward your goals!

Point-of-sale actions are about self-discipline and the willingness to stretch into uncomfortable territory. How else can things change for the better?

SLOW DOWN. GET ORGANIZED.

The problem in too many lives is chaos brought on by the failure to slow down enough to set goals and determine sensible strategies to reach them. Add to this the failure to make system-improvements when inefficiencies crop up (which would prevent those problems from recurring).

Yes, the key phrase is "slow down" and—let me guess—slowing down is what you are struggling with right now as you work your way through this book....

If at first slowing down doesn't feel right, that's normal. Be patient as you work your systems and the end result will be fast, efficient processes down the line.

I learned this potent mindset in high school while ski racing slalom courses, a sport that requires forethought, fast reflexes, strength, and balance. I used to slam through the gates with abandon, powering my way down the course, off balance, my arms and legs flailing. I was giving it everything, but my race results were mediocre because of the multiple errors and inefficiencies generated by my brute-force, Hell-bent-for-leather approach. I was making too many tiny mistakes that incrementally slowed me down, or I was outright crashing and not even finishing.

Then one day my coach told me to relax in my skiing, to think "smooth and slow" instead of "power." It felt wrong; at first it was frustrating because it seemed to me I was not *trying* hard enough. But I forced myself to hold back, to ski slowly and smoothly. My results dramatically improved. From then on, including two years on a college team, I seldom failed to finish a race and consistently ranked well. That single mindset adjustment changed everything and I never went back to my old tear-it-up comportment. The "slow down and be smooth" lesson spilled over into the rest of my life, too. (But, even after all these years, I occasionally struggle with this positioning because my natural inclination is to thrash things into orderliness.)

Measuring The Body

Eight years ago, in the depths of my workplace chaos, I was also dealing with a very sick body and an exhausted mind. I was delirious during the day and couldn't sleep at night. My doctor had me on antidepressants, and then Ritalin, convinced I was "depressed," my 100-hour workweeks notwithstanding.

But as a result of my mini-enlightenment regarding the systems of my business, I grasped that my body was likewise a collection of systems. I bore down on the revelation, and asked, "Of what are these systems composed?" It was obvious: my body's composition is of chemicals. With this realization, I asked my doctor to give me a wide range of blood tests. Convinced of my "depression," at first he balked at the idea, but then conceded.

The blood analysis showed my adrenal glands had shut down and my master hormone, DHEA, was not in evidence. The "stress hormone," Cortisol, was in the stratosphere, another important hormone was deficient, and to cap it off, I was chronically dehydrated.

My task was to work on each of the systems individually, and one by one, bring each back to normalcy. Once I got all all four dysfunctional systems back to efficiency, I would have a balanced, holistic body and an alert mind. How could it be otherwise?

For the next two years, I took the blood tests repeatedly, as I watched my bodily intake, added relevant supplements to my diet, and modified my lifestyle, bringing my various chemical systems back into balance. My chemical makeup was a mess at the beginning but was completely in tune at the end of those two years. I was physically strong again, and my thinking was clear.

Was it that simple? Yes and no. On the one hand, the road to recovery was obvious—*what* I had to do was clear. On the other hand, it was sometimes a struggle to be self-disciplined enough to do what needed to be done. I stumbled once in a while, but I succeeded enough to improve things dramatically. Do I still stumble? Yes!

How about you? Are you sure the chemicals that compose your body are OK? If they are not, could *this* be affecting your physical and mental performance? Consider taking your health into your own hands by directing your doctor to perform full-screen blood tests.

Then again, your solution may not require a doctor. If your chemicals are OK, maybe you just need to get regular exercise, eat better, and find more sleep.

A final thought about measuring your body. If you are addicted to a substance, however benign, an imbalance exists. Any foreign substance throws things off—so a good starting point is to quit those substances and face the world "cold turkey." It won't be easy, but you'll be in select company.

There is no better place than one's body to start getting things straightened out. Using systems strategy to analyze the physical body—the vehicle that holds and transports consciousness—is perhaps the most "outside-and-slightly-elevated" position one can take.

CHAPTER 20

EXTRAORDINARY SYSTEMS OPERATED BY GREAT PEOPLE

Most people, especially successful people, are hard working.
They want to participate. They want to do things well.

Annie Leibovitz

No Super Powers Required

I've discussed the importance of creating efficient, documented systems but have not sufficiently addressed a prime benefit: The people who work for (or with) you do not have to be mind readers or fortunetellers. Your superb systems are for regular people like you and me, people who do not have super powers.

People have said to me, "I'm sure you are successful because you've been lucky enough to find very good people to work for you." Translation: "You just bumbled into finding people who adore you, know your every thought, and will perform your every wish. You lucky guy!"

The idea that one must "find the right people" is a pervasive misconception. It is not that the statement isn't true; it's that the inference is backwards. At Centratel, we *do* have an extraordinary staff from top to bottom, but that is not because of plain dumb luck, or my prowess as a recruiter. It's because we attract and keep quality people due to the great work situation we offer. The great situation comes *before* the great people.

Plenty of hard working, disciplined, honest people are out there, quietly looking for a fair shake so they can put themselves on the line and show what they can do. And when they perform well, they want to be rewarded. You just need to find these people and then give them black and white instruction, good pay, and the promise of a bright future. As always, it's just simple mechanics.

Efforts to seek the perfect employee who will solve all problems—a from-the-top-down solution—is opposite of the systems-thinking solution. In the *Work the System* business, hard-working, loyal employees concentrate on enhancing sub-systems in order to improve the primary system—a from-the-bottom-up solution.

So these great people *become* great employees. You make it possible for them to shine by providing a forum for their innate skills and high motivation. You give them opportunity, and turn them loose.

ASSERTIVELY APPLY THE GUIDELINES

Avoid the danger of becoming bogged-down in the pros and cons of a decision. Accomplish this by assertively applying the guidelines of the three critical documents.

At Centratel, I love it when a new employee explains that he or she is taking a certain action because it is congruent with a guideline within the Strategic Objective, 30 Principles document, or a particular Working Procedure.

Another positive sign is a staff member's unsolicited request for a Working Procedure's modification—a sure indication he or she "gets" the systems-methodology.

To These People You Owe Your Best

You want smart, honest, clean-living, and enthusiastic people who will believe in what you have created; individuals who can become intrigued with your personal vision and who will want to continue into the future with you, at least for a while. These good people are the bedrock of your future. To them you owe the best—and the best's centerpiece is the carefully constructed system-based environment you provide. Then, if your people grow with your company and you teach them well, it will be a compliment to you if someday they go out and start their own businesses. On the other hand, it will be the supreme compliment if they stay with you over the long term.

IS THE FOCUS ON THE PRODUCT OR THE SYSTEM?

It seems logical the manager's total efforts should be focused on the product or service itself; that all energy be directed to the work that must be done, the customers who must be found, and the money that must be made.

And *this* is the problem! Focus entirely on these tasks without an overall strategy of system-improvement, and dysfunction is imminent. Failure to adopt an outside-and-slightly-elevated perspective is the primary reason only one business out of 100 will survive 15 years.

Here's good news: The bulk of those one percent survivors are doing very well indeed. Albeit morbid, here's more good news for you: The vast majority of your new competitors are doomed.

Understand what large successful businesses have in common: *The leader is not producing the product or service. He or she is holding court, observing and adjusting the systems that produce and sell the product or service.* To accomplish this, the leader insists management documents goals, methodology, and procedures—and ensures employees follow this documentation exactly.

By doing things this way—by providing extraordinary systems and then inspiring everyone to abide by those systems—leadership can employ real people, people who don't have super powers.

The CEO's job is not only to create foundational systems that are forthright and sensible, but also to hire managers who see the vision and understand it is their responsibility to oversee sub-systems in the same logical and well-explained way. If you wish to operate a successful business that will have intrinsic value, should your role be any different?

Large successful businesses don't have documented systems because they are large; they are large because they have documented systems! This is an absolute key point, one that is obvious once the systems-thinking epiphany strikes home.

Evaluating People

Your team must see things your way.

If you are going to embrace the *Work the System* method and you are in charge of staff, you will have to remove people who can't or won't deal with your vision. In their place, you will recruit new people who share your systems mindset.

In seeking system-oriented personalities, here are a few "hoops" that Centratel job applicants must negotiate. Note that clear-headedness and self-discipline are the common threads of these systems-thinking prerequisites:

1) Did the applicant show up for the interview on time?

2) Give the aptitude test. Is the minimum score achieved?

3) Does the applicant know about the business? Did he or she check out the web site before applying for the position? Are there questions about what goes on, or is the applicant just looking for *any* job? Is advancement important?

4) Do they smile? Do they seem happy? Generally, do they seem to be self-disciplined?

5) Do they *listen* to you or are your words sliding by unheard as they wait for the next opportunity to pitch their expertise?

6) Discounting for the standard nervousness of a job interview, can they carry on a reasonable conversation? Does he or she look you in the eye when speaking?

7) Do they look like they take care of themselves? If they don't, the raw truth is that in most cases there is a lack of self-discipline.

8) Job history: Did they bounce from job to job?

9) Is the applicant clear-headed? Did he or she pass the drug test?

10) Does the applicant naturally play by the rules? Did he or she pass the criminal background check?

By breaking down the subjective interview process into component parts, we transform it into an objective, "you must jump through the hoops," black-and-white test. Yes, gut-feelings can be important but they should never overrule your guidelines. Don't confuse feelings with logic; subjectivity with objectivity. However compassionate, the "this person needs a break" gut-feeling is often a mistake. *If there is a gut-feeling, use it to disqualify people, not to qualify them.* (That's a useful rule to follow elsewhere in life, too.)

At Centratel, it is critical the job applicant passes through ALL of the aforementioned "hoops." If he or she fails just one, we won't offer the position because that one negative probably can't be neutralized, even by all the other positive ones added together. We are hard-hearted about this and don't make exceptions.

College education? We don't worry too much about this although a college degree indicates someone who can stick through long-term challenges to reach a goal. Unfortunately, a college degree is no longer a reliable indicator of literate capability, or of a reasonable mindset.

I've touched on this already: Hiring and then firing someone is not just a bad investment for the company, it's an intense personal blow to the employee. For the job prospect, it's infinitely less painful to not get the job in the first place. Be compassionate by creating a thoughtful (and, of course, documented) hiring procedure.

Kill the Moles, Manage the Fleet

And what about the leader of a typical large, successful company? Most times, these people are not innately special. Beyond their willingness to work hard and an adequate degree of intelligence, their leg-up is they naturally operate from a systems-perspective—while the huge majority of people do not. *These leaders are heavyweights because they understand moles must be eliminated, not repeatedly whacked.*

Via managers who understand the process, the large-business leader focuses on perfecting systems and keeping them that way, constantly making efficiency adjustments while keeping up with trends and changes. It should be the same for you if you are to climb out of the morass within which 95 percent of the world struggles.

You have competitors. Do you think your product or service—or your personality—is so superior that people should flock to you? Unless you are a celebrity, it rarely happens that way. Don't make the naïve, arrogant mistake of operating from that premise.

For your business, you must find and keep employees and suppliers, supervise the creation and sales of your product or service, make payroll, pay taxes and steer the whole enterprise toward a profit. If you hold a job and your goal is to advance, you have equal challenges. To win in the long term you must do things more efficiently than your competition or your peers, and you can't do that by winging it, depending on personal charm, finding the perfect employee, or doing things like everyone else. *If you are to leap ahead, your product or service must be consistently superior, and that can't happen if you don't hyper-focus on the details of how that product or service is produced and distributed.*

In the short term, you must focus on creating extraordinary, well-defined systems. In the long term, you and your people must relentlessly tweak and maintain those systems. The by-product will be an extraordinary service or product that people want.

Another thought: *All* the ships in your fleet must be at peak efficiency: One slow boat will hold back the entire flotilla. This is a central tenet of the *Work the System* method, and it's the reason you will want to insure all of your people are on board with your systems methodology.

You'll want everyone in your organization working together—repairing, tweaking, and adjusting to outside changes. The fleet must move forward full steam, directly toward the common goal, and it is your job to make sure that happens. This is called "being a leader."

A Super Market

Being aware of the systems around you, and of distinguishing the efficient from the inefficient, keeps your systems-mindset front and center.

In southern California, you'll find a certain grocery chain. Walk into any one of these markets and the first impression is they are organized and relaxed. Look a bit harder and notice the rows of goods are full. Everything is clean and polished. In fact, the *people* who work there are clean and polished! Walk the aisles and catch the eye of a clerk. You can feel the pride.

Each store is efficient, confident in itself. If you are a Southern Californian you maybe have already guessed what grocery chain I am describing. I don't know the top management people, but it's obvious: Here is a perfect model of thought-out and documented systems strategy, directed from the top of the organization down to the customer-contact level.

Of course, other businesses just like this one exist. They are not common but you will find them. When you do, spend time there and think about the systems that are behind the efficiencies. Watch and learn.

It's easy to find floundering businesses. You can't help spending time in them because they are everywhere. In visiting *those* businesses, there is also much to learn: Get a visceral feeling for the lack of systems and vision, the lack of controls. Feel the chaos. This is the antithesis of what you want for your work and your life.

CHAPTER 21

CONSISTENCY
AND COLD COFFEE

My goal in sailing isn't to be brilliant or flashy in individual races, just to be consistent over the long run.

Dennis Conner, winner America's Cup sailing race

In the Northwest, the coffee kiosk is pervasive. Often fewer than 100 square feet in size, these tiny portable buildings inhabit parking lots adjacent to busy intersections and high-traffic streets. Typically operated by perky, bright-eyed "baristas," the kiosks are convenient for the drive-up, on-the-whim, coffee drinker. The concoctions they serve run the gauntlet of complexity and can range up to $8. Although the kiosks offer every coffee drink imaginable, I don't use them often. My infrequent coffee stops are made at one of two large, established downtown shops. One is part of a national franchise (guess who), while the other is locally operated and offers coffee every bit as good as the franchise. The infrequent times I drink coffee now, I go out of my way to buy it at one of these two businesses, with a preference for the local shop (because, well, it's local).

About 10 years ago, I experimented with patronizing a kiosk.

It was a new business located near my home. One morning in the midst of my serial 100-hour workweek phase, I pulled over, desperate for a hot, strong cup of coffee. (In those days, when I drank a lot of coffee, my usual "cuppa Joe" was a bit downbeat for someone living in the Northwest:

"Large black, please.")

At the kiosk, Ms. Brighteyes reached down to my car window and served me my paper-cup coffee. I set the cup in the cup holder, negotiated my car back onto the busy street, and was again on my way to the office. I was *so* ready for that first hot, strong taste! I took a sip, and…*YECK! It was tepid warm, and thin!* ARRGGGHHH! I instantly ratcheted 10 on the frustration level—and have always remembered the intensity of my annoyance with that particular cup of coffee.

I was not in the mood to go back to Ms. Brighteyes and grumble. What good would that do? I wanted a hot, black, strong cup *right now*, and it wasn't my job to point out what constitutes a decent cup of coffee. Anyway, what would she do with my cold coffee, microwave it to boiling and hand it back? Did she even have a microwave in her tiny building?

I drove downtown to one of my standby shops and with a ceremonial flourish, dumped the still full kiosk cup in the trash bin outside. I stepped inside and bought another cup.

As usual with this shop, the coffee was hot and strong. I also remember *that* particular cup….

Here's the aftermath that, to this day, still surprises me: I shy away from buying coffee at a kiosk. Why? Am I being too critical; too unforgiving? Neither—it's more self-serving than that. It's because I don't want to deal with the inconvenience again and, especially, don't want to feel like a fool for making the same mistake twice.

After all these years, my first impulse is to avoid using a kiosk if one of my regular coffee shops is within five miles. And, my visceral aversion falls on a number of other local establishments too, including half a dozen restaurants, as many retail stores, and more than one gas station. To be sure, my gut-level judgments are not completely fair or entirely rational…but they are real.

Conversely, Linda and I go out of our way to patronize certain other service providers. We find our way to favorite places and *every* time we get fast, high-quality service with a smile. For instance, we take the time to drive to a particular burrito shop clear across town. We base our loyalty on the ever-friendly staff, and the absolute consistency of the inexpensive, great food they serve. Of course, that consistent quality comes from an organization that understands systems.

In fairness to kiosk operators: Just before publication of this book, Andi informed me that Centratel's "Latte Monday" drinks (in which we buy coffee or cocoa drinks for everyone on busy Monday mornings), is now being provided by a kiosk, not one of the local shops, as has been our tradition. Our staff says the drinks are consistently superb. Could it be this particular kiosk has something special going on? Could it be it is being operated differently than the "cold cup" kiosk of so many years ago?

Watching Yourself Closely

I learned something from observing my over-reaction to that single cup of bad coffee: From the coffee kiosk incident onward, it was clear to me the success of Centratel was going to depend on our ability to provide *consistent* high quality.

What if you work for someone else? That's easy, and here's the mantra: "*My boss is my primary customer. At work, my number one task is to avoid letting my boss down.*" (Of course, if the boss is impossible, or the position is dead-end, exiting the situation is probably a better strategy.)

The bad news is true. In our culture, and despite the universe's propensity for efficiency, service quality is too often poor (mostly because of the human tendency to neglect systems). But the good news is it's easy to provide superb service if the focus is on creating and maintaining the systems that will insure consistent quality.

Here it is yet again: Creation, maintenance, and improvement of internal systems must be the manager's main objective.

A not so tongue-in-cheek "for instance:" You don't want a customer treated badly by an employee who has a hangover. What you want is a system that will cover the bases for someone who is having a bad day (presuming this someone is not a chronic problem employee). You can't stop the headache but you can create solid, fluid, and sensible procedures that will get this employee through the shift without alienating customers. Not providing guidance and leaving things up to your not-doing-so-well-today employee is a losing bet—the numbers do not bode well for you, the business owner or department manager.

(And what if *you* have a hangover? If you have worked your systems, you can lay back for a day or so, stay out of the way without gumming up the works with your sour disposition, and let your systems carry the load.)

It's a powerful human idiosyncrasy, this willingness to make snap, yet irreversible negative decisions based on one-time bad experiences. So beware: *When a customer is disappointed in service, they have a powerful predilection to go elsewhere next time, never to return.*

Your best bet is to not fail in the first place.

When Out and About

Centratel is a pure service operation, so quality of service is my natural mindset. When out and about, I find myself evaluating the service quality of restaurants, sandwich shops, retail stores, movie theaters, plumbers, bed and breakfasts, public transportation services, etc. It's an unconscious analysis until I encounter superb service or poor service, at which point I automatically get conscious. On the spot, I have offered jobs to friendly, smart, and upbeat servers or cashiers who can't keep smiles off their faces and who are paying attention. Then there are the other times when someone with a lousy attitude forever alienates me from that establishment.

Outside of work, my managers naturally do this evaluation, too. Once the systems mindset takes hold, it's impossible to avoid.

THE TIP SYSTEM

Here is an evaluation system, albeit waggish. It's about tipping in restaurants, and I'll preface things by saying I don't believe a tip is a diner's obligation. It's a *tip*—something extra that one earns if the service he or she delivers is at least good.

Linda and I sit down for a meal in a restaurant. At this point, before even saying a word, the waitperson, in this case a female, has earned a twenty five percent tip. It's downhill from there. If she greets us with "how are you *guys* today?" there is an immediate five percent deduction in the tip for off-handedly calling my wife a "guy." Now the tip can be no more than twenty percent. If the waitperson delivers the food and walks away with a semi-pretentious, air-headed "enjoy," there is another five percent discount. If she delivers the check along with the food (working man's diners excepted), there's another five percent off the top. If she checks to see how we are doing at mid-meal and blatantly interrupts one of us mid-sentence, yes, there is another five percent deduction. Now we're getting to no tip at all.

Although I don't sit there tallying things on paper, or even in my head, and seldom does a waitperson go without being tipped, the essence of my thinking process is in the above formula. Call me persnickety. It is systems-thinking both at its best and at its most ridiculous.

How does this relate? If I were the owner of a restaurant, understanding serving food is a process that repeats itself, I would be watching my own reactions while dining at someone else's restaurant. I'd take notes. In my own restaurant, I would produce a Working Procedure of "never use" phrases and actions and then would make sure every single one of my servers knew it by heart. It would be called the Forbidden Phrases and Actions Procedure. (Yes, really. That is exactly what I would call it.) This Working Procedure would be my obsession and my staff's center of attention. We would continuously update it, using my own experience as well as feedback from customers, open-eyed staff, or whomever. Only one or two pages in length, it would be *alive*; the continuous centerpiece of discussion and action, a document that old-hands and new people would study, discuss, and tweak. With everyone's input it would improve steadily over time.

For the owner of a restaurant, how much work is this? A simple document like this could quickly take a restaurant's service quality from mediocre to superb—an incredible payback for a tiny investment of time and effort.

To summarize: A propensity to analyze other's service quality has two benefits.

The first, I've already covered in the kiosk story: It is a reminder the customer has a visceral inclination never to return if there is a bad experience. (Conversely, a customer will dogmatically return when there is a good experience). The customer has a potent memory.

Second, one becomes inspired to devise ways to reduce their own customers' bad experiences.

We Watch and Learn

At Centratel, we watch and learn and we use that information in our work and in our personal lives. We try hard to avoid foul-ups, but when we do create error, we are finicky about fixing it. We bombard the unhappy customer with tender loving care to the point where he or she is happier after the error than before it. (Via our Complaint Procedure, we call the customer back a minimum of four times, at prescribed intervals of one day, three days, ten days, and thirty days to make sure the error has not repeated itself. Yes, that process of fixing things is via a 1-2-3 step documented system).

Our Complaint Procedure doesn't end there. We also inform the *entire* staff of *every* complaint, as well as the steps taken to remedy less-than-perfect situations.

So you don't operate a business? If you are someone's employee and your position has potential, apply these principles and watch your rapid ascent of the corporate ladder.

Tweaking and Maintaining

A primary commonality among large, successful businesses is the steady, concerted effort to maintain consistency in product and service quality. This means *in a prosperous business, the leader spends most of his or her time tweaking and maintaining systems.* The more successful a business is in gaining and retaining customers, the more one can be sure that business has a strict set of system guidelines for quality control. Again, for the successful employee aiming to climb the corporate ladder, this system-improvement process is also the center of attention (although confined to one's area of responsibility rather than to an entire company).

Just how hard can I beat this concept to death? *It's all about perfecting systems and then maintaining that perfection!*

What about your personal life? It's what mom told you: Always return a friend's phone call promptly. Say thank you, pay your bills on time, and pay attention to holidays. Don't forget birthdays. If you promise something, make sure you do it no matter how trivial. Do these things consistently and people will trust you. They will want to help you. They will know you are dependable and will want to spend time with you.

Oh, and why was the coffee so poor at the "cold cup" kiosk? You know the answer: The proprietor had no procedures installed to ensure consistent quality. She had no clue she had to consciously manipulate systems in order to keep customers. Further, she had no idea of the enormous negative impact of one bad cup of coffee. I am sure that particular proprietor winged it every day, hoping for the best but more often hitting-and-missing, depending on her emotions, the attitude of her customers, or even the weather.

By the way, that kiosk went out of business after just a couple of years.

A PLACE FOR EVERYTHING
AND EVERYTHING IN ITS PLACE

Work the System methodology relies on the personal habits of congruency and consistency, the children of self-discipline and character. Congruency and consistency are not hand tools one picks up from the tool bench to use only when needed. They are personal traits to pack around everywhere, traits to be used every minute, permanently imbedded in the fiber of your being.

To cultivate these traits, the largest challenge is to fight old habits, simple laziness, and procrastination, while manhandling moment-to-moment activities into being organized and efficient. However, by paying attention, good results come home quickly, and with those successes congruency and consistency soon become effortless while backtracking into old habits, dissatisfying.

It is no good to set up a system of organization at work and then return home to chaos. It doesn't work to exercise a few days of the month, be nice to your spouse most of the time, or to apply the *Work the System* principles sporadically. If life is to be efficient, it's a full-time job.

Fifty years ago, my aging grandfather told me, "Sam, there is a place for everything and everything in its place." I was eight years old when I first heard Grandpa's favorite platitude and I wondered how he knew it was true. Was there proof this was a good idea? Why did he tell me this with so few words but with such passion?

His explanation was…it's just…*true.*

It's just true that being organized is worthwhile. At first, if you must, take it on faith. Then, find the time tomorrow to clean that top drawer in your desk, and this weekend, go out to the garage and start the cleanup. Do some organizing every day even if it's for just 15 minutes each time. Work on the back-clutter but also, from this point forward, avoid creating new clutter as you move along through the day. Clean up as you go.

Accomplish this clean-up and then step back and ask yourself how you feel. There will be intense satisfaction, and the great thing is this satisfaction is addicting and you'll want to feel it again and again. You'll become a fanatic about preparation and systems-thinking.

It might take weeks or months to take care of getting things in order, but this is what you must do to drop into the groove of the systems mentality. Do a little bit every day and consider it a crusade. *Be consistent, and in consistency comes strength.*

Plow through the disorder in your life and you will find the process is exactly congruent with the other aspects of the *Work the System* method. Keep at it and soon disorder will bother you. You'll see it in the people and places around you—disorganization you can't fix—and you will shake your head as you understand the waste of it.

Will your new orderliness make you an uptight control freak? No, on the contrary, as I pointed out in the beginning of the book, you'll loosen up and feel relaxed and effective. You'll be a smooth operator with time and energy to spare.

Breaking the Rules and Job Security

This has nothing to do with "good" or "bad" employees, or about discipline or conflict resolution. Simply, it has to do with thorough documentation and staff buy-in. With clear-cut rules, no gray areas exist to cause uncertainty or anxiety.

At Centratel, several years ago we had problems with two employees.

The first's work was very good, but he failed a random drug test. (We drug test often at Centratel because TSRs must have 100 percent clarity as they handle emergency calls). The second violated our computer privacy policy. Her work quality was also exceptional. Both violations were serious breaches of policy.

What to do? For management, there was powerful incentive to sweep these major offenses under the carpet in order to spare unpleasantness and eliminate a time-consuming search for replacements. But we had to ask, if we keep employees who violate policy, wouldn't this render our policies impotent?

The system solution: We spell out rules, regulations, and guidelines in our Employee Handbook, viewing this collection of policies as a primary system in itself— a giant Working Procedure (you can see the entire 35,000-word document on the Centratel web site, **centratel.com**, under Resources). All employees are required to understand the Handbook policies and, with their signatures, accept them as a condition of employment.

In these two instances, employees violated portions of the thoroughly documented system of policies and, per the Handbook, these serious violations were cause for employment termination. And that's what happened. We ended their employment on the spot. There was no arbitrary, manipulative corporate judgment call. We simply followed the "conditions of employment" system that had been set up in advance.

Here, management remained completely outside the system: The Employee Handbook exactly spelled out the policies and explained the ramifications of not following them. These two employees knew they were gambling. They lost their respective gambles and their departures were simple and clean. Parties on both sides—and our remaining staff—understood why these terminations occurred.

Because we follow policies exactly, all Centratel employees know deliberate line-crossing will not be met with wishy-washy "don't let it happen again" platitudes, as interminable second chances are given. After a serious violation, does and employee deserve a second chance? Well, actually, no, as a matter of policy they don't. But because of this intractable position, policy violations seldom arise. We are not often faced with letting someone go.

Employees want rules to be consistent and fair, and in contrast to some conventional corporate wisdom, my partner and I believe when we let someone go for assertively violating clear-cut policy, our remaining staff feels *more* secure in their jobs, not less. Yes, we lost two valuable people, but the losses were outweighed by the positive, long-term effects on the remaining rule-abiding staff who always understand where things stand and that management is fair.

There is important subtlety here that I want to clarify: Did we terminate the employment of these two individuals to set an example? No. We terminated their employment because "that's the deal." If an example was set, it was a by-product of the action.

CHAPTER 22

COMMUNICATION:
GREASE FOR THE WHEELS

*"The quality of your communication equals
the quality of your life"*

Anthony Robbins

It seems sensible that a discussion of communication would parallel other *Work the System* protocols, protocols which dictate that quality supersedes quantity. However, with this I disagree. The sense I have developed over the years is that *quantity of communication is more important than quality of communication*. Of course, this refers to sensible discourse between two parties. It is no good if one spews unlimited information while ignoring the other side, or if the content is inane.

Quantity of communication connects to any success or failure. Is someone talking and someone else listening? Or, is there silence? Simply looking at world affairs confirms that between nations, the degree of cooperation is in direct proportion to the *amount* of two-way communication occurring. *Paranoia ensues if exchange is limited.*

It's the same in a marriage or a workplace relationship. More communication leads to better efficiency, stronger cooperation, and deeper trust. Between two people—or between two nations—if silence reigns, problems will arise in the relationship, or there will be no relationship at all.

If lots of communication occurs, the quality will take care of itself. For instance, sometimes I am at a loss for agenda topics for our weekly staff meetings because our regular communication is so thorough. Nevertheless, we have our Monday morning meetings even if we just chat about an impending marriage or someone's camping trip. It keeps us in touch and we feel like a team. We laugh, and that alone is worth it. We keep the meeting short, though. We have work to do.

Andi, Hollee, and I have ad-hoc get-togethers now and then, either in person, tele-conference, or by phone. Since the three of us have the deepest understanding of the company's overall systems strategy, these meetings go to the root of things. Our discussions are fluid and concise, and in a very few minutes we discuss a variety of issues. Like the weekly staff meetings, these are enjoyable sessions for me.

My partner and I have occasional quick check-in chats too, pointed and brief.

A caveat (there's always a caveat...) to the idea that quantity trumps quality: communication with oneself—one's own personal self-talk. Here, excessive internal communication is a problem, especially in Western culture. We examine, re-examine, dissect, and massage our personal thoughts, endlessly wondering, what *is* the problem? Is he (or she) angry with me? Did I say something wrong? Did I do enough? Do I need medication? *Am I a good person*? Arrgh! We could do well to act more and self-ruminate less.

DO WHAT YOU SAY YOU WILL DO

Keeping promises is a system in itself, a system with the end-purpose of maintaining solid relationships.

Don't distinguish between large promises and small promises. Keep them all. Keep them to everybody you make them to, including yourself. Keeping promises will set you apart from the crowd. Think about it. In the past couple of months, how many times have people failed to do what they said they would do, especially relating to the classic assurances, "I'll call you next week," and, "I'll take care of that right away!"

What if you become 100 percent reliable to friends, family, and work associates? What if you keep the promises you make, rather than leaning on them as manipulations intended to change the topic or exit the dialogue? What if people don't have to prod you into action? What if you do what you say you will do, exactly as promised and on time? The short answer is the people in your life will hold you in high esteem, as someone of high integrity, someone to be counted on. *They will want you to be part of their lives.*

Communication Mechanics

Discussing communication mechanics could be a monstrous proposition, so let's boil things down. This is basic stuff. Each point is sensible; each applicable to both business and personal life:

- If there is a problem with someone, have a meeting today. Talk things out one-on-one. If silence ensues, do something to promote dialogue. But be careful. If emotions are running high, put point-of-sale aside and wait for things to calm down.

- Be accessible. Give people an opportunity to leave a message if you are not available. Can the people who are important to you reach you readily, or are there mechanical, bureaucratic, and/or psychological barriers?

- Promote fluid discourse by making communication tools available to your staff—cell phones, digital recorders, voice mail, e-mail, and various meeting places for one-on-one, in-person dialog. Scheduled group meetings are prime tools that provide everyone a forum for communicating. However, keep meetings brief.

- Can your staff, clients, and potential clients find out more about you through a web site, hard copy, or other medium, or are you a mystery? Do you talk about your world to the people around you, or do you keep to yourself? Mysterious people typically don't do well in friendship or business.

- Yes, it's important to keep lines of communication open, but are you going back and forth with a person who consistently works against you? This could be in a personal relationship or with an employee or client. If the other side's intentions are too often contrarian or malevolent, it's irrational to continue to communicate. End the relationship. You are not in the business of being coerced. Do you have a close family member who is on the attack? If so, I sympathize. That's a tough one.

- Be concise. Get to the point. Unless you are at a barbecue on a Saturday afternoon, do yourself and those around you a favor by getting on with things.

- Be cordial and friendly, but don't overdo it.

- Never bash others behind their backs. It's low-class and any employee, client, or relative who has any degree of personal sophistication will devalue you.

- Talk up to people if that is the context. Your client, who is paying you, wants the bottom line—your personal friendship or clever witicisms are not part of his or her expectations. Likewise, with your boss. Again, while you take direction and provide information, be cordial, but not too cordial.

- Speak authoritatively and clearly to the people you manage. What they want from you is concise direction, respect, and paychecks that arrive on time.

- Your children? You aren't equal-footing pals with your kids. You are the parent. Act like one. It's what they expect and it's what works.

A SYSTEM FOR COMMUNICATION

At Centratel, based on our Strategic Objective and the efficiency thread that permeates the 30 Principles document, we employ the latest communications technology. It is an interesting paradox: The simple effectiveness of our internal communications hinges on highly complex technologies. (Somehow our IT manager, Dan, keeps all of it working with rarely any downtime.)

Right at the beginning of our transformation, we developed a Working Procedure for communication among ourselves and with the outside world. Because it's simple and easy, our managers communicate a lot.

Every Centratel staff member uses the same methodology. There is no confusion. This procedure has evolved with the technical and even social changes that have occurred in the last half dozen years. Here it is:

Internal Communications: Procedure and Fundamentals

The tools of active communications:

1. Voice Mail (VM)
2. E-mail (EM)
3. Instant Messenger (IM)
4. One-on-one via phone
5. One-on-one in person
6. Hard copy memo/procedure

What method of communication should I use?

1. Routine, not time sensitive: VM, EM
2. Time sensitive: IM, one-on-one in person or via phone
3. "Getting all my thoughts in order," detailed explanations: VM, EM
4. Personal and sensitive issues: one-on-one in person or via phone
5. Documentation is necessary: E-mail or hard copy
6. Information is complex/detailed: E-mail, hard copy, one-on-one in person or via phone
7. Procedures: Soft copy on Procedures drive and hard copy

Point-of-Sale

Point-of-Sale protocol for our internal communications means, most of all, that when someone asks a question, the response is immediate. For instance, avoid saving a voice mail message for a future response. If you must delay your reply, immediately take the time to answer the message sender to say you will get back with a detailed answer later (be sure to provide an approximate time he or she can expect your response). Understand this approach is just as applicable to e-mail: The most basic rule is to keep your inbox empty by dealing with the issue *now*, via our point-of-sale mandate.

Microsoft Outlook

The Centratel Microsoft Outlook information system is the heart of our administration's internal communications. The task list, contact list, and calendar are critical to staying organized and maximizing efficiency. Have the program open all day and use it often. Use the task list both to remind yourself of your own tasks, and of tasks delegated to others.

Instant Messenger

If you are on the job, it must be active. Be sure you configure it to turn on automatically when you log in.

E-mail

Thoroughly read messages you receive. Reread and double-check each outgoing message before you send it. Is your outgoing e-mail clear, concise, and brief? Are there grammatical errors? Does your message make sense, or are you presuming you are communicating with a mind reader, or maybe, someone who is fond of deciphering puzzles?

Giving (Delivering) a Message Via Any Medium

- Consider quantity before quality. In fact, Centratel's definition of quality communication includes high quantity. But note, *the quantity aspect has more to do with frequency than with volume of content.* Generally, if there is enough communication, quality will evolve. If in doubt about whether to communicate or not, you should communicate.

- Rambling dispatches that contain more information than necessary, or messages that keep repeating the same detail, are a waste of two people's time. The voice mail medium is particularly susceptible to fatiguing, inefficient messages. But then, sometimes a voice mail message is faster and more meaningful than an e-mail message. *Sometimes a 30-second voice mail will deliver the same message as a fifteen-minute e-mail.* Whatever the communication method, remember this when sending a message: "A great message is a short message."

- Not many people think about the quality of their communications. At Centratel, since our entire purpose is to provide the very best communication services, we have to be good at it! We are "The highest quality telephone answering service in the United States" because we unceasingly refine and improve the communication services we provide, as well as our own internal communications. We think about communications all the time. It is a primary system that we relentlessly analyze and refine.

- We have many communication tools. At any given time, is the best method being used? Before leaving a message for someone, what preparation is necessary for the message to be complete, clear, and concise? While leaving the message, is too much being said, or too little?

- An effective training process is to record and review conversations with callers and clients. For most of us, there is incongruency between how we think we sound and how we actually sound. This self-analysis can eliminate "yeahs" and "ya'knows," deepen one's voice, promote conciseness, and point out annoying flaws that otherwise go unnoticed.

Personal Communications

You can improve the quality of communication with yourself.

Eight years ago I devised a personal point-of-sale communication system that is enormously efficient. Using a cellular phone, Microsoft Outlook, and a voice recorder, it is ironic that the genesis of the system was my 100+ hour workweeks. The tools, working together, help me cover a lot of ground, easily doubling my overall effectiveness. (See **www. workthesystem.com/tools** for detailed information).

Other Aspects of Great Communication

In the typical work situation there is a lot of room for improvement. See if any of the following suggestions stimulate new ideas for your own situation.

In perfecting the primary communication system for staff, at Centratel we didn't limit ourselves to sub-system devices, methods, and policies. Our physical office is part of our communications strategy.

Burning up time looking for each other is utterly wasteful so we provide a sub-system to prevent it: glass walls between offices. Each administrative office has windows on all sides so managers can always see each other. To determine the availability of another manager, all we do is raise our heads to see if the manager we need is busy talking to someone in person, or if they are on the phone. There is no need to make a call, or to get up and search.

The TAS operations department—the place where calls are processed—is in the center of the office space, with administration offices around the edges of the room. It's a psychological reminder for all employees that the main purpose of our business is in taking messages and delivering them.

Our office is an energizing space, too; open and bright—and it promotes positive group chemistry, as each of us sees the rest of the team quietly hammering away. *We're all in this together!* Form follows function and the function is the result of our systematic approach.

Dan made it possible for Linda and me to do our part of management without having to be in the office. Our in-office capabilities are duplicated from anywhere in the world because of the data and video-conferencing capabilities of our laptops. I've worked my Outlook task list and led staff meetings from all over the United States, as well as Europe, South America, China, and Pakistan. Online, Linda has performed her CFO tasks from Thailand, Taiwan, Seattle, New York, Hawaii, and Southern California.

Intense system management means freedom.

Gone Missing

Several years ago we had our house remodeled. Immediately after, we "flipped" another house. In both cases, numerous subcontractors, both experienced and inexperienced, did the work.

Linda was the interior designer. I was the general contractor.

In this world of framers, plumbers, electricians, roofers, and concrete specialists, there is an interesting commonality among inexperienced subcontractors: It is difficult to communicate with them. Phones go unanswered, messages are left but no return call is forthcoming, or voice mailboxes are full.

Generally, the contractor has "gone missing."

How do these people stay in business?

The dysfunctional communication system is a reflection of the new contractor's chaotic personal methodology in which he or she is so wrapped up in fire-killing and "doing the work," that insidious inefficiency remains invisible while it gobbles up the bottom line. It's a subconscious miscalculation in which unhappy customers are relegated to the list of "those things that can't be measured, and therefore have no value." The owner of this business must make a perspective adjustment or the business will fail. (And, per the statistics, the huge majority of them *do* fail).

CHAPTER 23

PRIME TIME

*It has been my observation that most people get
ahead during the time that others waste time.*

Henry Ford

Two Kinds of Prime Time

Prime time is about maximizing productivity during the period brainpower is at peak capacity.

The prime time viewpoint aims at the most fundamental of systems: our own actions. Here is the opportunity to exert tight control over the most potent primary system at your disposal—yourself.

Prime time has two components. The first has to do with your most effective time of day due to biological makeup. Let's call it "biological prime time," or BPT. The other component has to do with *what* you do with your time. This is "mechanical prime time," or MPT.

The prime time concept is mind-numbingly simple and has everything to do with Ockham's foundational premise that the "simplest solution is invariably the correct solution." Like all *Work the System* fundamentals, the unadorned logic makes it easy to understand.

The Ephemeral Nature of Biological Prime Time

First, let's talk about BPT.

We function at maximum effectiveness just a few hours within a 24-hour day. It is important to take advantage of this interesting facet of human performance. To illustrate, I am a "morning person," and over a period of two years, six days a week, I have written 95 percent of this book between the hours of 5 a.m. and 11 a.m. I write at this time because my energy level is at a peak and I can think clearly. But, that's me. Your BPT could occur later in the day.

Compared to afternoon or evening, my BPT quality and speed are never better than during early and mid-morning, so I avoid squandering it on television news, exercise, or reading, spending it only on my most important projects—the projects that lead to freedom and peace. By noon, my critical thinking ability is declining and my energy slumps. By 2 p.m. it's hard to keep my eyes open.

If I miss or squander my daily 6 hours of BPT, that's a full day's peak creative allotment wasted.

I avoid doing anything that requires crisp thinking in the early-to mid-afternoon. Then, yard work, reading for entertainment, napping, meditating, or watching the news are among the activities I can pull off with no problem. I am humble about my afternoon downturn because it's just a mechanical phenomenon—a sine wave low point—a decreased performance period that has nothing to do with my overall intelligence or worth. Because my car is out of gas does not mean it needs repair.

If peak performance is necessary in my low-ebb timeframe, I exercise or find some other non-chemical way to hold my peak.

I get a second wind at 4 p.m. that lasts a few hours. Your BPT may orchestrate a later second wind.

In all probability, these ebbs and flows are genetic. (Not surprising, both my mother and father share the same pattern).

Linda's BPT lags behind mine by about five hours: She is devastatingly effective from 9 a.m. to 3 p.m., but a zombie (her words) at 6 a.m. Her second wind comes in the evening around 8 p.m. and lasts until 11 p.m. or beyond. So, as we go through the day, there is an overlap. It can be amusing as we simultaneously hit our individual highs and lows: For the one "bottoming out," it's an exercise in humility; for the one reaching "peak," it's a demonstration of mental incisiveness.

We joke about it.

Managing your BPT

It is important to know precisely when your BPT occurs and then to use it wisely. Six hours out of a 24-hour day is not much. If it is true that BPT is hard-wired into our individual biological systems, then permanently modifying BPT by sheer force of will is impossible. For most people in northern latitudes, if it is necessary to be at peak reasoning ability outside of BPT's natural range, caffeine enters the picture. In South America, it's Yerba Matte.

Presuming you wish to reach your goals sooner rather than later, *it is best to perform the tasks that contribute most to your primary goals during your BPT hours and that you protect those hours from interruption.* Avoid squandering BPT on the frivolous.

BPT is when you should create your Strategic Objective, General Operating Principles, and Working Procedures. Of course, after your initial *Work the System* documentation is complete, BPT will continue to be there for whatever takes focus, whatever takes the most concentration. You will learn to cherish these golden hours.

Every day, the remaining non-BPT hours are available to take care of less demanding activities and for recharging the biological, psychological, and social batteries. These are the hours for iPods, periodicals, movies, exercise, and time with friends.

The afternoon non-prime time hours are a reward for the earlier prime time hours that were well spent. Both periods are equally gratifying.

The *Work the System* methodology calls for breaking complexity into workable components, so it makes sense to reduce time into one-day manageable chunks. *It is easier to master one day at a time.* Plan each day carefully, pay attention to details, and watch the hours quickly pass as you work toward your goals, riding the ebb and flow of your energy cycle. At the end of the day, look back and evaluate your accomplishments. Take what you learned and apply it in your "next day chunk."

When is Your BPT?

Analyzing the "why" of personal BPT is not important. What is vital is to know *when* it occurs.

If you are a "night person," you'll slowly wake up in the morning, cruise gently into the day, and gradually work up your head of steam. If this is you, be implacable about protecting those late morning or afternoon BPT hours because, unlike early morning BPT, the world's demands and distractions will be in your face, making it a chore to concentrate. Turn the cell phone off and shut the door, or disappear to the library or coffee shop. Protect yourself.

What is your BPT? Stand outside yourself and observe your energy level over the course of a week or so. Note when you are most motivated, positive, and energized—and when you do little more than stumble around. You must be rested, relaxed, and healthy when you do this.

You'll figure it out with no problem unless you are a habitual user of mood adjusters such as coffee, alcohol, anti-depressants, or other legal or illegal substance. Caffeine, for instance, thoroughly masks the energy cycle. If you are addicted and wish to stop drinking it in order to pinpoint your personal BPT—you know this already—expect some mental depression. Headaches often accompany the depression.

My experience with caffeine is that it is a 16-hour top-to-bottom drug. People who are mildly addicted need it in the morning to counteract the withdrawal symptoms of the previous day's indulgence, but after their morning dose, they can get through the afternoon and evening without it. Removing 90 percent of the withdrawal effects of mild addiction takes three to four weeks of total abstinence. If you are a heavy caffeine drinker—you drink it all day—my condolences. Quitting is going to be tough. But if you can abstain for those three or four weeks, you might decide to quit permanently. Hang tough because if you can quit, you will learn to ride your body's natural rhythms and find downtimes are best addressed with more sleep, not a chemical boost.

There is another benefit to getting though the day without dependence on a state-of-mind adjuster: Personal pride in facing the world "cold turkey." (In *my* life, am I completely clean? No. I enjoy a cup of coffee now and then, and in my trips to Pakiston for NGO work—a jet-lag body slam of twelve time zones—a small dose of Valium helps me to sleep).

WALLOW IN IT

Here's a wild card: Some days, biological prime time will take off with more than the usual torque. When those days appear, energy surges with unusual strength. I stick with work as my intense energy level churns through the morning and deep into the afternoon, sometimes not letting up until late evening. I wallow in these rare opportunities and can cover three day's ground in one epic, single-day effort. I'm clueless as to why it happens.

Is This You?

For too many, this is the 24 hour day-cycle: By 7 a.m., external demands of work and family kick in. A dose of caffeine generates an artificial morning prime time no matter the natural BPT cycle. The fray begins and the schedule takes over. The mindset is, "There aren't enough hours to do what must be done!" The day is spent killing fires and any plans for system improvement remain amorphous and ill-defined. There is *so* much to do and so little time to do it!

In the evening, the caffeine buzz has transmuted into nervousness, and alcohol is applied to calm things down.

That night, deep sleep suffers because of the lingering effects of the day's mood adjusters. (This is a serious consideration because every night some quantity of deep sleep is necessary for solid mental and physical functioning the next day. As time goes on, sleep debt increases and, until it is paid back hour-for-hour, performance and mood suffer).

The next morning, the repercussions of long-term sleep deprivation, combined with alcohol and caffeine withdrawal, begins anew, and another caffeine pick-me-up is mandatory if anything is to be accomplished. It goes on and on, day after day, and…whew! The result is a wired, nervous, and exhausted "treadmill" human being.

Just another rat in the rat race.

It is understandable why many Western adults take yet another step, trying to find peace in anti-depressants. Here is where things really begin to get shaky: Notwithstanding sleep deprivation, how can anyone be cutting-edge effective with caffeine, alcohol, *and* anti-depressants circulating in the system?

With the classic Western world day-cycle, is there any hope for an unadulterated BPT focus each day? Not without some serious effort. So, for most, the magical BPT hours remain a mystery, muddled by uncontrolled external demands, exhaustion, and mood-altering substances.

But not for you! If you don't want it to be that way, you can clean things up, discover when your BPT occurs, and then discipline yourself to use it properly. Never waste your BPT!

UNIVERSAL UPS AND DOWNS

> For the population as a whole, and despite individual variations, a general surge of energy occurs during two periods of the day. The first is in the morning around 9 a.m. and extends maybe another four hours. Then, the early afternoon to late-afternoon hours are low key (which is the reason much of the world takes a nap after

lunch). Around 5 p.m., things pick up again and a secondary surge begins, lasting several hours. At around 9 p.m., mental sharpness begins to decline again and it's time to get ready for bed. This universal cycle is part of human biology, and whether you are a morning person or night person, your personal sine-wave peaks and lows will intermingle with the universal pattern.

Mechanical Prime Time and the Real Business

The second form of prime time has to do with *what* you do with your time. Mechanical Prime Time (MPT) is the time spent in system improvement, building primary systems such as a business or career. With some notable exceptions we will discuss, it is not the time spent doing a job for money, or producing the product or service.

Whatever you do, if you wish to find freedom along with prosperity, you must spend as much time as possible in the MPT zone.

Unlike BPT, which happens automatically whether we are ready to take advantage of it or not, MPT exists only if we create it. Many people never experience MPT because they don't know what it is, or if they do, they are too busy killing fires to go there. Most just stumble into it occasionally.

Let's define MPT through the back door by discussing my rather strict definition of a "real business." This interpretation presumes there are but two positions in life: Either one is the boss or one isn't the boss. One either owns the enterprise or one works for the enterprise. The obligatory caveat: Can a person be both? Sort of. We'll get to that.

We've talked about this already: *In a real business, the owner is not the one physically doing the production of the product or service. This can be a bitter pill to swallow, but it is difficult to dispute that if you are doing the work of creating the actual product or service, you don't own a business, you work a job. You "own" a job.* Yes, even with attendant high income and prestige, doctors, attorneys, consultants, celebrities, and professional athletes have *jobs*, not businesses. (Don't get me wrong here. A job is not a bad thing, offering some real advantages over my strict definition of a "business." We'll get to that soon, too).

So, a key indicator of a job is one has to "show up." Not so with a business: A true business operates with cursory supervision from the owner, churning out profits as its own primary system; its own organism, self-sufficient and independent. Think, "The dollar bills keep materializing while the owner is elsewhere."

If you are a professional and have other professionals working *for* you—and without your direct input they are accomplishing goals you have set out for them—this portion of your life is a business and the cursory management time you spend dealing with it is MPT. In contrast, the time spent with patients or clients is production work, so that part of what you do is a job, not MPT. If you must trot out into left field at specific dates and times as a New York Yankee or a Boston Red Sox, or be on-location as the star of a feature film, that's a job. Indeed, these are very good jobs!

Here's another example of a job versus a real business: Real estate sales. If the real estate professional is selling property and living on the income, that's a job. However, if a portion of those commissions are being invested in rental properties or bare lots, that part is a business. MPT is the time spent doing the legwork of acquiring property for the personal portfolio, not time spent "showing up" to sell or list property.

THE DEFINING QUESTION

During the work day, no matter what you are doing, look at each action you take and ask yourself if it is contributing to "working less and making more." As you analyze your actions, it's the moment-to-moment mindset that matters most. The day you "get it," and switch your focus to the blow-by-blow mechanics of daily life, while leaving aside theory and wishful thinking, freedom and wealth will begin to materialize.

It's Your Job *and* Your Business

Let's look at this a bit closer. If you are a creative person making a living in art or performing; a professional athlete, doctor, attorney, consultant; or if you are the centerpiece in some endeavor or another, yes, you have a job—but, yes, you also have a business. *You* are the business and you carry it everywhere. You have a unique skill that is a blessing—you are a "creator"—but as you create, you must deal with the "showing up" challenges *and* the business requirements of managing the enterprise.

You not only must do what you do as a creator, you must manage accounting, purchasing, accounts receivable, advertising, customer service, public relations, and so on. If you make your living as a celebrity, there is also the extra notoriety-baggage that comes along with the package.

This is the reason why, in a business where the creator is doing the production *and* managing the details, life can be exhausting at the least, and at the worst, nightmarish. The goal is to use the MPT mindset to find ways to minimize the management tasks/burdens so focus can remain on creative efforts.

A FIRST TASTE OF MPT

If you are a charter boat captain taking fishermen out on the ocean every day, while every night you must hunker down to do the books, recognize you have a job. And if this job makes you unhappy because of lack of freedom, then only by taking the outside-and-slightly-elevated "this is job, not a business" vantage point will you be able to devise a future in which others are piloting the boat and doing the books. This mental positioning will allow you to visualize assembling the pieces in a way that will remove you from the production, thus ending the long hours and securing the peace and prosperity you want. Asking the question, "what must I do *right now* to start to build this job into a business?" is your first taste of MPT.

The Beauty of Holding a Traditional Job

Most people have jobs, and as of this writing, there is not a general revolt against the concept. In any society, it is a revered position, one that carries a certain "it's a good feeling to be part of the team" camaraderie. Whether a democratic or a socialistic state, it is understood that the people who are out there working jobs are the bedrock of the society. They keep the wheels turning.

For you, having a traditional job is ideal if any one or more of the following are of high importance:

- Freedom: It is a luxury to be able to leave the job at the end of the day and not have a single work-related worry on your mind.

- You abhor the idea of managing the extra degree of financial risk, uncertainty, and headaches that can come with a business.

- In your job, you are doing what you love, feel a high sense of self-esteem, and simply don't want things to change.

- You are building something of value in your job, and the future looks bright.

- The job situation is the only way you can obtain the necessary resources to do the thing you love (flying a jet, or politics, for example).

- You value the social aspect of being surrounded by peer employees.

- For the moment, you must survive as you prepare for independence down the line.

- You are making more money than you require, creating a future of freedom just from the assets you are stashing away.

- With your skill set, because of your physical location, or for whatever reason, there is no opportunity elsewhere.

- You crave the security of insurance, retirement fund, savings plan, etc.

If you enjoy your job and don't want to be on your own, know the MPT mindset is a tremendous asset. It will provide you a better understanding of the big picture of the organization and, with a clear vision of where the organization is headed, you can make a more potent contribution. Presuming advancement is your goal, the MPT mindset will energize the process.

Beware Falling Off the Roof

Presume you are the sole proprietor of a chimney sweep company, and every day you climb up on a different roof. This makes you an integral component of the "chimney sweep business system." You're gambling with the long-term because when you least expect it, you may fall off the roof and be seriously injured. As the business owner/worker, who will perform the production work when you are out of commission? Your time on the roof is not MPT. It's a job, and a dangerous job at that.

MPT is time you spend finding someone else to climb up there on those roofs to clean chimneys; *it's the time you spend thinking about how to extricate yourself from the mechanism in order to build it and make it self-sufficient.*

A Self-Contained Entity of Worth

Here's the great thing about owning a real business: Someday it can be sold as a packaged entity, a self-contained primary system.

The ability of a business to generate income without the owner doing the actual production work is what endows a business with value beyond everyday cash flow. *If you are a critical element in the generation of the product or service, the need for your presence is going to be a problem when you want to sell what you've built.* If you are a chimney sweep and wish to retire, with just a customer list to sell as an asset and no one to climb up on those roofs to perform the service, how much is *that* worth? Unquestionably, much less than you want it to be.

But if you have people doing the production work up on those roofs, and the organization cranks out a good monthly bottom line without physical input from you, your business will have solid, tangible worth to someone else. It will be a dollar bill machine for you while you own it—and for someone else who buys it later. *The ability to churn out a black-ink bottom line without the owner's immediate contribution means the business is its own organism, separate from the owner, with tangible worth as an independent entity.*

No, this doesn't mean you will create a business that won't need you. There will always be some MPT work for you to do if the business is to grow. You will have to give it direction and make it efficient.

YOUR NEW BUSINESS

If you are interested in forging your own way and finding maximum freedom, you must be in charge of an enterprise. This means operating your own business.

A fast way to go about it: Find a small business that is in trouble. When you investigate it, more often than not you will see mismanagement. Decide if the product and the market is viable, and if so, buy the company for what it is worth. Then, fix it.

Creating MPT

The charter boat captain or the chimney sweep can turn 80 hour weeks into 40 hour weeks, and then into 2 hour weeks. Proper use of MPT gets one out of the boat—or off the roof—and turns a business/job into a real business, a stand-alone entity that has intrinsic value.

For those in corporate management positions, the same MPT strategy accelerates the ladder-climb.

At the root of MPT, *the owner/manager must spend the majority of time focused on building the business into self-sufficiency and on making it grow. Executing production is a distraction from what must be done to achieve independence and/or ascend the corporate ladder.*

To maintain MPT through the day, ask the following questions moment-to-moment: What should I be doing *right now* in order to grow the company, or get a promotion? And, for the efforts required to create my product or do my job, how can I delegate or automate those efforts so they are done with maximum efficiency while taking as little of my time as possible?" Again, the time spent delegating and/or automating is MPT.

Centratel, as a telephone answering service, is a business providing an intangible service to business clients. We take incoming calls, record messages, and then deliver those messages. Then we charge the client for those services. I spent 15 years assisting with this work, many times processing calls as a TSR. At the time, it seemed heroic, as I jumped into the melee whenever the incoming call traffic became too much for the TSR staff. What a stand-up guy! But as a result, and although I thought my multi-tasking performance was terrific, in reality I did only a mediocre job in bookkeeping, sales, receivables, payables, customer services, human resources, etc.

In those years, no time was spent fashioning a company that would someday operate without me; a company that would have tangible value without the requirement of my presence. I was working 80-100 hours every week, personally performing the production and administration work. This is why, after fifteen years, the market value of Centratel was zero, and why my income was at the same subsistence level every single year for that decade and a half. It was also why the business almost killed me.

MPT wasn't a concept for me back then. I didn't understand my time should have been spent building the company into independence, and "doing the work" could be my undoing. I understood time could be spent either wisely or unwisely, but what I didn't understand was what defined "wise," and "unwise."

Overlooking the important, I was frittering away my days while building no value for the future. I was majoring in minors while Rome was burning.

How about you? Today, how are you spending your time and energy?

Steering the Ship with BPT and MPT

Now, in my business, I simply steer the ship. There is a great income, and the asset base grows.

My BPT is carefully allocated to the actions that are most important for long-term gain—MPT tasks, including reviewing and suggesting system refinements, occasional brief meetings with managers to provide whatever guidance or input they need, and envisioning and planning.

My non-MPT tasks include handling payables (because overseeing expenditures is the smart thing for me to do), and updating and maintaining our web site and blog (because I enjoy doing it).

So now, my workweek is two hours long and my monthly earnings exceed my previous yearly earnings. Of the brief time I spend on business issues, 90 percent of it is MPT and, no, I don't answer the phones or take deposits to the bank anymore.

Here is the crux of Prime Time: Enormous advancement comes from spending the most alert periods of the day doing the most important system-building tasks.

When you are *not* in BPT, if you feel like it, it's OK to focus on MPT tasks—the tasks that have to do with improving and growing your business and your life. High energy or low energy, keep your work activities pointed toward primary business-building or career-advancing activities per your critical documents. In your day, stay in MPT as long as possible, but remember you must be balanced in order to avoid burn-out. *Have a life outside your work.*

IN THIS MOMENT, BE WARY

Once there is some progress, there will be no going back to the old ways. You will see *you* are in control; *you* are building something good, and never again will you be the victim of unpredictable circumstance!

Nevertheless, in this moment, be wary. You have not yet developed new, good habits, while you are still prone to old bad habits. If the "my world is composed of systems!" lightning bolt hasn't struck yet, all you have right now is feel-good theory. If this is the case, maybe go back and read chapters seven and eight again.

Even after the "ah-ha" strikes, you will sometimes have to muscle your way through the initial documentation, especially when your energy levels are low. It takes maybe eight weeks to form a new habit, so give yourself time. But then again, positive results will probably come sooner and then your motivation will be powered by plain common sense, the most powerful impetus there is.

It's All about How You Spend Your Time

Once you begin to see a reduction in time demands, you will be inspired to use BPT and MPT more and more efficiently. It's that "cycle of increasing returns" concept.

But later, in your prime time, maybe it will be your choice to write a book or to get that easel out and paint again. You will have lots of time to do those kinds of things once the *Work the System* methodology does its magic.

A Point-of-Sale Appreciation of Life

I sit here writing these words on a Wednesday in November.

It's noon, and I have been on-task for eight hours, working through and then past my usual BPT, and am still at maximum throttle. It's one of those rare and exquisite maximum-BPT days, perhaps because that is my topic today. I will work for a while more, and then plug into my iPod and rake the lawn because that is both relaxing and satisfying.

After that, Linda and I will go for a walk in the neighborhood. Then, we'll see a movie. After the movie, we'll have dinner out.

There is a Zen proverb: "Before enlightenment, chop wood, carry water. After enlightenment, chop wood, carry water." It's perfect, really, as we immerse ourselves in the simple mechanics of what needs to be done *right now*: creating, adjusting, and maintaining systems.

Chop wood, carry water.

Sometimes we say to each other, *"This is it!"* It's a simple, happy way to remind ourselves *this* is the life we've envisioned and there is no need to brood for anything more. Life is as tangible as it can be when we just acknowledge it in the moment and agree it's good. No matter where we are or what we're doing, this instant in time—this right now—*is it!* Any other time is not real; either a memory or conjecture.

So, for fleeting moments in the middle of working our systems, we withdraw a bit in order to celebrate the only true reality there is—this *right now*—and we're grateful.

PTO: Taking Time off from Work

Here we altogether eliminated a complex process (as always, a delightful event), and replaced it with an automatic point-of-sale system. Linda, as Centratel Chief Financial Officer, is in a bird's-eye position now, no longer in the middle of things.

In the systems-revision discussed here, we went back to a premise: Paid Time Off (PTO) is an employee benefit designed to keep employees satisfied and happy, but most of all, to encourage them to continue to work for Centratel—and working means showing up for work!

There was a problem with our paid-by-the-hour staff's PTO arrangement. (PTO is an earned time-off allowance that employees use for sick days and vacation days. Depending on the employee's seniority, the allowance is the equivalent of two or three workweeks per year.)

In theory, it sounded great when we first offered the benefit, but in the real-world application it was terrible.

First, it was a nightmare to calculate and administrate. Did our managers do their weekly job of tallying all eligible employee PTO hours and then submitting them? For example, did Tony report his absence yesterday as PTO time, and beyond that, just how many hours are now available for him to use? Did the books start accurately accumulating Carmella's PTO after her 90-day probation was finished?

Second, our employees used PTO hours in ways we did not intend. We had designed it for vacation time off—for employees to get away from work once or twice a year in a way we could plan and schedule around. And our intent was it would also be available to use for occasional sick days or appointments. But, for many staff members, PTO was used as soon as it was accumulated—a few hours here, a few hours there.

Many times, it was an excuse to be absent from work under the pretense of "I don't feel good today and I think I have accumulated enough PTO to take the day off, so I am going to call in sick." It turned out that too often the hourly-paid TSR did *not* have enough PTO available and so did not work 40 hours for the week. For the staff member, this resulted in a smaller paycheck than expected. Furthermore, Centratel was understaffed.

Third, errors in the complex administrative system invariably led to the granting of too much paid PTO, and over the years, it had been a substantial loss to the company's bottom line. What should we do?

We dropped the old system altogether, adopting another much simpler one. Our point-of-sale principle was key in developing the new policy. We stopped the long-term accumulation of PTO. Instead, on each paycheck, we pay it as it is earned. It is paid by the hour, the hourly amount determined by that staff member's pay rate and length of employment. We note this earned PTO as a separate line-item on paychecks.

Based on the number of hours worked in a given pay period, our accounting system automatically determines the paycheck's PTO amount. There is no more manual record keeping and the employee knows where he or she stands at all times. There are no more errors.

Can employees take vacations? Yes, they can take time off as they wish, but they know the time off has been paid in advance and there will be no paycheck while they are gone.

Now, since employees earn their pay only when they work, absenteeism is reduced 80 percent, manual administrative paperwork is eliminated, and there is no confusion.

An outside-and-slightly-elevated solution? Absolutely.

CHAPTER 24

THE TRAFFIC CIRCLES
OF PAKISTAN

Confusion is a word we have invented
for an order which is not understood.

Henry Miller

In Lahore, Pakistan, the traffic circle is the epicenter of the driving experience. Like traffic circles anywhere, the Pakistani version absorbs vehicles from various points and then spews them out at other points. However, these circles differentiate themselves from the more civilized circles of the West, with each Pakistani driver's unspoken proclamation: "Enter here but *beware*! I do not care what you want. Your existence is an obstacle to me! May the best man win and know that man is me!"

The driving is instinctual and primal.

Some of the circles are huge, with five concentric lanes of traffic, each with vehicles voraciously roaring around and around the pock-holed pavement. The circles are beautiful, really: Raw, closed, no-nonsense systems in which an observer can generalize about how third-world systems operate.

A Dearth of Guidelines

In the Pakistani traffic circle there are two rules: Go as fast as possible and avoid colliding. That's it. It's every man for himself (in Pakistan it is almost always a man behind the wheel) with the whole thing propelled by an invisible frenzy of mocking desperation. As a Westerner standing on the sidelines, it is clear that for each driver it's a matter of life and death; that each must reach his destination just a bit sooner than what is humanly possible. Within the seething circle—indeed, a living organism—there is no rule for which vehicle has the right of way, unless one considers intimidation a rule.

It's amazing.

The drivers revel in the silent pact that no organizing guidelines shall interfere. It is similar to most third-world gatherings of people: Queuing into a single-file line just doesn't happen as everyone agrees survival-of-the-fittest is the single guideline for securing whatever is to be had. In the circle, no one is insulted or irritated by the hyper-assertive jostling and the line crashing. *It's the nature of the game,* and within the Pakistani traffic circle, you will cut me off while blowing hard on your horn and that's OK!

The traffic rages around and around, with all participants frustrated the general vehicle velocity isn't faster than it is. Competing for space are fragile donkey carts, huge ornately decorated trucks, tiny Chinese cars, cantankerous bicycles, and hoards of darting, weaving motor scooters. When a car or truck breaks down, the driver simply stops his vehicle without any attempt to pull over to get out of the way. In nonchalance, he lies down on his back under his disabled vehicle and makes repairs. Nobody cares or pays attention as the driver escapes being crushed by no act of his own.

Within the circle there is no cooperation or consideration and everyone agrees that's fine.

Cooperate or Challenge?

Comparing the traffic circles of Pakistan to those in the West illustrates a stunning contrast.

To flatten the playing field for my forthcoming theory, I am presuming all drivers everywhere share the same desire—to travel without physical damage from point A to point B in a minimum amount of time.

Here's the question: To get what one wants—in this case, traveling from one place to another as rapidly and as unscathed as possible—shall it be by group cooperation (an intricate and formal system) or shall it be by independent, single-minded challenges to one another (a rudimentary, free-for-all system)?

In Bend, Oregon, USA, one follows many rules of the road. If not, there will be problems. For instance, the cars already within the Bend traffic circle unquestionably have the right of way. Incoming drivers rarely violate this rule but if they do, a physical altercation could ensue, with the vehicles pulled over, the drivers making fools of themselves. The Western right-of-way rule is ironclad and 99.9 percent of drivers follow the rule exactly. Of course, there are other Western rules too, having to do with speed, signaling, etc. And no one would ever think of changing a tire anywhere near a traffic circle. The mindset is on the other drivers and no one thinks of impeding traffic for any reason. One does not see this oh-so-sensitive driver persona in Pakistan.

In Pakistan, as in most third world countries, one driver does not consider the other driver and each charges into the fray without forethought, the opposite of the conservative driver's culture of the United States.

At the risk of being culturally judgmental, it is my contention that in getting from point A to point B, cooperation is better than a competitive free-for-all.

My guess is that despite the Pakistani frenzy, more traffic flows through the staid Bend traffic circle than flows through the Lahore traffic circle. It's also my bet there are fewer accidents in the Western traffic circle.

So, again, at the risk of making a stupid, bellicose East-West judgment, it is obvious to me that if the goal is to move huge volumes of traffic from point A to point B, the cooperative social agreements of a rigid-rule traffic circle beats the frenzy of a traffic circle that has no guidelines. The West's higher capacity traffic circle is an illustration of the importance of mutual consideration, as well as rules participants understand and agree upon. And, away from the traffic circles, in the social process, it is more productive for each participant to consider the welfare of other participants, and to follow simple rules that deal with common contingencies. For individual drivers, and for the culture as a whole, it just works better. It's a matter of mechanical efficiency.

But there is more to this than mechanics. Ignoring the efficiency aspect, which traffic circle is the most *fun*, the most satisfying? The most innovative and free-form? Clearly, it's the Pakistani circle. The flair and competitiveness in Pakistani streets is a remarkable thing, with a colorful, good-natured jousting that is fascinating to watch. For a Westerner on the periphery looking in, it's a spectator sport that is in direct contrast to the uptight, boring military orderliness of the streets of the West. When I'm in Pakistan, I just stand there on the edge of the frenzy, watching those traffic circles. It makes me feel alive.

These people are not just going somewhere; they're free-form artists, creating and surviving and having a Hell of a good time doing it.

We Westerners could learn something from that.

From this Rigid Framework, Take Your Risks

So the drivers in Lahore, Pakistan, and Bend, Oregon, *do* arrive at their respective destinations. Like any business or any life—with individual comportment and social expectation being major influences—strategies for making those journeys range from pedantic rule-following to vainglorious self-interest. It's my guess most Westerners find themselves somewhere in the middle, but leaning toward rule-following.

The two culture's traffic circles beautifully illustrate the extremes of how one can go about getting what one wants. But is there a middle ground? In life outside of the traffic circles, could it be that a staid, conservative foundation could be the launching pad for surges of innovation and leaps of faith?

Think about traffic circles as you plan for getting yourself through the day. And consider the circles as you contemplate the *Work the System* methodology in which you will create a thoughtful, planned framework—a framework that is safe-harbor for later off-the-wall new ideas that will propel you into the life you want.

So, today, slow down and begin the process of finding order and creating structure. Later, from this framework, take your risks.

Why Can't We Find Employees?

It's our greatest challenge: Centratel's pay and benefits are very good, but no matter how aggressively we advertise our positions, we don't have many job applicants. Because we have a hard time finding qualified people, we are fortunate our current staff sees little turnover. But the irony of simultaneous recruitment challenges and staff stability is understandable. If one digs a bit deeper, it becomes clear why we have problems finding job applicants—and the good fortune of having high staff stability. It's our drug-testing policy.

Before we instituted drug testing, we had plenty of job applicants, but there was also high staff turnover. A staff that uses drugs is flighty, and a flighty staff means quality achieved through long-term individual experience can never happen.

Our brutal judgement is that only a limited number of service-industry job candidates are drug free. It's a painful, almost unbelievable conclusion, but we must operate on that basis because the statistics bear it out. The choice seems to be, "I'd rather smoke dope and earn minimum wage with no benefits at a menial job, then *not* smoke dope at Centratel, where I could earn more than double minimum wage with full benefits."

Ouch.

Many business owners understand the truth of this so they don't invoke drug testing. Of those who do, it's a gamble. I know of one local restaurant that had to close its doors after an impromptu drug screening of all its employees. They had to terminate employment for nine of their twelve people. Another local business, a new, huge "box" store, selected twenty people for its automotive department. Sixteen of the twenty failed the drug testing.

Did our decision to use drug-screening stem from an outside-and-slightly-elevated perspective? There is no question. Per our Strategic Objective, we looked down on our business and decided we required a stable workforce. We decided to trade the chaos of high staff turnover for the staid challenge of finding drug-free people who are steady, superb performers.

To be sure, the introduction of a drug-testing policy must be handled with care, supported by a well-thought-out written policy.

CHAPTER 25

SYSTEM IMPROVEMENT AS A WAY OF LIFE

Dogs bark, but the caravan moves on.

Arabian Proverb

The Systems-Perspective Must Be Part of You

In Part One, I described the system-improvement concept in a nutshell. Here it is again, verbatim: *For a given primary system, in order to ensure the desired result occurs over and over again, the task is to adjust that primary system's sub-systems so the correct components are being used and they are sequenced properly. This is the goal of any manager, the work of "system-improvement."*

The *Work the System* process is about preparation. If you pay attention to the mechanical details of your world and make proper adjustments to the key systems that compose it, you can construct a life that is un-encumbered with fire-killing; a life seldom dictated by urgency. Flexible, strong, and resilient, it's a life of smooth, calm days; days that have lots of room for thinking and planning, for friends and family, and for just being yourself. It's a life that deals with road bumps, not earthquakes.

Whatever your station in life, if your days are frustrating—crammed to the max—and you're not getting ahead, know things can be fixed if you focus on system-improvement: It is the crux of the *Work the System* method.

It is one thing to gain a deeper understanding of the mechanics of how this material world functions, but it is another thing to apply this understanding in every instance, to have the system-improvement methodology so ingrained that it modifies even the smallest decision of the day. For this, the systems-perspective must be part of you.

Also in Part One, I discussed—in fact, belabored—the *Work the System* epiphany. For you, it's possible it has happened already. In any case, the change in perspective has to do with abandonment of the vision that random events make up the day. Instead, it becomes clear beyond any doubt that fluid 1-2-3 step systems make up the events of life, and that 99.9 percent of everything does indeed work perfectly. *Along with this perspective change there must be mechanical action,* otherwise it's too much like a psychedelic drug trip: One ingests the drug and then experiences profound new insights. Then, one crashes and things are bleak beyond words and the questions must be asked, was anything gained? Was the insight worth the price?

Here is a final summary of the mechanics of the system-improvement/Work the System methodology:

1. It starts with your change in perspective, the "ah-ha!" insight arriving in a moment of time. Deep down, you permanently internalize your new vision. You see each life event as the product of the unfolding system that engendered it, and not as an isolated happening; a product of luck, fate, God's justice, karma, the stars, or the benevolence or wrath of someone else. When the insight arrives, your next mechanical moves are obvious.

2. You establish your goals and strategy through the creation of the Strategic Objective and General Operational Principles. You do this for permanence, so there is continuity in your thoughts and efforts.

3. You examine the mechanics of the sub-systems that make up your business, job, health, and relationships. With the systems isolated, one by one you analyze their components, looking for opportunities for improvement.

4. You make the system improvements, moving each sub-system to peak efficiency. If you're in a business or job environment, you create documented Working Procedures to describe the protocols. Following the protocols exactly, but open to making further incremental adjustments when necessary, you and your people repeat the system-improvement process in all recurring situations. In the end, scores, if not hundreds, of perfected Working Procedures will emerge.

5. A more positive attitude toward life comes naturally because you have developed faith in the reliability of the systems that are at work everywhere. You are powerful and serene because you have successfully harnessed your systems, directing them to do what you want them to do. With sub-systems isolated, perfected, and then combined together again, you preside over stunningly efficient primary systems—your business, job, relationships...*you*. At the gut level, without putting your head in the sand regarding the many things that are not perfect in this world, you grasp the great truth that 99.9 percent of everything works just fine.

Singles and Doubles

Forget about making that one big swing that will save the day. The numbers are more than a little against you, and your big swings will be a distraction. Instead, hunker down, preserve what you have, and go for the sure-fire, incremental system-improvement advances: the singles and doubles. Go slowly at first. Be patient. Pay attention to the small yet permanent improvements that will add up to something big down the line. It's the little things that add up.

Always offer a positive regard for those around you and do what you say you will do. Demonstrate quality and do it consistently. Keep your goals in mind and relentlessly work toward them through thick and thin. Don't try to fool yourself or others around you. Start and finish things on time. Don't complain.

Your life will get better sooner than you think.

Focus on the systems that produce results, not the other way around, and never doubt that a superb collection of sub-systems will produce a superb primary system.

The reality is that most people look for results without considering the mechanisms that produce those results. They don't understand the system-improvement concept. In thinking locally, this gives you great advantage. Thinking globally, you know there are a whole lot of people out there not getting what they want.

Remember, *you* are a system of systems and your body and mind are the most important primary systems of your life, fortunately the ones you can control best. Improve your personal systems at every opportunity; maintain them always.

In everything you do, perform the basics, focusing hard on the pragmatic details. Keep things simple but don't take shortcuts.

With finesse, take life as it comes.

The largest problem with swinging for the home run is that all those hammer-swings will cause you to strike out too often. And those strike-outs, added together, will make life a struggle, or take you down altogether.

Instead, you've heard this before: Swing steady, one swing at a time. Relax, keep your eye on the ball and make contact. Funny thing, your steady and controlled swing, combined with the right pitch, will effortlessly send the ball over the fence when you least foresee it, and more often than you could predict.

See that each swing is a closed entity unto itself; each has the singular goal of making contact with the ball. When you miss the ball, and of course you sometimes will, calmly accept it as a natural outcome in the numbers game of life and then, undistracted, give 100 percent focus to the next swing.

One last time, I remind you *the mandatory adjustment is in your moment-to-moment perception of things. All your actions stem from this new, on-the-ground vision: Your world is composed of systems that function flawlessly 99.9 percent of the time. All you need to do is climb on board!*

Every day has its flavor, its tone. Learn to work with your individual days and to savor them as they slide by.

Understand that most people wake up in the morning with only a vague sense of their ultimate, primary goals. Events quickly peel back the layers of control and the day becomes a Whac-A-Mole® epic that dictates reaction to bad results while disallowing efforts at system improvement.

In contrast, you *carve* through the hours, directing sub-systems with confidence and precision, constructing the primary systems you desire.

By filling your days with accomplishment, the negatives that previously dragged you down will no longer factor into who you are and what you do. They will just annoy you occasionally.

Will you become blind to the dysfunction around you? Not a chance. In fact, you'll be in a position to do something about dysfunction as it comes within your ever-increasing circle of influence.

The *Work the System* mindset is focused, deliberate, and organized.

It's about action, not reaction.

CHAPTER 26

A VISION
TO CULTIVATE

The individual who wants to reach the top...
must appreciate the might of the force of habit and
must understand that practices are what create habits.
He must be quick to break those habits that can break him
and hasten to adopt those practices that will become the habits
that help him achieve the success he desires.

J. Paul Getty

Most of us have at least one process in which we excel. For you, what is it, and why are you good at it? It's probable that when you are in the midst of performing this process, you experience a delicious taste of precision and confidence. What you do well is your passion and you take every opportunity to do it. It's a positive addiction.

There are a couple of things I do well. One of them is system structuring—the *Work the System* method. I am ardent about it, and I wonder, *for this thing I do well, do I love doing it because I am good at it, or am I good at it because I love doing it?* The black-or-white answer is elusive but a third possibility intrigues me: Do the two go together without distinction?

Again, what do you do well? What makes you passionate?

Leaving aside the chicken-or-the-egg question, and *while continuing to hone your particular passion, now extend that fire to the perfection of the mechanical workings of the other facets of your existence.*

Get visceral about it. Wallow in it. Enjoy the flow of it.

Be outside the events of your day and treat those events as elements of an overall game, a game that your proper management will make perfect.

That game, of course, is your life.

Few people understand the magnificence of the systems around them—but now you do. From this point forward you will reject escapism as you appreciate the here and now for the miracle it is. You will find control and freedom because you understand the mechanisms that determine the events of your life.

You will never go back.

Appendix A

Note to the reader:
I originally wrote this article in 2002 for a telephone answering
service trade journal. It was directed to answering service owners
but the message is simple and is applicable to any business with
employees. I have updated it slightly for this book.

—SC

Ockham's Razor is a principle attributed to the 14th-century English philosopher William of Ockham. It states that "entities should not be multiplied beyond necessity, or that one should choose the simplest explanation, the one requiring the fewest assumptions and principles." (from the *NY Public Library Desk Reference*).

Ockham's Law and the Long-Term Employee

Exactly, *what* is the problem?

What attributes do telephone answering service (TAS) owners seek in their telephone service representatives (TSRs)? The short list includes cheerful and constructive attitudes, high-quality performance, and long-term employment.

Employee performance and turnover are *the* major topics in our trade meeting get-togethers, both in general sessions and in one-on-one discussions. In our industry, it's a fact that most TSRs don't stick around for the long term, and for those who do, there are sometimes "negative comportment" problems.

Why is there such tumult within answering service TSR operations departments? Why are owners and managers constantly trading tips and secrets in an attempt to stem the tide of incessant staff turnover, and why do these owners and managers berate themselves, their employees, and the telecom industry in general?

The problem is not due to unqualified job applicants or a general lack of work ethic. Instead, it's the owner/manager's failure to address the real-life requirements of staff, while proffering gimmicky and manipulative incentives and/or punishments.

I knew an answering service manager who claimed staff turnover was *not* his largest problem (although it was his number two problem). He told me the largest challenge is the state government's mandated increases in the minimum wage. He complained, "it keeps going up"!

There was another owner who had a well-thought-out, documented employee punishment procedure for non-performance and "bad attitude." (The floggings will continue until morale improves!) And here's a comment I overheard from a TAS operations manager: "We can't do drug testing. I would have to fire everyone and then there would be no one to answer the phones!"

None of those three people are in the industry anymore—and all three of the businesses they operated are defunct.

So, what about TSR compensation? Here's the ubiquitous industry excuse for offering meager pay: "You just don't understand. This is a competitive, cutthroat, low-income industry and we *can't* pay a better wage. Telephone answering service is a commodity and although quality is important, in the end, success is more a function of low price. If we raise our rates, we'll lose our customers."

Of course, client service rates are a factor, but what if we could pay our TSRs more while making their work environment more stable and logical? If this produced a long-term staff that provided better service quality, could we charge clients more?

So, why is there so much staff turnover? What are the root, no-frills, no-cover-up, no Band-Aid, *causes* of the problem? The causes *are* simple and, in their simplicity, they expose unsuccessful attempts to cultivate stability for what they are—smoke screens that offer initial excitement but have nothing to do with a TSRs' fundamental needs.

I will interject a simple yet vital concept: Long ago, when I had just started in the business, Sandy, the owner of a large and successful TAS in Portland, Oregon told me, "Your TSRs *want* to do a good job. It is *your* job to make that easy for them. Don't ever second guess their motivation. *They want to do a good job!*"

If an owner or manager begins with the premise "all employees are lazy," or "there is no work ethic anymore," or "I can't pay enough to find and hold quality people," where will that lead?

(And, I pointedly ask, how *stupid* is this mindset?)

If these are your fundamental beliefs, you must change them. If you don't, you are doomed.

Here are the three primary reasons why most answering services can't keep people long-term. They are disarming in their simplicity: First, employees aren't getting what they want in terms of pay and benefits. Big surprise. Second, they don't know what ownership expects. They have to be mind readers in order to stay out of trouble. Third, with knee-jerk irregularity, owners manipulate TSRs in subtle and not-so-subtle ways, while seldom acknowledging their good work.

So, here's what we have: the money is not good, requirements for performance are mysterious, and childish reward and punishment schemes erupt sporadically. On top of all that, good work goes unnoticed.

Not a terrific work situation, and hence, relentless staff turnover. It's so simple when stated on the written page.

A Philosophy and a System of Employment

Again, incentive plans that don't address the fundamental needs of employees will fail. These programs are worse than a waste of time and money. They crush morale. And what about punishment? Don't even think about it.

Instead, develop a philosophy of employment that will address the true needs of your employees. If you worked for someone, would you want it any other way? Could anything be more simple?

Remember this: There are no super-human people out there, but there are plenty of great people who are looking for solid opportunities.

You need stable employees—ones with backbones; ones who are reliable, honest, and hard working. There are lots of people out there like that, and if you do things right, they will find their way to you, be committed, perform superbly, and stay long-term. All you must do is satisfy people's reasonable needs and not ask them to be mind readers. Tell them exactly what you want them to do, and treat them like the adults they are. If you do this you will have an extraordinary employment system; one that acknowledges your TSRs' worth as it fulfills their personal requirements.

Be crystal clear about the employer-employee arrangement without being afraid to throw up a challenge—this is the "deal" between the employer and the employee. At Centratel, the deal we offer TSRs is simple—"we will pay you very well if you give us 100 percent."

You must put your extraordinary employment system down on paper so your people know what it is. It will take time to do this, but so what? You are already breaking your back dealing with chronic staff turnover. Isn't *that* hard work? Doesn't *that* take time? Just channel the same time and energy and money in this different direction. Swallow the pill: Documentation is a prerequisite for long-term staff stability and if you create it, stability is what you will have.

What to Leave Out

Before discussing what to include in your new employment vision, it is important to consider what *not* to include. By dropping ineffective actions, you will promote simplicity as you gain time and energy.

Here are some "motivators" I've heard about in other answering services: Useless gifts (as exemplified by a huge bag of plastic Mickey Mouse ears brought back to TSRs after the owner visited Disney World), complicated formulas to award cash bonuses for perfect attendance; at staff meetings, "fun" games and rewards for attending those meetings. I've heard of gift certificates for having a "good attitude," and movie theater tickets as prizes for making it through initial training, or for "good behavior." Also useless: long, drawn-out conversations with problem employees in attempts to reason with them, perhaps to convince them to show up for work on time.

What do all of these strategies have in common?

First, they have nothing to do with the real, long-term needs of people. Arriving inconsistently, they are of low intrinsic value. They are ineffective Band-Aids.

Second, TSRs perceive motivational gimmicks and heart-to-heart chats for what they are: manipulative and childish, management's thinly veiled efforts to maneuver them into being good little girls and boys.

This is "infantilizing." It is insulting in a low-key way. This is carrot-on-a-stick, Bugs Bunny methodology, and within your staff it will breed an underlying disrespect because it is disrespectful.

Good People from the Start

At Centratel, we have little staff turnover in our operations department. Only occasionally will a TSR call in sick or arrive late. Everyone makes it to staff meetings. These are exceptionally positive, solid, good people—and they were that way before they showed up at Centratel. Our success was in being able to find them and convince them to work for us.

Rather than attempting to cultivate the personal attitudes and work ethic we seek, we carefully pick good people and then we don't alienate them.

In addition to giving TSRs what they need for compensation and treating them like the adults they are, we work hard to give them a stability that, occasionally, is in contrast to their personal lives. It may be just a job, but Centratel is a place that is safe, calm, and predictable. This stability is rooted in our rigorous documentation: In exact detail, we have written down what we want them to do.

As a sidebar: In the history of my own business, the ground-shaking paradigm shifts came at the blackest of times. It was usually "do something dramatic right this minute, or file for bankruptcy tomorrow morning." In these on-the-edge times, a huge and immediate change in philosophy and operating policy was exactly what was needed.

Be thankful, I say, for the hard times we survive.

Getting Specific

Please. No more Band-Aids.

What would Sir William of Ockham do if he owned a telephone answering service? Following is my best-guess list. None of these strategies are new or revolutionary, but what they have in common is they meet the needs of both TSRs and owner/managers. Remember to presume the good intentions of each TSR. OK. Let's get to it.

1. You've already presumed the number one item: Pay a generous wage. Money is why people come to work. Forget the convenient theory, "pay isn't the most important part of a job; it's the feeling of being valued," etc. How '60s is that? Don't ask college campus psychologists and sociologists what is most important to your people. Ask your people! *Ask your employees what is most important to them!* Long ago, I submitted a written questionnaire to our TSRs asking what was most important to them regarding their positions with Centratel. The overwhelming response was that *pay* is what is most important—and so I was delighted to find I had "a firm grasp of the obvious." Remember that a high pay scale has benefits that are not always obvious and measurable—high quality performance from long-term employees. Have faith these non-measurable benefits will more than compensate for the extra cost.

2. I'll get some argument on this one: No part-time people. All full-timers. Part-timers won't have the same experience on the phones. They can't get the same workout with the accounts and the techniques. How can a 20-hour per week employee attain the same degree of expertise as a 40-hour per week employee? Also, for part-timers, the job tends to rank a too-low priority in their lives. We want career-minded, serious people who consider their jobs important enough so what *we* want, and what *they* get, really matters to them. My partner and I don't take our business in a casual way and neither does a full-time employee.

3. No paid sick days. Why? Because paying people when they are not at work is a reward for not being at work! We provide PTO, but it is a cash payment that shows up as TSRs earn it, as a separate line-item on their biweekly paychecks. TSRs can take time off—two to three weeks each year, depending on length of employment—but because PTO is paid in advance, there is no pay while they are gone.

4. Health insurance? Yes, and an IRA, too.

5. If an employee does a good job, say so, publicly. If an employee does a poor job, also say so, privately.

6. We put shift schedules out to bid and award them by seniority. Inevitably, the most senior TSRs occupy the best weekday

daytime shifts, with everyone understanding this is the reward for long service. The less tenured TSRs will also value their time with the company, seeing their accumulating work histories as assets that grow more valuable every day. The seniority method is logical and fair.

7. Put the job down on paper. This includes a clear and concise operational manual, an employee handbook, and individual job descriptions. It's a stressful occupation as it is: Do TSRs also have to be mind readers and fortune tellers in order to survive? To the very last detail, instructions for performing the work should be in black and white, hard copy, and online.

8. "Pay by performance" with an objective method of measurement. At Centratel, we have a full-time independent quality specialist who rates call quality and reviews performance weekly with each TSR. TSRs can boost their take-home pay by up to twenty five percent with this plan. For the TSR, that additional twenty five percent is the "fun-money or get-ahead money that lies beyond the necessary money."

Cultivating a long-term, loyal staff begins with a mindset change. Stop looking for the perfect employee, inserting gimmicks, or blathering away with impotent excuses about unmotivated employees, a declining work ethic, or nonsensical theories of human motivation. Instead, per Sir William, "choose the simplest explanation, the one requiring the fewest assumptions," and document a plan that addresses the real needs of your people—people who want to do a good job.

Appendix B

Not in any particular order, here's some reading I've found interesting

— S C

Emotional Intelligence, Daniel Goleman

Influence, Robert Cialdini

Ubiquity, Mark Buchanan

The Dumbest Generation, Mark Bauerlein

The Blank Slate, Steven Pinker

The Moral Animal, Robert Wright

Full House, Dinosaur in a Haystack, Stephen J. Gould

Born That Way, William Wright

Manliness, Harvey C. Mansfield

The Decline of Males, Lionel Tiger

The World is Flat, Thomas Friedman

Three Magic Words, The Secret of Secrets, U.S. Anderson

Unlimited Power, Awaken the Giant Within, Anthony Robbins

Synchronicity, The Bridge Between Matter and Mind, F. David Peat

The Holographic Universe, Michael Talbot

The Power of Now, A New Earth, Eckhart Tollee

New Passages, Predictable Crises of Adult Life, Gail Sheehy

The Death of the Grown-up, Diana West

The 7 Habits of Successful People, First Things First, Stephen Covey

Wherever You Go, There You Are; Full Catastrophe Living, Jon Kabat-Zinn

Looking Out for #1, To Be or Not To Be Intimidated? Robert Ringer

How to Win Friends and Influence People, Dale Carnegie

Choice Theory, William Glasser

Glimpses of a Golden Childhood, Bhagwan Shree Rajneesh (Osho)

The Power of Positive Thinking, Norman Vincent Peale

Where I'm Calling From, Raymond Carver

Me Talk Pretty One Day, Naked, David Sedaris

The Demon-Haunted World, Shadows of Forgotten Ancestors, Carl Sagan

Future Shock, Alvin Toffler

What I Saw at the Revolution, When Character Was King, Peggy Noonan

Mean Genes, Terry Burnham and Jay Phelan

On Writing, Stephen King

Being Digital, Nicholas Negroponte

Natural Acts, The Flight of the Iguana, David Quamman

Bobos in Paradise, On Paradise Drive, David Brooks

Megatrends 2000, The Extreme Future, The Global Paradox, John Naisbitt

The Book, Alan Watts

The Best of Times, Hanes Johnson

The Rise of the Creative Class, Richard Florida

Under the Banner of Heaven, Into the Wild, Jon Krakauer

Kings of Creation, Don Lessem

Raptor Red, Robert Bakker

A Brief History of Time, Stephen W. Hawking

Nature and Nurture, Matt Ridley

Pride in Performance, Les Schwab

It's Not About the Bike, Lance Armstrong

A Short History of Nearly Everything, Bill Bryson

The Tipping Point, Blink, Malcom Gladwell

America Alone, Mark Steyn

The True Believer, Eric Hoffer

Information Anxiety, Richard Saul Wurman

Breaking Open the Head, Daniel Pinchbeck

Flow, Creativity, Mihaly Csikszentmihalyi

The Looming Tower, Lawrence Wright

Deep Survival, Lawrence Gonzalez

Real Change, Newt Gingrich

The Six Pillars of Self Esteem, Nathaniel Branden

Pulling Your Own Strings, Wayne Dwyer

Lone Survivor, Marcus Luttrell

Rich Dad, Poor Dad, Robert T. Kiyosaki

The Promise of Sleep, William C. Demet

The E Myth Revisited, Michael E. Gerber

The Zone, Barry Sears

Treating Type A Behavior and Your Heart, Meyer Friedman and Diane Ulmer

Listening to Prozak, Peter D. Kramer

Driven To Distraction, Edward M. Hollowwell

Beyond Prozac, Michael J. Norden

Scattered, Gabor Mate

American Soldier, Tommy Franks

Good to Great, Jim Collins

How to Think Like A CEO, D.A. Benton

Thriving on Chaos, Tom Peters

Losing My Virginity, Richard Branson

Freakonomics, Steven Levitt and Stephen Duvner

Business at the Speed of Thought, Bill Gates

What Will Be, Michael Dertouzos

The Progress Paradox, Greg Easterbrook

Nuts, Kevin Freiberg and Jackie Freiberg

Straight Man, Richard Russo

—SC

Appendix C
Other offerings from North Sister Publishing:

Work the System Easy Template Software™
This software will quickly guide the business manager through the process of creating the three vital *Work the System* documents: The Strategic Objective, General Operating Principles, and Working Procedures. The system is simple (as you might have guessed), with a fill-in-the-blanks format. See **workthesystem.com/easy** for details. (Avail. Oct. 2008)

Work the System Boot Camp™
Held in Bend, Oregon, the two-day small-group program goes to the heart of the process with the intention of launching your business or department into an organized, efficient, self-sufficient, and profitable organism. Bend is *the* Northwest resort town, a perfect vacation destination with opportunities for golf, hiking, rock and mountain climbing, skiing, cycling, river rafting and trout fishing. Stay for a week! Logistics permitting, Sam will join you outside. See **workthesystem.com/bootcamp** for details, or call us at 1-800-664-7448.

Keynote Speaking & Personal and Corporate Consulting
Sam will occasionally travel for presentations or consultations. Call us at 1-800-664-7448.

Audio: An unabridged version of this book. (Available Oct. 2008)

Appendix D
Kashmir Family Aid

On short notice, and just after the October 8, 2005 earthquake that devastated great swaths of Azad Jammu Kashmir (AJK) and the North-West Frontier Province of Pakistan, I traveled alone to Muzaffarabad, Azad Kashmir, the epicenter of the quake. I was taken in by local Kashmiris and did independent relief work. Also, I wrote articles and took photos in order to publicize the plight of the millions who were homeless. The dazed survivors wandered the tent camps and streets, wondering what to do next. It was devastation, with 80,000 dead—a disproportionate number being children trapped in schools when the quake struck just after they had been seated in their classrooms. Nearly every family I met had lost one or more members in the quake. Not restricted to a guarded encampment, I was probably the only Westerner to roam freely through the area, not attached to an official NGO or the U.S. military. Since that visit, I created Kashmir Family Aid, a 501c3 non-profit. It's narrow purpose is to provide assistance to the school children of the region. I had been to Pakistan several times before the earthquake, on business, and have returned a number of times since. With me, Linda's been there too. These are wild places but I love going there, especially to the back country regions. Why? It's the beautiful children who have little more than the clean, pressed school uniforms they wear, but nevertheless are hopeful, smiling, and optimistic. Go to the web site (**kashmirfamily.org**) and view the slide presentations and photos. You will find some of my newspaper articles there, too. Please consider helping us. A 200 student school with a faculty of 12 can be totally supported for less than $1,000 U.S. dollars a month, but any size donation goes a long way. Thank you. —sc

Index

Note: At the end of most chapters is an illustration, a short true story that reflects the *Work the System* methodology. You will find a list of these stories under the main entry, "illustrations." Also, any main entry with page numbers in italics indicates an end-of-chapter illustration.

mental posture of, 8
systems perspective, 123–125
vantage point of, 24

P

Paid Time Off (PTO), 244–246
pain
    inefficiency and, 56
    self-generated personal, 53
Pakistani traffic circles, 247–251
paranoia, 23–24, 64–65
parsimony in scientific explanation, Ockham's
        principle of, 182
paying attention, consciously, 7–8
Paying the Bills, *70–71*
peak performance, 230
"99.9 percent of everything works fine," 30
98 percent perfection, 177–178
perfect
    definition of, 30
perfection
    as an anomaly, 51
    definition of, 30
    98 percent, 177–178
performance, 172–175
permanence, 81–82
personal communication, 226–227
personal pain, 53
personal system analogy, 111–112
personal systems, 76, 119–120, ix–x
philosophy and a system of employment,
        266–267
point-of-sale
    affect of procrastination on, 197
    appreciation of life, 243–244
    communications and, 196
    overview, 192–193
    personal life decisions and, 195
    protocol for, 225
poly-phasic activity, 77
the power and the why, 52–53
power line/clock metaphor, *179*
power outages, 183–186
Power Outage Working Procedure, 186
pragmatism, 5
primary system, definition of, 28
prime time. *See* Biological Prime Time
Procedures
    adherence to protocol, 161
    Centratel's Procedure for, 156–157
    creating, 155–157
    definition of, 29
    design, 158–159
    documentation, 164–166
    Power Outage Working Procedure, 186
    ruthlessness and flexibility in, 160–161
procrastination, 190–191, 193

project engineer, 9
    definition of, 30
    personal systems, 119–120
promise keeping, 221–222
providing consistent high quality, 211–212
PTO. *See* Paid Time Off

Q

quality, consistent, 211–212
quiet courage, demonstrations of, 187–188

R

random errors, 82
REA (Rural Electrification Administration),
        113–120
reading resources, 271–272
recurring, definition of, 30
recurring systems, 28
relationship maintenance system, 84–85
resources, reading, 271–272
respect for cultural systems, 95–96
responsibility, ethical, 166
Rural Electrification Administration (REA),
        113–120
ruthlessness and flexibility, 160–161

S

self-generated personal pain, 53
self-talk, 221
semi-enlightenment, component failures and,
        55–56
service quality, 212
simplicity, 94
Small Good Thing, A (Carver), 152
social systems, 175–176
spirituality, let-it-be brand of, 15
staffing strategies, 269–270
staff turnover, 268
start objectivity, 189
statistics
    on new business start-ups, 39
    on power failures, 116–117
    on substance abuse, 20
Strategic Objective
    Centratel's, 135–137
    creating, 134–135
    definition of, 29
    document, 100
    overview, 133–134
streaming video, 22–23
strength and resilience, 61
stress
    action items for reducing, 68–69
    and chaos, 4–5
    sleep deprivation and, 42
sub-systems
    definition of, 28